NUMBERS AND NERVES

Numbers and Nerves

*Information, Emotion, and
Meaning in a World of Data*

EDITED BY
SCOTT SLOVIC AND PAUL SLOVIC

OREGON STATE UNIVERSITY PRESS
CORVALLIS

The paper in this book meets the guidelines for permanence and durability of the Committee on Production Guidelines for Book Longevity of the Council on Library Resources and the minimum requirements of the American National Standard for Permanence of Paper for Printed Library Materials z39.48-1984.

Library of Congress Cataloging-in-Publication Data

Names: Slovic, Scott, 1960- editor. | Slovic, Paul, 1938- editor.
Title: Numbers and nerves : information, emotion, and meaning in a world of data / edited by Scott Slovic, Paul Slovic.
Description: Corvallis, OR : Oregon State University Press, 2015. | Includes bibliographical references and index.
Identifiers: LCCN 2015032793| ISBN 9780870717765 (pbk.) | ISBN 9780870717772 (ebk.)
Subjects: LCSH: Information society--Psychological aspects. | Big data. |BISAC: SOCIAL SCIENCE / Media Studies.
Classification: LCC HM851 .N868 2015 | DDC 005.7--dc23
LC record available at http://lccn.loc.gov/2015032793

Oregon State University Press
121 The Valley Library
Corvallis OR 97331-4501
541-737-3166 • fax 541-737-3170
www.osupress.oregonstate.edu

To Roz Slovic

There are 1,198,500,000 people alive now in China. To get a feel for what this means, simply take yourself—in all your singularity, importance, complexity, and love—and multiply by 1,198,500,000. See? Nothing to it.

—ANNIE DILLARD, *For the Time Being*

In the entire history of biology, every species that outgrows its resource base suffers a population crash—a crash sometimes fatal to the entire species. The issue may be not just whether we need to stop growing, but whether, for our own survival, we must humanely bring our numbers down from where they are now to a figure we can, literally, all live with. . . . Either we decide to manage our numbers . . . or nature will do it for us.

—ALAN WEISMAN, *Countdown: Our Last, Best Hope for a Future on Earth?*

Contents

Foreword

Headbone and Hormone:
Adventures in the Arithmetic of Life

ROBERT MICHAEL PYLE

You have in your hands a book that glides gracefully between two stand-points, logical and emotional, illuminating as it does the broad and murky territory in between. Scott and Paul Slovic, in designating the ends of this particular teeter-totter as "numbers and nerves," lay out an elegant template for mapping the poles of our proclivities. We know from the start that we are creatures of compassion and feeling, but also animals of analysis and mea-surement. Which way of seeing and expressing the world actually achieves our desires, meets our needs, and satisfies our lives to a greater extent? Which makes more things happen? Which can heal the wounded world?

Maybe both. As Scott and Paul state in their Introduction, "Despite the compelling power of quantification, despite our sense of the usefulness of numbers, there persists an underlying skepticism toward numbers as a medium of communication and as a gauge of reality." This is certainly so, for as they continue, "There is a space in all people, even in the scientists and economists whose daily currency is the worldview we call 'quantifica-tion,' that 'cries out for words,' and for images and stories, for the discourse of emotion." And yet we need our numbers, too: acres cut, barrels spilled, degrees risen, hectares flooded . . . people killed. How, then, to navigate between these two ways of relating to the facts of life?

My friend Neil Johannsen served as director of Alaska State Parks for fourteen years, during which he grew the system from one to four million acres. When I asked him how he did it, with a sometimes hostile public, hundreds of employees, and four different governors from two political par-ties, he answered with pithy concision.

"Bob," said Neil, "it takes the right combination of headbone and hormone."

In the pages that follow, you will find a remarkable community of writers brought together to carry the conversation between the two further, perhaps, than ever before.

For my part, the earliest murmurs of that dialogue came long ago, from the butterflies. Butterflies had hold of my heart from an early age. I fell for their colors, shapes, and changes, their secrets, their beguiling ways. And not long into my love affair with butterflies and their haunts, I began to see that there were different ways of taking in and speaking of the objects of my delight.

My gospel, *Colorado Butterflies*, by F. Martin Brown, furnished a heady mixture of colorful description, exciting storytelling, and taxonomic detail. There was room, it seemed, for both the imagination and factual precision to come into play. At twelve, as one of the younger members of the Lepidopterists' Society, I read its journal with more avidity than comprehension. I was somewhat befuddled, for example, by a spirited exchange between F. M. Brown himself and Vladimir Nabokov, about the importance of statistics in evaluating the patterns of ringlet butterflies. Nabokov, known for his butterfly work at Harvard even before the then-recently published *Lolita*, argued that keen aesthetic impressions could discern important evolutionary patterns, while Brown insisted on sophisticated statistics to prove their validity. I came away with the strong sense that maybe both approaches were equally important.

Yet I was far from being able to *do* both. In my sixteenth summer I received a small grant from the Colorado-Wyoming Academy of Science to study variation in wood nymph butterflies (relatives of those same ringlets) along my beloved High Line Canal and in other Colorado locations. Their variability proved radical, matching several named subspecies. But I also found that fully a quarter of the dramatically eye-spotted satyrs had bird strikes on or near their ocelli, which demonstrated how natural selection acts to make bigger, brighter, expendable bull's-eyes on butterflies' wings. (*The Origin of Species* had been my hip-pocket companion for years.) I had a powerful data sample from my fieldwork, but I was utterly innocent of the statistical tools necessary to test and express my results in any scientifically meaningful way.

This lapse was driven home when I offered my own first contribution to the august journal. On a field trip with my mother, not long after high school graduation, I witnessed "an extraordinary swarm of butterflies in Colorado"—which became the title of my article. The spectacle really was astonishing: a vast assembly of several species of blues in a milkweed gully near the Black Canyon of the Gunnison. The arroyo was a'shimmer with a living blanket of butterflies. I could go on like that all day about them—and did, in my manuscript, calling them "an azure fog." But how to count them? I couldn't just net a clump of the insects, tally, and extrapolate out over the whole area, as is done with wintering monarchs, for these were mostly moving targets. Even though the adroit editor of the *Journal of the Lepidopterists' Society*, Professor Jerry A. Powell of UC Berkeley, helped me achieve slightly more precise language, the best I could manage was this: "Our consensus could not be finalized to a greater degree of precision than 'many thousands,' although my own estimate proclaimed 'At least ten thousand, and perhaps a hundred!'" To this day, Jerry teases me about my combo of Muirian words and muddy numbers: "An azure fog . . . at least ten thousand, and perhaps a hundred!"

Clearly, if I was going to progress as a lepidopterist (and a conservationist, for by this time, rare butterfly conservation had become my main interest), I was going to have to become something of a mathematician as well—just as lepidopterists must be botanists too. But there was a problem: I was no mathematician.

But this book is not *about* innumeracy. As several of the essays to follow will show, numerical numbness can afflict the sensibilities of us all, whether we embrace math or not. The most advanced mathematician might be just as put off by the mere quantities of crisis, and just as moved by their emotional counterpart, as the most rarefied artistic intellect. Yet numbers matter. Understanding the eyespots of brown butterflies might seem an arcane and inessential whim. But the survival of ecological conditions that allow those butterflies to live and evolve is clearly related to our survival too. I saw that, if we were to conserve those conditions, along with much that we love of the world as it is, we would need to engage with both quantities and qualities.

My dissertation problem not only proved this to me, but also showed me the way around it. The intention was to use Washington state butterfly

distribution to reveal gaps in the state's nature reserve system. Through
studies in England, I had seen the power of applied biogeography for conservation. In my first book, I proposed the existence of "butterfly provinces," or regions of natural distribution, but these were erected strictly by
gut feelings about the insects and their whereabouts. The challenge now
became, how to prove that these patterns held water?

By paying attention in every conference and seminar I attended, every
paper I read, I learned through osmosis how figures came to the necessary
service of science—and how to use them. The fieldwork went well, and I
was able to demonstrate that my butterfly provinces had numerical reality—to calculate their acreage and distinctness, using a formula and resem-
blance trellis drawn from mammalogy. In the end, the butterflies revealed
dramatic inequalities in conservation coverage between distinctive regions
that had been lumped by managers—gaps that have since been filled with
new reserves and wilderness areas, thanks in part to the butterflies and the
numbers. My hunches had proved mostly correct; but hunches seldom
affect policy.

And so—mirabile dictu!—I came out able to perform field science after
all. Yet, along the way, though I shed both my antipathy for math and my
resistance to analytical techniques, I also learned that the poet in me was
stronger than the scientist. My inclination lay more toward the descriptive
and personal response to things. I still do some science, and when I do, I
use numbers. But much more, I write; and I am not afraid to mingle a
lyrical or emotional response with empirical detail. In fact, almost all of
the conservation campaigns and issues with which I have been involved
have drawn deeply from both sides. My book *Wintergreen* gives chapter
and verse of certain less-than-sustainable logging practices in my hills of
home, including acres of stumpage, board feet of timber cut, and number
of jobs lost and families fractured along with the woods. Weyerhaeuser was
unable to discredit my criticism, because I took care to get the facts and
numbers right. But it may have been the book's lyrical qualities that affected
readers more.

Likewise, in *Chasing Monarchs*, I described both numerically and emotionally the astonishing overwintering colonies of the migratory butterflies
in Mexico and California, a threatened phenomenon. It is one thing to
speak of twenty hectares of clusters involving millions of monarchs, quite
another to read of Homero Aridjis's richly poetical and visceral reactions to

the spectacle, elsewhere in this book. And as for the Xerces Society for Invertebrate Conservation, which I founded in 1971, which one makes more impact: to talk about the biggest job in the world, trying to save ten or twenty million species, or to hear former Xerces president E. O. Wilson utter the simple but elegant profundity that insects are "the little things that run the world"?

If there is almost a chuckle in that elemental (and critically important) truth, it is no accident.

~

Numbers and Nerves is full of stories of overwhelming importance to us all: hard lessons of human and more-than-human behavior that are seldom funny and often to weep for. Yet when the tale-teller can find a shred, a mote, a moment of human wit or natural humor in the midst of harsh realities, so much the better for the listener—who may be all the more moved thereby. I have always tried to relate what I have to say in narrative, to find the stories in the page-pictures; and sometimes, the humor. *Mariposa Road* is really a catalogue of the current plights of our butterflies (and, by extension, of life) thanks to the compromised state of the American landscape. But the litany of loss is leavened, and maybe better assimilated, when interrupted by a Louisiana sheriff's deputy who slowly examines my Xerces Society calling card and asks me, "So, you belong to this *Exorcist Society*?"

So it seems we need to invoke all of our powers on behalf of these parlous times. That suits me fine, for I like to stride that "high ridge" that Nabokov believed to exist between "the mountainside of scientific knowledge and the opposite slope of artistic imagination." And Nabokov is just the one to bring up here, for though he is known chiefly as a superb literary artist with little quantitative education, he performed durable science based on what was then known among butterfly folk as "a good eye"—a trait that often counted for more than mere math. Just how good an eye he had was demonstrated recently by sophisticated DNA work—coordinated at Harvard, right where Nabokov counted scales and dissected genitalia of blues—that has shown his systematic ideas and conclusions to have been remarkably correct, given his simple tools and training. Nor are these just bits and bobs of butterfly esoterica: they involve species at risk for which it is vital to know both who and what they are. Such as the famous Karner Blue, which became the cause célèbre for a whole biome, decades after Nabokov discerned it as a separate species of delicate needs. Life's very survival may depend upon both the poet-naturalist's "good eye" *and* the hard scientist's numbers. Nabokov liked to confound doubters by speaking of "the precision of poetry, the art of science." Wouldn't we always like to have each on hand?

Mind you, the balance can swing too far, either way. I have lately listened to earnest graduate students, ignorant of both the lifeways and the poetry of their butterfly subjects, not so much massaging their figures as Rolfing them, in order to squeeze significance out of weak data. On the other side, far too many pastoralists and poets think they can save a place or a population or a people solely through an outpouring of art and heart. Is not the desired state surely to live, speak, debate, and act out of the richness of both heart and head, as the whole people we are?

Yes, it does take both headbone and hormone, if we are going to perceive and respond to the world aright. As I finally understood for myself, we need all the math we can marshal for our case, which is the case of the Earth and its living things, including ourselves. And we also need all the song, dance, poetry, and emotion we can muster, when we go forth to make that all-important case.

Numbers and nerves, headbone and hormone, abacus and emotion: they all *count*, after all. Let the conversation begin.

Acknowledgments

Colleagues, friends, and family members have known for many years that something called "Numbers and Nerves" was in progress whenever the two of us went out for a run together. We appreciate the interest and support we have received from so many people who've caught wind of the core ideas of this project, recognizing intuitively the significance of how the brain processes numerical information and that a convergence of social science and the humanities might help to illuminate this phenomenon.

We particularly thank Roz Slovic for always reminding us that there are real people in real need out in the world and that our work as scholars should count for something beyond academia. Susie Bender and Brigid Flannery were often present as we tinkered with this manuscript, probably wondering if an actual book would ever emerge from our efforts. Harold Slovic was particularly helpful in directing our attention to the unique numerical art of Roman Opalka. We would also like to acknowledge the support of the rest of the Slovic clan: Steve, Rhonda, Lauren, Spencer, Cameron, Jia, Oblio, and Sol Jacinto.

Leisha Wharfield, Andrew Quist, and John Silvey, of Decision Research, provided essential help with preparation of the final manuscript and assistance with permissions. Robin Gregory, David Frank, and Daniel Västfjäll contributed in important ways to the ideas underlying Chapter 3. Mary Braun, of Oregon State University Press, took an immediate interest in this project and shepherded the manuscript toward its final shape, as did copyeditor Susan Campbell.

Of course we are particularly indebted to the scholars, writers, and artists who have contributed their own words, images, and ideas to *Numbers and*

Nerves. Robert Michael Pyle crafted a beautiful and witty foreword for the book. Homero and Betty Aridjis, Vandana Shiva, Sandra Steingraber, and Chris Jordan, whose professional work and personal commitments to social justice and environmental protection are profoundly linked to this subject, took the time to meet with Scott and participate in interviews that offer a special dimension to *Numbers and Nerves.*

We are grateful to the William and Flora Hewlett Foundation and its president, Paul Brest, for supporting the early stages of conceptualizing the book and to the National Science Foundation for additional support under Grants SES 1024808, 1227729, and 1427414.

SCOTT SLOVIC

PAUL SLOVIC

Credits

"Datasets and Trends of Genocide, Mass Killing, and Other Civilian Atrocities," by C. H. Anderton. Copyright 2015 by C. H. Anderton. By permission of Oxford University Press.

Figure 1.2 showing a psychophysical-collapse function describing the value for saving lives adapted from "Compassion Fade: Affect and Charity Are Greatest for a Single Child in Need," by Daniel Västfjäll, Paul Slovic, and Marcus Mayorga, in *PLOS ONE*. Copyright 2014 by Daniel Västfjäll, Paul Slovic, and Marcus Mayorga. Reprinted in accordance with Creative Commons Attribution License CC BY 4.0.

"Pseudoinefficacy and the Arithmetic of Compassion" adapted from "Pseudoinefficacy: Negative Feelings from Children Who Cannot Be Helped Reduce Warm Glow for Children Who Can Be Helped," by Daniel Västfjäll, Paul Slovic, and Marcus Mayorga, in *Frontiers in Psychology*. Copyright 2015 by Daniel Västfjäll, Paul Slovic, and Marcus Mayorga. Reprinted in accordance with Creative Commons Attribution License CC BY 4.0.

"The Age of Numbing," republished with permission of Robert Jay Lifton and Greg Mitchell, from "The Age of Numbing," by Robert Jay Lifton and Greg Mitchell, *Technology Review* (August/September 1995), copyright 1995; permission conveyed through Copyright Clearance Center, Inc.

"Epidemic Disease as Structural Violence," excerpt from *Never Again? Reflections on Human Values and Human Rights,* by Paul Farmer, published by The Tanner Lectures on Human Values. Copyright 2005 by Paul Farmer. Reprinted by permission of The Tanner Lectures on Human Values.

Photographs of man undergoing treatment for AIDS and tuberculosis by David Walton. Copyright 2003 by David Walton. Reprinted by permission of the photographer.

"Save the Darfur Puppy," by Nicholas D. Kristof, from *The New York Times,* May 10, 2007 © 2007 The New York Times. All rights reserved. Used by permission and protected by the Copyright Laws of the United States. The printing, copying, redistribution, or retransmission of this Content without express written permission is prohibited.

"A Student, a Teacher and a Glimpse of War," by Nicholas D. Kristof, from *The New York Times,* June 21, 2007 © 2007 The New York Times. All rights reserved. Used by permission and protected by the Copyright Laws of the United States. The printing, copying, redistribution, or retransmission of this Content without express written permission is prohibited.

Introduction

The Psychophysics of Brightness and the Value of a Life

SCOTT SLOVIC AND PAUL SLOVIC

As WE ENTER THE TWENTY-FIRST CENTURY, many of the important issues that occupy news headlines and capture the attention of world leaders and ordinary citizens require us to use the best available statistical information—gallons of oil spewing into the Gulf of Mexico, numbers of fisherman put out of work by the disaster, billions of dollars made available in an effort to stem the economic damage and compensate the local residents—to assess various situations and mitigate problems. Without numbers, how could we evaluate what's happening in the world and know how to react? And yet it has become clear as well, to scientists and policy makers, that numerical information often fails to register on audiences an effect forceful enough to lead to significant action. Social scientists who study human thought processes and literary artists and scholars who specialize in communication strategies have increasingly found themselves trying to explain and overcome the paradoxical need for numbers and the numbing, desensitizing effects of quantitative discourse. We require data in order to describe such phenomena as contamination, genocide, species extinction, and climate change. But the data alone, while bolstering the authority of journalists and scientists, tend to wash past audiences with minimal impact. What is the visceral, emotional meaning of thirty-eight parts per million of a potentially cancer-causing chemical in the desert air of central Nevada? What do hundreds of thousands of impoverished, homeless Sudanese villagers mean to residents of the Upper West Side of Manhattan?

In recent decades, social scientists, journalists, and literary and visual artists have become increasingly attuned to the ubiquity of numerical information in the daily lives of North Americans and citizens in other industrialized countries. We've come to believe that truth inheres in numbers, and people who speak (and write) the language of numbers *appear* to know what's going on in the world. In the past decade and a half, American writers have offered several powerful investigations of this numerical fetish of ours.

One of the particularly potent meditations on how meaning accrues, or fails to accrue, through quantification is Annie Dillard's 1999 book *For the Time Being*, in which she imagines, at one point, what it would be like to multiply our unique personal qualities—our "singularity, importance, complexity, and love"—by the number of people in the world's most populous country in order to fathom the "meaning" of China's vast population. Who among us can perform such a simple act of multiplication? "Nothing to it," jokes Dillard. Simply do the math. We have used Dillard's memorable statement as the first epigraph for this book because it states so graphically that we struggle to understand big numbers, whether these numbers describe quantities of *things* or the kinds of vast processes—either sudden cataclysms or slow, barely perceptible systemic changes—that we're told are occurring in the natural world or in the arenas of public health, the economy, or human demographics. Anything that happens on a large scale seems to require that we use numbers to describe it, and yet numbers are precisely the mode of discourse that, in most cases, leaves audiences numb and messages devoid of meaning.

Dillard clearly understands the need for numbers to convey feeling to be meaningful. Referring to the population of China, she says, "To get a *feel* for what this *means*, simply take yourself . . . and multiply by 1,198,500,000" (italics added). She knows that we cannot feel the humanity beneath the statistic and thus cannot truly understand that reality. Psychologists studying the link between affect (jargon for "feelings") and meaning concur. Numerous laboratory studies have demonstrated that information must convey affect to be meaningful and to play a role in judgment and decision making (Slovic et al., 2002).

The second epigraph comes from journalist Alan Weisman's *Countdown* (2013), which offers a litany of ecological and social pressure points, contexts in which we can feel the risk our entire species now faces as we enter the Anthropocene, the era we have helped create. Weisman says, "Either we decide to manage our numbers . . . or nature will do it for us" (p. 40). Although he means literally that we must learn to understand and manage the impact of human population upon the planet, the phrase "manage our numbers" might also imply managing our ability to fathom and feel the meaning of numbers—managing our ability to respond to and communicate quantitative information.

A good illustration of what happens when we try to respond to quantitative information about social or environmental information comes in Terry Tempest Williams's statement in the "Getting It Right" symposium in the pages of the January/February 2000 issue of *Sierra* magazine. She emphasizes what might well be a common response to information presented in abstract or numerical form. "When I hear all of the statistics," writes Williams,

> the losses we are incurring, the truth and weight of issues like genetically manipulated foods, a population of 6 billion and rising, the loss of diversity of species and land, the control wielded by global corporations, I become mute, my spirit crushed by information that becomes abstracted into despair. My human frame cannot accommodate it all. I become listless, apathetic, impotent, and turn inward, turn to pleasure, to distraction, to anything that will move me away from what I perceive to be the true state of the world. (Pope, 2000, p. 45)

Even when one does understand the problems represented by numbers, there are barriers to effective action. It is all too easy to be overwhelmed by the size of such problems and to feel that one's efforts will be insignificant in the face of such magnitude. As the writer puts it, her "human frame cannot accommodate it all." The "accommodation" of such information requires both cognitive apprehension of data that defies our human-sized frames of reference and emotional resilience in the face of dauntingly vast problems. Although Williams suggests focusing on her own local experience, on the good, constructive work that her neighbors in small-town southern Utah are doing, or that people in other specific communities are doing, to restore and protect their immediate environments, this sense of solace seems like whistling in the dark. It can make us feel better for the moment, but it seems simply to avoid the bigger issues, to defer or deflect them. And perhaps the most fundamental issue is that we need to understand how the human mind uses (or *struggles* to use) numerical information if we are to contemplate some of the most important challenges of our time.

Many people in industrialized societies accept without question the special form of veracity that seems to attach itself to numbers. But this is the result of cultural determination, not an inevitable and permanent truth of human nature. In *The Measure of Reality: Quantification and Western Society, 1250–1600* (1997), historian Alfred W. Crosby documents the emergence of quantitative measurement as a forceful gauge of truth in thirteenth-century Europe. "What shall we call this devotion to breaking down things and energies and practices and perceptions into uniform parts and counting them?" asks Crosby,

> Reductionism? Yes, but that is a baggy category; it does not help us to place in relation to other developments Niccolo Tartaglia's answer in the 1530s to the question of how much a cannon should be tilted upward to fire a ball the farthest. He fired from a culverin two balls of equal weight with equal charges of powder, one at 30 and the other at 45 degrees of elevation. The first went 11,232 Veronese feet, the second 11,832. This is quantification. This is how we reach out for physical reality, push aside its darling curls, and take it by the nape of the neck. (pp. 11–12)

Despite the compelling power of quantification, despite our sense of the usefulness of numbers, there persists an underlying skepticism toward numbers as a medium of communication and as a gauge of reality. W. H. Auden once stated, with a tinge of bitterness, that we live in societies "to which the study of that which can be weighed and measured is a consuming love" (Crosby, p. 12). Activists such as Bill McKibben and Paul Farmer have expressed their frustration at the limitations and impenetrabilities of numerical discourse in the context of contemporary American environmental and social discussions. But what's even more interesting is how social science and contemporary journalistic and artistic expression have developed parallel strategies for responding to this apparent impasse: the need for numerical information and the difficulty that the human mind has in attaching visceral, emotional meaning to numbers.

In the past two decades, cognitive science has increasingly come to support the claim that we, as a species, think best when we allow numbers and narratives, abstract information and experiential discourse, to interact, to work together. Psychologist Seymour Epstein, in the article "Integration of the Cognitive and the Psychodynamic Unconscious" (1994), argues that humans apprehend reality, including risk and benefit, by employing two interactive modes of processing information: the deliberative, logical, evidence-based "rational system" (known as System 2) and the "experiential system" (called System 1), which encodes reality in images, metaphors, and narratives associated with feelings, with affect. In other words, we need numbers and we need nerves.

In recent years, many writers have corroborated the findings of cognitive science, expressing their frustration at the numbing effects of numerical discourse. In an essay called "The Blood Root of Art," published in his 1996 volume *The Book of Yaak*, Montana author Rick Bass gets right to the heart of this discussion, stating, "The numbers are important, and yet they are not everything. . . . We quickly grow numb to the facts and the math" (p. 87). Yet Bass also frets in this essay about the possible inadequacy of art, of language, for the communication of solid information that might have the power to sway government and corporate officials away from excessive harvesting of natural resources, the destructions of wild places and nearby communities. He writes: "I had . . . meant for this whole essay to be numbers, a landslide of numbers, like brittle talus. But I cannot tolerate them at present. There is a space in me this short winter day that cries out for words" (p. 93). There is a space in all people, even in the scientists and economists whose daily currency is the worldview we call "quantification," that "cries out for words," and for images and stories, for the discourse of emotion. What is the function of language—chiefly, "narrative" language—in helping us, scientists and laypeople alike, appreciate the meaning of society's quandaries?

Over time, we have noted the emphasis that both social science and literature have placed on emotion and the language of story in the apprehension and communication of social and environmental issues. We have repeatedly observed the parallels between writers' intuitive understanding of human psychology and the empirical findings of contemporary psychologists. Our conversations, as a psychologist and a literary critic, inspired us to embark upon a father-and-son collaboration, joining forces to explore the place where our professional interests coincide. We believe that scientists, activists, and members of the public who wish to communicate important ideas about social and environmental issues will bolster the power of their own language by understanding the psychological complexities inherent in apprehending and transmitting quantitative information without succumbing to numerical numbness.

∽

Take a look at the images in Figure 0.1 of candles flickering near a work of art.

These images, taken from a six-minute documentary film on risk perception made by students in a University of Oregon film course, illustrate a phenomenon we describe as "the psychophysics of brightness." Think of each candle as representing an individual human life and the brightness of the scene illuminated by that candle's light as analogous to the value of life. The dark scene of the first image is clearly brightened by the first candle. The second candle adds noticeably to the brightness, but not to the degree that the first candle did. The third image shows thirty candles. When the thirty-first candle is added in the fourth image, there is no noticeable change in illumination. Just as the eye loses sensitivity to changes as the brightness of a scene increases, research on *psychophysical numbing*, described later in

FIGURE 0.1 The psychophysics of brightness—and valuation of human life. Courtesy of Aflleje, Foss, and Palfreman, University of Oregon documentary film 2008.

this book, shows that the value of a human life decreases similarly against a backdrop of an increasing number of lives. The very first life at risk is enormously important. But we feel very little difference in thinking about the possible loss of eighty-eight lives rather than eighty-seven. In some circumstances we fall prey to *compassion fade,* actually becoming less concerned and less prone to take appropriate action as the number of lives at stake increases. This desensitization or numbing occurs when we contemplate numerical information about cancer clusters, casualties of war, environmental change, and a host of other phenomena that crowd the headlines of today's news publications. In her popular writing textbook *The Passionate, Accurate Story* (1990), Carol Bly corroborates this idea by referring to "the psychological law: only one thing can be imagined at one time" (p. 172). The answer for writers, she says, is to "have *as few plurals as possible*" (p. 173). But what if writers hope to convey and invest with meaning the vast processes of the world that call for our attention and engagement?

In Part I of this book, we describe psychological tendencies, such as psychic numbing, that are profoundly relevant to our efforts, conscious or not, to appreciate everyday information expressed quantitatively. The implications of such work, often unspoken, are momentous: if we do not come to terms with these tendencies, we will not achieve the sensitivity required to make careful judgments, as individual citizens or as societies, about some of the most vital concerns of the day. Even more worrisome, perhaps, is the possibility that the desensitizing inundation of vaguely worrisome information will result in (or continue the ongoing trend of) a collective shutting down of compassion that will be difficult to overcome. Perhaps the first thing to realize, however, is that we are all, to some degree, "innumerate." Even the most mathematically gifted human beings are psychologically limited when it comes to attaching feeling to numerical information. The ability to sense the meaning of quantitative information does not come down to computational talent. When Annie Dillard describes a fabulous emotional calculus by way of which we might multiply the intricacies of the human individual by the number representing the current population of China—or, for that matter, tiny Pitcairn Island (population fifty-six)—she is gesturing toward an impossible cognitive task. But one of our essential ideas in this book is that understanding how the human mind works when faced with quantitative information enables us to better counteract our innate insensitivity to certain kinds of information and to better compose multidimensional communication strategies that will be salient for our own readers, listeners, and viewers.

We also learn from the studies below, and from the literary and visual examples elsewhere in this book, that the ability to communicate numerical information effectively, sometimes by sidestepping collective information and emphasizing individual examples, is a way to empower audiences as engaged citizens. Instead of numbing audiences with blizzards of nerveless information, skilled communicators can navigate accurately and vividly between large-scale phenomena and small-scale illustrations, between the remote and the proximate. The purpose of such discourse, of course, is to foster audience *attachment* to the issues and phenomena being described, and crucial to the formation of attachment are *proximity* and *scale*. Rhetorician Matthew J. Newcomb, in a 2010 article titled "Feeling the Vulgarity of Numbers," points out the complicated role of statistics in communicating information about the Biafra crisis of the 1960s and the Rwandan genocide of the 1990s, concluding that numbers can be both empowering and dreadfully desensitizing. He uses the term "vulgar statistics" to describe data about tragic phenomena that trigger both emotive responses (affect) and a sense of helplessness among audiences. What's particularly needed, he finds, is a way to bring together "the global and the individual" (the abstract understanding of the situation in question and a sense of attachment to individuals who are suffering or experiencing the crisis).

For some scholars, such as Susanne Kaul and David Kim, the editors of *Imagining Human Rights* (2015), the goals of human rights, social justice, and greater international cooperation may be achieved by exploring how the *imagination* functions in moral, political, and aesthetic contexts, among others. The present volume, too, touches on not only the perception and processing of information, but also the imaginary expansion of this information in pursuit of "meaning." In this sense, "meaning" comes to indicate a kind of emotional and informational equilibrium, whereby we feel an emotional reaction to information we have gathered—in many cases, emotion prompted by information (not only abstract information, but information that comes to us by way of images, stories, and experiences) leads us, in turn, to imagine actions we might take, actions in the form of thoughts, expression, and sometimes direct intervention. Such actions are "meaningful" to the extent that they constitute emotional and moral gestures somehow equivalent to the informational prompts.

A recurrent theme in several of the scholarly and literary writings that follow is the problem of human empathy—empathy toward other human beings and empathy toward others more generally. What habits of mind and expression obstruct or support empathetic reaches of the human imagination? Some might argue that without the ability to care for someone or something other than ourselves, human beings are not fully human. And yet, when faced with the need to empathize with numerous beings worthy of our concern, the human ability to feel compassion tends to diminish. Psychological, philosophical, journalistic, and artistic analyses of this problem are central to the numbers and nerves project.

The reason to be aware of these tendencies of the human mind, these potential limitations, is to develop ways of supplementing the status quo of technical, journalistic, and other categories of communication, particularly in situations that seem to call for numbers, for numerical language. We are certainly not proposing that quantitative forms of expression must be avoided altogether—to do so would be to nullify the evidential force of data. But in order to make the data *mean* something (and perhaps even to *count* for something), it seems vital that quantitative discourse be complemented with other modes, such as story and image, which so forcefully inspire human audiences and shape our moral compass. Many of the crises that face individual societies and that challenge all of humanity today are either preventable or correctable. In other words, we hope in this project not merely to describe a static condition by which the human mind is ill suited to comprehend the numbing complexities of the modern world. Instead, we offer these inquiries into the nature of our responses to numbers as a path toward intervention. Some of the research offered in the following pages was inspired by the failures of existing laws and public policies to compensate adequately for how the mind struggles to comprehend social and environmental crises. This research highlights the need for further efforts in the areas of law and policy in order to overcome major problems resulting from this lack of comprehension.

∼

We have organized the material that follows into three broad categories, hoping to clarify the parallel concerns and insights among social scientists (Part I) and humanities scholars, journalists, and artists (Part II), and to show the diverse range of contemporary issues often represented with "numbers" but calling out for "nerves." Part I includes Robert Jay Lifton and

Greg Mitchell's overarching discussion of our contemporary era, a time of vast social and environmental change and crisis, as an "age of numbing," much of which can be attributed to the meta-human scale of the current challenges. The phenomenon of psychic numbing is related to the psychology of efficacy and pseudoinefficacy, which psychologists and social activists have applied to a variety of real-world contexts; another key psychological concept, the "prominence effect," helps explain why individual and collective action often fails to match the values people espouse. The contexts presented in these articles include such issues as genocide, the use of natural resources, and policy decisions concerning public health. Paul Slovic, Daniel Västfjäll, Marcus Mayorga, and Paul Farmer consider the psychological and ethical dimensions of these issues in their essays in this section of the book.

While Part I focuses on social and psychological perspectives on sensitivity and meaning, Part II seeks to demonstrate narrative, analytical, and visual strategies for prompting sensitivity and meaning. Many of the articles in this section offer analyses of how humans respond to numerical information, but there is also a particularly concrete emphasis on *strategies* for overcoming our insensitivity to important phenomena—strategies in the classroom, the lecture hall, and the pages of books, newspapers, and magazines. Nicholas D. Kristof's *New York Times* columns help bridge the psychological and narrative sections of this project, demonstrating how awareness of the human tendency to experience psychic numbing might be overcome by strategic use of story and image focusing on individual examples. His two articles make compelling use of narrative in the context of the Darfur genocide and recent famine in the eastern Congo as a result of civil war—and show "the power of one." Landscape architect Kenneth Helphand explores the spatial and visual display of complex information in his essay, focusing on various sensory dimensions of meaning, particularly with regard to memorial sites. Ironically, even the sadness and bitterness associated with war and genocide can erode toward numbness when we try to fathom large numbers of casualties and victims, so artists, urban planners, and others have resorted to extraordinary strategies for instilling such numbers with visceral meaning. Annie Dillard's essay, which later became part of her 1999 book *For the Time Being*, also explores the psychology of numbers by asking, mostly through narrative examples, how meaning attaches itself to information or slides off the glass walls of abstract statistics. Scott Slovic, working

with two examples of climate change fiction, uses the medium of li
criticism to question narrative discourse as an inevitably trustworthy alternative to technical or quantitative discourse in the context of large-scale
environmental phenomena such as climate change. These pieces in Part II
directly discuss numbers and alternative modes of processing and communicating information.

Part II also offers several powerful demonstrations of nonquantitative
treatments of large-scale issues. Terry Tempest Williams's essay on the
"healing" of Rwanda in the aftermath of the genocide uses the mosaic trope
from the visual arts as a metaphor for her collage-like narrative style. Much
of Bill McKibben's writing, in works ranging from *The End of Nature* to
The Age of Missing Information, highlights the telescopic alternation of personal, narrative information with abstract, quantitative information in order
to approach highly technical and politically sensitive topics ranging from
climate change to human population. McKibben's essay in this book, however, shows how words and numbers can work in concert with each other
to educate the public and mobilize action on complex issues—numbers can
crystallize complex ideas, while words are needed to unpack the numbers
and offer context and human salience. Rick Bass also weaves together data
and emotional plea in considering the varieties of language needed to touch
a nerve among voters and decision makers with regard to logging the forests of northwestern Montana, and this weaving together of oppositional
modes of discourse highlights the ultimate complementarity of numbers
and nerves. As thinkers going back to Immanuel Kant have realized, the
human mind consists of rational and extra-rational dimensions. Numerical
data and other forms of rational analysis, in tandem with emotional stories
and arresting images, may be our best way of assessing the meaning of the
conditions and situations we find ourselves facing in our individual lives
and as larger communities.

This balanced or multidimensional approach to communicating "data"
accords well with the thinking of statistical evidence guru Edward Tufte,
whose books include *The Visual Display of Quantitative Information* (1983)
and *Envisioning Information* (1990). In his 2006 publication titled *Beautiful
Evidence*, Tufte states: "The world to be explained is indifferent to scholarly specialization by type of evidence, methodology, or disciplinary field. A
deeper understanding of human behavior may well result from integrating
a diversity of evidence, *whatever it takes to explain something*" (p. 131). While

Tufte's emphasis appears to be on the appropriate description of the world's complexities, what we hope to show in the materials collected here is how writers and artists intuitively appreciate the human mind's tendencies and limitations in apprehending quantitative information—the numerical discourse often used to describe phenomena, large and small, that elude sensory apprehension. From Kristof to Bass, we find that writers frequently rely on an "integrative," comprehensive approach to communication, one that provides context and tangibility for quantitative abstractions. In his textbook *Writing Naturally: A Down-to-Earth Guide to Nature Writing* (2001), David Petersen underscores this idea, stating simply, "'Wholeness of outlook.' *That's* the ticket" (p. 6). Literary critic Heather Houser strikes a similar theme in her essay on "managing information" in contemporary literature and visual art, noting that we have arrived at a state of "information saturation" during the second decade of the twenty-first century. She observes: "No one cultural form shoulders the full burden of disseminating information to media consumers today. In movies and maps, verse and visualizations, artists experiment with the aesthetics of information management as an end in itself and as a spur to social, political, and environmental critique" (Houser, 2014, p. 742). We hope our commentary and examples in this book help to illuminate the significance of such "diversity of evidence," "wholeness," and experimentation with "the aesthetics of information management" across a range of media—and will also inspire and facilitate socially engaged communication in contexts where numerical information might otherwise inhibit public attention and concern.

Finally, in Part III, we offer four in-depth interviews with prominent writers, artists, and social activists from Mexico, India, and the United States, experts in the communication of sensitive and even volatile information to the general public, who have thought deeply about the issues explored in this book. Homero and Betty Aridjis, the founders of El Grupo de los Cien (the Group of 100), an organization of environmentally concerned scientists and artists in Mexico, make it clear that the key to their use of technical information is to find points of "emotional connection" and to confront the moral dimension of the information they present, from their own perspectives. Information is not morally neutral, and teasing out their own moral interpretation of information is not merely a rhetorical strategy (a way of bringing readers into agreement with them) but a means of triggering readers' interest and engagement with particular issues, such as air pollution, degradation of gray whale breeding waters, and deforestation of the mountains where monarch butterflies overwinter.

Vandana Shiva, the New Delhi–based leader of the environmental justice organization Navdanya, gets right to the heart of this book when she claims that "quantification is the anesthesia of destruction" and describes her own efforts, as a physicist by training, to deconstruct numbers and place them in a meaningful context that will "touch people's hearts." She emphasizes her use of her own voice "as a human being" as a vital strategy for injecting heartfelt import into her social arguments.

American science journalist and activist Sandra Steingraber, who has both a master's degree in poetry and a doctorate in biology, shares Shiva's familiarity with natural science and her tendency to use personal narrative, a central technique for humanizing potentially abstract, dull, and confrontational topics. In her interview statements, Steingraber discusses not only what she learned about writing in the process of producing her books *Living Downstream* and *Having Faith*, both of which concern the human health effects of environmental contamination, but also the moral imperative for science writers to spur social change. She offers nuts-and-bolts suggestions for science writers regarding the use or avoidance of technical jargon and statistical information—and the use of humor—in writing for the general public.

An avant-garde form of visual sleight of hand occurs in photographer and digital artist Chris Jordan's meticulous arrangement of common consumer items, from plastic cups to cell phones, as a way of commenting on North American habits of consumption. Jordan's experimentation with the visual experience of "scale" (from the big picture seen at a distance to the close-up revelation of individual objects within the collective) promotes a unique experience of introspection that energizes the meaning of consumption-related data. In the interview for this book, he also explains the "trans-scalar imaginary," a flexible mode of thought that transits between small and large, individual and many, as a cognitive process or condition toward which we should aspire in order to apprehend the meaning of information, and which his own work coaches viewers to accomplish.

In the Introduction to *Environmental Communication and the Public Sphere* (2013), Robert Cox argues that how we communicate ideas about the world fundamentally influences how we perceive the world. Many laypeople and policy makers assume that with accurate information, it should be possible to make good decisions as individuals and as communities about issues pertinent to social and environmental well-being. However, the form in which we receive information profoundly affects our understanding of that "data" and our determination of its relevance, importance, and urgency. Cox writes:

> Why communication? . . . Our understanding of the environment, our efforts to alert, educate, or persuade others, and our ability to work together can't be separated from the need to communicate with others. Indeed, our language, visual images, and modes of interacting with others influence our most basic perceptions of the world and what we understand to be a problem itself. (p. 1)

Although he does not explicitly discuss the challenge of communicating— or translating—numerical information into human terms, Cox makes it clear with a variety of environmental examples that how we package perceptions and beliefs makes all the difference in capturing the attention and interest of audiences.

The section of Cox's book devoted to "narrative framing" is particularly relevant to our focus on meaningful communication of complex, quantitative ideas in this volume, but the author and other communication specialists focus primarily on the idea of "interest" rather than on the intrinsic accessibility, or comprehensibility, of information when presented in the form of numbers. M. Jimmie Killingsworth and Jacqueline S. Palmer, for instance, in their foundational work *Ecospeak: Rhetoric and Environmental Politics in America* (1992), offer a lengthy chapter devoted to "Transformations of Scientific Discourse in the News Media," but their focus is on questions of scientific objectivity, the intrusion of "values" into the processes of conducting and communicating science, and what it takes to capture media attention (and, by extension, the attention of the reading public). Killingsworth and Palmer state, at one point, "Human interest is the leading factor in determining what scientific activities will be covered as big stories" (p. 134). In other words, this elusive "human interest" factor, which is never quite defined in *Ecospeak*, is apparently essential in bringing technical and quantitative information (about any topic) to the attention of audiences. Presumably, making information interesting to human audiences involves revealing the relevance of the material to salient human experiences and concerns. But capturing the attention of readers and listeners is not the same thing as enabling audiences to capture the meaning of such material—and research suggests the latter part of the process may be the most challenging.

Introducing a section in *Environmental Communication and the Public Sphere* devoted to narrative framing in journalism, Robert Cox states that "news media communicate not only facts about the environment but also wider frames or guides for understanding and making sense of these facts." He continues by pointing out that there is a current "focus on such sense-making or frames to help explain the role of news reporting in organizing our experiences of the world and our relationships to the environment" (p. 164). When scholars of environmental and other socially relevant modes of communication speak of "making sense" of information, they are often referring specifically to the challenge of securing attention to complex and elusive phenomena, not to the challenge of bringing meaning to information about such phenomena. In this book, however, we seek to explore the use of specific communication strategies both to attract audiences' interest/attention and to facilitate the apprehension of ideas and feelings associated with various topics.

Awareness of the intrinsic human struggle to balance reason and emotion is nothing new. Scholars of persuasive language look all the way back to the fourth century B.C., to Aristotle's *Rhetoric*, which lists ethos, pathos, and logos as the building blocks of argumentation. "Ethos" emphasizes the authority of the speaker, while "logos" highlights the logical arrangement of information—both of these ideas correspond to the modern use of technical and numerical information and the appeal to readers' and listeners' rational modes of thinking. "Pathos," on the other hand, suggests Aristotle's appreciation of the power of emotional appeal as a way of reaching and convincing audiences to think in particular ways. It is commonplace for rhetoricians, discourse analysts, and even literary and film critics to talk about the reliance on particular Aristotelian modes of communication in specific contexts or texts. But the quest to strike appropriate balances between ethos, pathos, and logos—or reason and emotion—has proven to be an elusive challenge; the significance of this process has only increased over time.

In the eighteenth century, German philosopher Immanuel Kant took on this basic aspect of human cognition in one of his major works, *Critique of Pure Reason* (1781), which sought to explain how human beings understand

fundamental aspects of reality, such as space-time and cause-effect, by relying on both reason and experience. Writing in the wake of Western culture's
new prioritizing of quantitative information as the ultimate "measure of
reality," Kant nonetheless understood the limitations of reason as an exclu-
sive cognitive tool for understanding the world. He thus anticipated the
work of twentieth- and twenty-first-century psychologists, who have refined
our understanding of the mental processes, or systems, that enable us to
grasp the meaning of our own lives and the complex phenomena, large and
small, that coexist with us in the world. For Kant and for modern psychologists and writers, the balance of reason and emotion is not merely a matter
of persuasive communication, but an underlying problem of apprehension,
a crucial aspect of our ability—and often, our inability—to perceive and
understand what's happening around us. Readers of this book will gain
familiarity with psychological descriptions of important thought processes
that dictate our species' apprehension and communication of information.

So why does this matter? Most of us fancy ourselves to be "good people"—
conscious and conscientious, eager to help out when we become aware of
situations where we have the ability to make positive contributions. But we
tend to feel numbed by the sheer bombardment of information we receive
on a daily basis. The psychological concepts and demonstrations of scholarly, journalistic, and artistic engagement offered in this book will, we hope,
enable readers to feel less daunted by information overload—and, particularly, by the overload of quantitative information. Knowing what's happening in our own minds is a form of empowerment. Even being able to describe
our condition with terms like "psychic numbing," "pseudoinefficacy," "the
prominence effect, " or "the asymmetry of trust" enables us to push back
against such cognitive tendencies. Without necessarily having access to the
formal concepts of contemporary psychology, the writers and artists included
in the book have developed strategies for perceiving and engaging with
situations in the world that have drawn their attention. Just as the psychological articles in this book empower us by helping to explain why we think
as we do, the communication balancing acts offered here show how some
of our leading writers have sought to compute what Polish poet Zbigniew
Herbert has called "the arithmetic of compassion."

One of the first steps we took in developing this collection of responses to
the numbers-and-nerves phenomenon was to contemplate Herbert's 1974

poem "Mr Cogito Reads the Newspaper." We began our cross-disciplinary discussion of this poem informally, merely chatting about the psychological insight of this literary work. Eventually we produced this layered reading of the text:

On the first page
> ss: Indicates importance.

a report of the killing of 120 soldiers
> ss: But the statement is perfunctory, vague—a summary, not an image. Devoid of emotion.

the war lasted a long time
> ps: Duration leads to normalization and accommodation.

you could get used to it
> ps: Thus loss of attention.
> ss: Use of pronoun "you" engages and challenges the reader—"getting used" to something implies that the poem is concerned with lack of sensitivity.

close alongside
> ss: Refers to location on front page, but also implies vivid proximity— a kind of emotional proximity to the story.

the news of a sensational crime
> ps: High emotion.
> ss: Could the numbingly dispassionate presentation of 120 deaths also be a kind of informational crime?

with a portrait of the murderer
> ps: An individual.
> ss: The word "portrait" also refers to visual representation/information. This poem is strikingly devoid of visual imagery—its absence is a kind of experiment in how information takes on meaning or loses meaning when deprived of a visual (or sensory) dimension.

the eye of Mr Cogito
> ss: Emphasis on the eye—on the visual/sensory process of taking in information—yet there is nothing visual about the representation of the many dead soldiers.

slips indifferently
> ps: Without attention or feeling.

over the soldiers' hecatomb

ss: Strange word—"hecatomb"—which refers to ceremonial slaughter of one hundred oxen in ancient Greece/Rome, so there is a gap between Cogito's indifference and the ritual care of the traditional hecatomb.

to plunge with delight

ps: The strange positive feeling linked to curiosity and excitement.

ss: Again, an emotional slippage, implying Cogito's failure of response, but inciting the reader's compensatory response (we feel what we think Cogito *should be* feeling).

into the description of everyday horror

ps: Focused attention—"everyday" means it is common and one can understand and relate to it.

ss: The phrase "everyday horror" could also imply a different sort of numbness that results from familiarity and routineness.

a thirty-year-old farm labourer

ps: Vivid imagery triggering strong feelings.

ss: The relative power of this little summary results largely from its juxtaposition with the less potent summary of the 120 soldiers—even a vague statement of a small-scale phenomenon becomes more interesting when placed side by side with a large-scale phenomenon.

under the stress of nervous depression
killed his wife
and two small children

ps: Multiple victims unitized as a family to produce singularity effect (the power of one).

ss: This mini-narrative is rather abstract and non-sensory, but nonetheless it is more vivid in our imaginations than the mention of the 120 soldiers—and we feel an interest here because this information is individualized and thus apprehensible.

it is described with precision

ps: Again details creating vivid imagery.

the course of the murder
the position of the bodies
and other details

ss: Odd that this stanza mentions the types of information offered in the news story, but does not really give the details—the language here is strangely analytical, not narrative, not traditionally poetic.

for 120 dead

ss: Repetition of the large number in order to juxtapose the many with the few and to create a symmetrical structure for the poem—start with the large number, end with the large number. This symmetry is a kind of "map," a pattern that gives a kind of satisfying "meaning" to the reader.

you search on a map in vain

ps: Hard to relate to, connect, or understand this number 120.

ss: Invoking the idea of a map suggests that our effort to make sense of numerical information (120 soldiers, one thirty-year-old, one wife, two small children) is a process of orientation. Without being able to reduce the many to the few, we are essentially lost—we may possess information, but be without meaning.

too great a distance

ps: Distance is central to loss of understanding, connectedness, and feeling.

ss: Again, a geographical idea (extending the image of the map).

covers them like a jungle

ps: Great line.

ss: And one that invokes vision, as above, suggesting that lack of meaning (information in the form of large numbers) is akin to blindness, like being consumed by a jungle's dense foliage.

they don't speak to the imagination

ps: Another important line; imagination (imagery) needs to be present and linked to feelings to achieve meaningfulness.

ss: But, strangely, this poem is relatively lacking in vivid imagery, yet even non-detailed individuals (or small numbers, as in "two small children") appear vivid by comparison with large-numbered information ("120 soldiers").

there are too many of them

ps: Psychic numbing as numbers increase.

the numeral zero at the end
changes them into an abstraction

ps: Great lines.

ss: But it's not only the numeral zero at the end that matters, as we learn from recent psychological studies: the two in the middle ("120") also transforms a vivid individual into a vague dozen, which is an abstraction that defies the imagination.

a subject for meditation:

> PS: Slow, deliberate thinking needed rather than fast, intuitive thinking, which does not appreciate scale.

the arithmetic of compassion

> PS: The arithmetic of compassion doesn't follow the rational calculus of arithmetic unless you free yourself from fast, shallow impressions and think carefully about the reality of the event. Leaving the last line without a finishing period keeps it open to meditation.

> SS: The power of this concluding phrase comes from the fact that it's an apparent oxymoron, a paradox, a koan (which is a Buddhist prompt for meditation). We assume that compassion is essentially nonquantitative, requiring the mind of the perceiver to contemplate poignant specificities. When the poet calls for meditation on "the arithmetic of compassion," we realize he is suggesting that compassion somehow requires us to think both non-arithmetically and quantitatively, to *meditate* about an arithmetic phenomenon.

In a sense, this entire book constitutes an extension of our commentary on Zbigniew Herbert's poem, a series of essays, some by us and others by kindred spirits, meditating on "the arithmetic of compassion"—how we come to care about that which is presented to us in the form of quantitative information or which, in other ways, defies our human-scale sensory apparatus and cognitive processes.

～

Much of this project evolved during morning runs along the sun-speckled bike paths of Sunriver, Oregon, where we told each other stories of travels and conferences and research projects. Over time, we came to realize that we were telling similar stories, but in the separate vocabularies of psychology and literature. We hope this collection of diverse writings from empirical social science and experiential literature and journalism will reveal the fundamental unanimity among these writers regarding the importance of coming to terms with the strengths and limitations of numerical discourse in our public discussions of contemporary issues.

The process of dispersing to the general public new perspectives on socially and ecologically crucial topics requires the development of new modes of discourse—new ways of describing experience, new strategies for translating statistics into stories, new tools for contextualizing data, and new ways of articulating the meaning of both numbers and nerves. We need entire forests as much as we need individual trees, entire species as much as individual birds, intact villages as much as individual refugees fleeing devastation in their homelands and waiting for relief. Numbers are essentially means of describing "the big picture." And stories and images have the power to help us understand large, complex problems that we cannot comprehend through quantitative information alone. This convergence of story, visual image, philosophy, journalism, and psychology suggests the value of collaboration among thinkers in a wide range of disciplines. We are all in this together.

REFERENCES

Bass, R. (1996). The blood root of art. *The book of Yaak*. Boston, MA: Houghton Mifflin.

Bly, C. (1990). *The passionate, accurate story: Making your heart's truth into literature*. Minneapolis, MN: Milkweed Editions.

Cox, R. J. (2013). *Environmental communication and the public sphere* (3rd ed.). Thousand Oaks, CA: Sage.

Crosby, A. W. (1997). *The measure of reality: Quantification in western society, 1250–1600*. New York, NY: Cambridge University Press.

Dillard, A. (1999). *For the time being*. New York, NY: Alfred A. Knopf.

Epstein, S. (1994). Integration of the cognitive and the psychodynamic unconscious. *American Psychologist, 49*, 709–724.

Herbert, Z. (1974/1993). Mr Cogito reads the newspaper. *Mr Cogito*. John Carpenter & Bogdana Carpenter (Trans.). Hopewell, NJ: The Ecco Press.

Houser, H. (2014). Managing information and materiality in *Infinite Jest* and *Running the Numbers*. *American Literary History, 26*, 742–764.

Kant, I. (1781/1999). *Critique of pure reason*. Paul Guyer & Allen W. Wood (Eds. and Trans.). New York, NY: Cambridge University Press.

Kaul, S., & Kim, D. (Eds.). (2015). *Imagining human rights*. Berlin, Germany: Walter de Gruyter.

Killingsworth, M. J., & Palmer, J. S. (1992). *Ecospeak: Rhetoric and environmental politics in America*. Carbondale: Southern Illinois University Press.

Newcomb, M. J. (2010). Feeling the vulgarity of numbers: The Rwandan genocide and the classroom as a site of response to suffering. *JAC, 30*, 175–212.

Petersen, D. (2001). *Writing naturally: A down-to-earth guide to nature writing*. Boulder, CO: Johnson Books.

Pope, C. (2000, January/February). Getting it right. *Sierra, 117*, 40–47.

Slovic, P., Finucane, M. L., Peters, E., & MacGregor, D. G. (2002). The affect heuristic. In T. Gilovich, D. Griffin, & D. Kahneman (Eds.), *Heuristics and biases: The psychology of intuitive judgment* (pp. 397–420). New York, NY: Cambridge University Press.

Tufte, E. (2006). *Beautiful evidence.* Cheshire, CT: Graphics Press.

Weisman, A. (2013). *Countdown: Our last, best hope for a future on Earth?* New York, NY: Little, Brown and Company.

PART I

Social and Psychological Perspectives on Sensitivity and Meaning

Introduction

PAUL SLOVIC AND SCOTT SLOVIC

P ART I LAYS THE FOUNDATION OF THIS BOOK, addressing fundamental social and psychological challenges to understanding the reality of extreme tragic events.

In Chapter 1, Slovic and Västfjäll bring psychic numbing directly to bear on the repeated failure of powerful nations and their citizens to prevent or halt genocide and other mass harm to people and the environment. They draw on the work of Jonathan Haidt (2001), who has articulated the distinction between moral intuition and moral reasoning:

> Moral intuition can be defined as the sudden appearance in consciousness of a moral judgment, including an affective valence (good-bad, like-dislike) without any conscious awareness of having gone through steps of searching, weighing evidence, or inferring a conclusion.
>
> One sees or hears about a social event and one instantly feels approval or disapproval. (p. 818)

Haidt finds that moral intuition comes first and usually dominates moral judgment unless we make an effort to use judgment to critique and, if necessary, override our intuitive feelings (see also Kahneman, 2011).

Slovic and Västfjäll argue that moral intuition is particularly prone to psychic numbing, and thus it misguides us in the face of genocide and other disasters that threaten people and nature on a mass scale. They point to strategies for overcoming this shortcoming, based on creative use of images and narratives, consistent with the work described later in this book. They also argue for the need to design laws and institutions that commit states to respond to mass tragedies rather than being silent witnesses.

Chapter 1 draws on psychological research to show how fast, intuitive thinking, guided by feelings, produces a questionable arithmetic of compassion, where one life plus one life is valued less than two lives and sometimes even less than one life. In Chapter 2, Västfjäll, Slovic, and Mayorga demonstrate another odd and disturbing form of emotional arithmetic. Numbers representing people who are in need but who cannot be helped (or even images of such people) are found to intrude upon and diminish the warm glow of good feeling associated with helping others. The resulting "illusion of inefficacy" thus inhibits assistance that would otherwise be offered. In terms of the arithmetic of compassion (to use Zbigniew Herbert's resonant phrase), this can be seen as allowing an irrelevant negative quantity to be subtracted from (or more likely averaged with) one's positive motivation. Research is needed to explore the potential for eloquent argument, narrative, or visual imagery to counter this insidious illusion and stop it from hijacking the precious commodity that is efficacy. (Later parts of this book, however, do demonstrate that there is a strong feeling among writers and visual artists that their literary and artistic efforts to overcome the numbing and demotivating effects of numerical information may well bear fruit in the form of individual and public action.) In Chapter 3, Slovic introduces "the prominence effect," a concept that helps complete the psychological picture of human responses to complex, values-laden information. The three key concepts here are psychic numbing, pseudoinefficacy, and the prominence effect.

In his landmark book *Death in Life,* Robert Jay Lifton coined the term "psychic numbing" to describe the diminished capacity to feel that enveloped survivors and aid workers after the bombing in Hiroshima. Such insensitivity has the benefit of defending the mind from being overwhelmed by the dreadful and unimaginable images confronting it. In Chapter 4, Lifton and Mitchell extend psychic numbing to those who created and used the bomb, aided by intentional censorship and cover-up to ward off feelings of guilt. Lifton and Mitchell point to this strategic blocking of emotion as enabling numbing in the face of other mass atrocities such as genocide.

Paul Farmer, renowned for his heroic efforts to bring medical care to the destitute poor in rural Haiti, contemplates the harm caused by social and economic inequities that bring danger, disease, and death to tens of millions of people (Chapter 5). Recognizing that numbers often lack the ability to shock or move us, he looks to stories and images as powerful motivators of action against this structural violence. But much as Slovic and Västfjäll call for better laws and institutions to overcome the deficiencies of unstable moral emotions, Farmer cautions against relying on the "politics of pity" and argues for policies that respect the rights of the poor to health care, clean water, education, and other basic entitlements. Serious social ills, he concludes, require in-depth analyses, "troves of attention."

REFERENCES

Haidt, J. (2001). The emotional dog and its rational tail: A social intuitionist approach to moral judgment. *Psychological Review, 108,* 814–834.

Kahneman, D. (2011). *Thinking, fast and slow.* New York, NY: Farrar, Straus and Giroux.

Lifton, R. J. (1968). *Death in life: Survivors of Hiroshima.* New York, NY: Random House.

CHAPTER 1

The More Who Die, the Less We Care

Psychic Numbing and Genocide

PAUL SLOVIC AND DANIEL VÄSTFJÄLL

A DEFINING ELEMENT OF CATASTROPHES is the magnitude of their harmful consequences. To help societies prevent or mitigate damage from catastrophes, immense effort and technological sophistication are often employed to assess and communicate the size and scope of potential or actual losses. This effort assumes that people can understand the resulting numbers and act on them appropriately.

However, recent behavioral research casts doubt on this fundamental assumption. Many people do not understand large numbers. Indeed, large numbers have been found to lack meaning and to be underweighted in decisions unless they convey affect (feeling). This creates a paradox that rational models of decision making fail to represent. On the one hand, we respond strongly to aid a single individual in need. On the other hand, we often fail to prevent mass tragedies—such as genocide—or take appropriate measures to reduce potential losses from natural disasters. We believe this occurs, in part, because as numbers get larger and larger, we become insensitive; numbers fail to trigger the emotion or feeling necessary to motivate action.

We shall address this problem of insensitivity to mass tragedy by identifying certain circumstances in which it compromises the rationality of our actions and by pointing briefly to strategies that might lessen or overcome this problem.

Background and Theory: The Importance of Affect

Risk management in the modern world relies on two forms of thinking. Risk as feelings refers to our instinctive and intuitive reactions to danger. Risk as analysis brings logic, reason, quantification, and deliberation to bear on hazard management. Compared with analysis, reliance on feelings tends to be a quicker, easier, and more efficient way to navigate in a complex, uncertain, and dangerous world. Hence, it is essential to rational behavior. Yet it sometimes misleads us. In such circumstances we need to ensure that reason and analysis also are employed.

Although the visceral emotion of fear certainly plays a role in risk as feelings, we focus here on the faint whisper of emotion called "affect." As used here, affect refers to specific feelings of "goodness" or "badness" experienced with or without conscious awareness. Positive and negative feelings occur rapidly and automatically; note how quickly you sense the feelings associated with the word "joy" or the word "hate." A large research literature in psychology documents the importance of affect in (1) conveying meaning upon information and (2) motivating behavior. Without affect, information lacks meaning and will not be used in judgment and decision making.

Facing Catastrophic Loss of Life

Risk as feelings is clearly rational, employing imagery and affect in remarkably accurate and efficient ways. But this way of responding to risk has a darker, nonrational side. Affect is a compass that may misguide us in important ways. Particularly problematic is the difficulty of comprehending the meaning of catastrophic losses of life when relying on feelings. Research reviewed below shows that disaster statistics, no matter how large the numbers, lack emotion or feeling. As a result, they fail to convey the true meaning of such calamities and they fail to motivate proper action to prevent them.

The psychological factors underlying insensitivity to large-scale losses of human lives apply to catastrophic harm resulting from human malevolence, natural disasters, environmental degradation, and technological accidents. In particular, the psychological account described here can explain, in part, our failure to respond to the diffuse and seemingly distant threat posed by global warming as well as the threat posed by the presence of nuclear weaponry. Similar insensitivity may also underlie our failure to respond adequately to problems of famine, poverty, and disease afflicting large numbers of people around the world and even in our own backyard.

Genocide and Mass Atrocities: The Scope of the Problem

Over the past century the world has been shocked to learn of many horrific incidents of mass collective violence. The Holocaust of World War II stands out and, in recent years, atrocities in Rwanda, the Balkans, and Darfur have gained the world's attention. Today, humanitarian catastrophes in Syria and the Middle East are in the news.

Yet, these memorable cases are only a small part of the problem, as shown in Table 1.1. Mass atrocities, defined as the intended death of at least one thousand noncombatants from a distinct group in a period of sustained violence (Ulfelder & Valentino, 2008), are not rare. Since 1900, 201 distinct cases resulted in an estimated eighty-four million fatalities, an average of about 470,000 each! The atrocities death toll is comparable to that from interstate wars and vastly greater than that from terrorism.

In addition to the stunning frequency and scale of mass atrocities, what stands out in historical accounts of these abuses is the inaction of bystanders. In her prizewinning book *A Problem From Hell: America and the Age of Genocide,* Samantha Power documented the inadequacy of the U.S. government's response to numerous genocides dating back to 1915 (Power, 2003). She concluded: "No U.S. president has ever made genocide a priority and no U.S. president has ever suffered politically for his indifference to its occurrence. It is thus no coincidence that genocide rages on" (Power, 2003, p. xxi).

TABLE 1.1 Comparative measures of seriousness for state-sponsored mass atrocities (genocides and mass killings), intrastate and interstate wars, and terrorism.

| | | | Seriousness | |
Conflict Type	Number of Distinct Cases	Time Period	Total Estimated Fatalities for the Cases	Estimated Fatalities per Case
Mass Atrocities	201	1900–2012	84,183,410	470,298
Interstate Wars	66	1900–2007	30,698,060	465,122
Interstate Wars Excluding WW I and WW II	64	1900–2007	5,485,122	85,705
Intrastate Wars	228	1900–2007	5,469,738	28,192
Terrorism (Domestic and International)	113,113	1970–2012	241,480	2

SOURCE: Anderton, C. H. (2016). Datasets and trends of genocide, mass killing, and other civilian atrocities. In C. H. Anderton (Ed.), *Economic aspects of genocide, mass atrocities, and their prevention* (Table 3.5). New York, NY: Oxford University Press. By permission of Oxford University Press, USA.

Nowhere is the problem of apathy and inaction more starkly apparent than in the Darfur region of western Sudan. Since February 2003, hundreds of thousands of people in Darfur have been murdered by government-supported militias, and millions have been forced to flee their burned-out villages for the dubious safety of refugee camps. This has been well documented. And yet the world looks away.

The United Nations (UN) General Assembly adopted the Convention on the Prevention and Punishment of the Crime of Genocide in 1948 in the hope that "never again" would there be such odious crimes against humanity as occurred during the Holocaust of World War II. Eventually, some 140 states would ratify the genocide convention, yet it has been invoked infrequently to prevent a potential attack or halt an ongoing massacre. Darfur has shone a particularly harsh light on the failures to intervene in genocide. As Richard Just (2008) has observed,

> We are awash in information about Darfur. . . . No genocide has ever been so thoroughly documented while it was taking place . . . but the genocide continues. We document what we do not stop. The truth does not set anybody free. . . . How could we have known so much and done so little? (pp. 36, 38)

Affect, Analysis, and the Value of Human Lives

This brings us to a crucial question: How should we value the saving of human lives? An analytic answer would look to basic principles or fundamental values for guidance. For example, Article 1 of the Universal Declaration of Human Rights asserts that "all human beings are born free and equal in dignity and rights."[1] We might infer from this the conclusion that every human life is of equal value. If so, then—applying a rational calculation—the value of saving N lives is N times the value of saving one life, as represented by the linear function in Figure 1.1a.

An argument can also be made for judging large losses of life to be disproportionately more serious because they threaten the social fabric and viability of a group or community (see Figure 1.1b). Debate can be had at the margins over whether one should assign greater value to younger people versus older people, or whether governments have a duty to give more weight to the lives of their own people, and so on, but a perspective approximating the equality of human lives is rather uncontroversial.

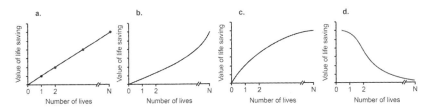

FIGURE 1.1 Normative models where (a) every life is of equal value and (b) large losses threaten group or societal survivability and descriptive models of (c) psychophysical numbing and (d) the collapse of compassion.

How do we actually value human lives? Research provides evidence in support of two descriptive models linked to affect and intuitive thinking that reflect values for lifesaving profoundly different from those depicted in the normative (rational) models shown in Figures 1.1a and 1.1b. Both of these descriptive models demonstrate responses that are insensitive to large losses of human life, consistent with apathy toward genocide.

The Psychophysical Model

There is considerable evidence that our affective responses and the resulting value we place on saving human lives follow the same sort of psychophysical function that characterizes our diminished sensitivity to changes in a wide range of perceptual and cognitive entities—brightness, loudness, heaviness, and wealth—as their underlying magnitudes increase.

As psychophysical research indicates, constant increases in the magnitude of a stimulus typically evoke smaller and smaller changes in response. Applying this principle to the valuing of human life suggests that a form of psychophysical numbing may result from our inability to appreciate losses of life as they become larger. The function in Figure 1.1c represents a value structure in which the importance of saving one life is great when it is the first, or only, life saved but diminishes as the total number of lives at risk increases. Thus, psychologically, the importance of saving one life pales against the background of a larger threat: we may not "feel" much difference, nor value the difference, between saving eighty-seven lives and saving eighty-eight.

Fetherstonhaugh, Slovic, Johnson, and Friedrich (1997) demonstrated the potential for psychophysical numbing in the context of evaluating people's willingness to fund various lifesaving interventions. In a study involving a hypothetical grant-funding agency, respondents were asked to indicate the number of lives a medical research institute would have to save to merit receipt of a $10 million grant. Nearly two-thirds of the respondents raised their minimum benefit requirements to warrant funding when there was a larger at-risk population, with a median value of nine thousand lives needing to be saved when fifteen thousand were at risk (implicitly valuing each life saved at $1,111), compared with a median of 100,000 lives needing to be saved out of 290,000 at risk (implicitly valuing each life saved at $100). Thus respondents saw saving nine thousand lives in the smaller population as more valuable than saving more than ten times as many lives in the larger population. The same study also found that people were less willing to send aid that would save forty-five hundred lives in Rwandan refugee camps as the size of the camps' at-risk populations increased.

In recent years, vivid images of natural disasters in South Asia and the American Gulf Coast, and stories of individual victims there, brought to us through relentless, courageous, and intimate news coverage, unleashed an outpouring of compassion and humanitarian aid from all over the world. Perhaps there is hope that vivid, personalized media coverage featuring victims could also motivate intervention to halt the killing.

Perhaps. Research demonstrates that people are much more willing to aid identified individuals than unidentified or statistical victims. But a cautionary note comes from a study in which Small, Loewenstein, and Slovic (2007) gave people who had just participated in a paid psychological experiment the opportunity to contribute up to $5 of their earnings to the charity Save the Children. In one condition, respondents were asked to donate money to feed an identified victim, a seven-year-old African girl named Rokia. Respondents in a second group were asked to donate to Rokia, but were also shown statistics of starvation in several African countries—millions in need. Unfortunately, coupling the statistical realities with Rokia's story of need reduced contributions to Rokia by about 40 percent!

Why did this occur? Perhaps the presence of statistics reduced the attention to Rokia essential for establishing the emotional connection necessary to motivate donations. Alternatively, recognition of the millions who would not be helped by one's small donation may have produced negative feelings that inhibited donations. Note the similarity here at the individual level to the failure to help forty-five hundred people in a larger refugee camp, with greater numbers not being helped. The rationality of these responses can be questioned. We should not be deterred from helping one person, or forty-five hundred, just because there are many others we cannot save! (See Chapter 2 for a more extensive discussion of this point, in the context of pseudoinefficacy.)

In sum, research on psychophysical numbing is important because it demonstrates that feelings necessary for motivating lifesaving actions are not congruent with the normative/rational models in Figures 1.1a and 1.1b. The nonlinearity displayed in Figure 1.1c is consistent with the devaluing of incremental loss of life against the background of a large tragedy. It can thus explain why we don't feel any different upon learning that the death toll in Darfur is closer to four hundred thousand than to two hundred thousand. What it does not fully explain, however, is apathy toward genocide, inasmuch as it implies that the response to initial loss of life will be strong and maintained, albeit with diminished sensitivity, as the losses increase. Evidence for a second descriptive model, better suited to explain apathy toward large losses of lives, follows.

The Collapse of Compassion

American writer Annie Dillard (1999) reads in her newspaper the headline "Head-Spinning Numbers Cause Mind to Go Slack." She writes of "compassion fatigue" and asks, "At what number do other individuals blur for me?"[2]

An answer to Dillard's question is beginning to emerge from behavioral research. Studies by social psychologists find that a single individual, unlike a group, is viewed as a psychologically coherent unit. This leads to more extensive processing of information and stronger impressions about individuals than about groups. Consistent with this, a study in Israel found that people tend to feel more distress and compassion and to provide more aid when considering a single identified victim than when considering a group of eight identified victims (Kogut & Ritov, 2005). A follow-up study in Sweden found that people felt less compassion and donated less aid toward a pair of victims than to either individual alone (Västfjäll, Slovic, Mayorga, & Peters, 2014). The blurring that Annie Dillard asked about begins for groups as small as two people.

The insensitivity to lifesaving portrayed by the psychophysical-numbing model is unsettling. But the studies just described suggest an even more disturbing psychological tendency. Our capacity to feel is limited. To the extent that valuation of lifesaving depends on feelings driven by attention or imagery, it might follow the function shown in Figure 1.1d, where the emotion or affective feeling is greatest at $N = 1$ but begins to fade at $N = 2$ and collapses at some higher value of N that becomes simply "a statistic" (Västfjäll et al., 2014). Whereas Robert Jay Lifton (1967) coined the term "psychic numbing" to describe the "turning off" of feeling that enabled rescue workers to function during the horrific aftermath of the Hiroshima bombing, Figure 1.1d depicts a form of psychic numbing that is not beneficial. Rather, it leads to apathy and inaction, consistent with what is seen repeatedly in response to mass murder and genocide.

Perhaps both psychophysical and collapse valuations are activated within the same decision context as the number of lives at risk increases, resulting in a hybrid, inverted-U-shaped function such as that shown in Figure 1.2. There is considerable evidence for a value function following such an inverted-U-shaped function (Grant & Schwartz, 2011; Reutskaja & Hogarth, 2009; Smith, 1983). For example, food consumption often follows this trajectory where the value of initial food intake is very high. After attaining some level of satiation, further food intake may no longer be attractive. Importantly, at some point (that may vary with individuals and over time and contexts) the value of further intake is going to decline, perhaps precipitously (Blundell et al., 2009). We believe that such a model applies as well to how we often value lives and thus contributes to the failure to respond adequately to genocide and mass atrocities (Västfjäll et al., 2014).

The Failure of Moral Intuition

Thoughtful deliberation takes effort. Fortunately, evolution has equipped us with sophisticated cognitive and perceptual mechanisms that can guide us through our daily lives efficiently, with minimal need for "deep thinking."

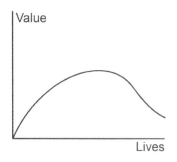

FIGURE 1.2 A psychophysical-collapse function describing the value for saving lives. Adapted from Västfjäll et al. (2014).

For example, the natural and easy way to deal with moral issues is to rely on our intuitive feelings We can also apply reason and logical analysis to determine right and wrong, as our legal system attempts to do. But, as Jonathan Haidt (2001), a psychologist at the University of Virginia, has demonstrated, moral intuition comes first and usually dominates moral judgment unless we make an effort to critique and, if necessary, override our intuitive feelings.

Unfortunately, moral intuition underlies the descriptive models of life-saving described above, where the importance of saving lives lessens or even declines as the number of people at risk increases. As a result, intuition, unschooled by analysis and deliberation, fails us in the face of genocide and other disasters that threaten human lives and the environment on a large scale. We cannot trust it. It depends on attention and feelings that may be hard to arouse and sustain over time for large numbers of victims, not to mention numbers as small as two. Left to its own devices, moral intuition will likely favor individual victims and sensational stories that are close to home and easy to imagine. Our sizable capacity to care for others may be demotivated by negative feelings resulting from thinking about those we cannot help. Or it may be overridden by pressing personal and local interests. Compassion for others has been characterized by social psychologist Daniel Batson as "a fragile flower, easily crushed by self-concern" (Batson, O'Quin, Fultz, Vanderplas, & Isen, 1983). Faced with genocide and other mass tragedies, we cannot rely on our intuitions alone to guide us to act properly.

What Should We Do?

Behavioral research, supported by common observation and the record of repeated failures to arouse citizens and leaders to halt the scourge of genocide and to prevent thousands from perishing in natural disasters, sends a strong and important message. Our moral intuitions often seduce us into calmly turning away from massive losses of human lives, when we should be driven by outrage to act. This is no small weakness in our moral compass.

Educating Moral Intuitions

A natural response to the growing awareness of our insensitivity to problems of scale is to consider ways to educate moral intuitions. But how can we modify our gut instincts to better understand and respond to problems large in scope? This is not an easy question to answer, but we can speculate about possible ways forward.

One way of infusing intuition with greater feeling is by changing the way we frame information. The affective system primarily deals with the here and now and with concrete images. We speculate that reframing a large-scale problem may be a way of increasing affect, attention, and action. For instance, "Eight hundred thousand killed in the last one hundred days" can be broken down and reframed as "one life lost every eleven seconds." Both the "one life lost" and the near-time horizon of "every eleven seconds" induce accessible images and thus are likely to create more affect and different information processing (Trope & Liberman, 2003).

More generally, if statistics represent, as is said, human beings with the tears dried off, tears and feeling can be increased by highlighting the images that lie beneath the numbers. For example, organizers of a rally designed to get Congress to do something about thirty-eight thousand deaths a year from handguns piled thirty-eight thousand pairs of shoes in a mound in front of the Capitol (Associated Press, 1994). Students at a middle school in Tennessee, struggling to comprehend the magnitude of the Holocaust, collected six million paper clips as a centerpiece for a memorial (Schroeder & Schroeder-Hildebrand, 2004). In this light it is instructive to reflect on the characterization by Holocaust survivor Abel Hertzberg: "There were not six million Jews murdered: there was one murder, six million times." (Additional examples of the use of imagery to convey numerical meaning are provided by Kenneth Helphand in Chapter 7.)

When it comes to eliciting compassion, psychological experiments demonstrate that the identified individual victim, with a face and a name, has no peer, providing the face is not juxtaposed with the statistics of the larger need (Small et al., 2007). But we know this as well from personal experience and media coverage of heroic efforts to save individual lives. The world watched tensely as rescuers worked for several days to rescue eighteen-month-old Jessica McClure, who had fallen twenty-two feet into a narrow abandoned well shaft. Charities such as Save the Children have long recognized that it is better to endow a donor with a single, named child to support than to ask for contributions to the bigger cause.

The face need not even be human to motivate powerful intervention. A dog stranded aboard a tanker adrift in the Pacific was the subject of one of the most costly animal rescue efforts ever (Vedantam, 2010). Hearing this, columnist Nicholas D. Kristof (2007) recalled cynically that a single hawk, Pale Male, evicted from his nest in Manhattan, aroused more indignation than two million homeless Sudanese. He observed that what was needed to galvanize the American public and their leaders to respond to the genocide in Darfur was a suffering puppy with big eyes and floppy ears: "If President Bush and the global public alike are unmoved by the slaughter of hundreds of thousands of fellow humans, maybe our last, best hope is that we can be galvanized by a puppy in distress" (see Chapter 6).

Further, to this last point, Paul Farmer (2005) has written eloquently about the power of images, narratives, and first-person testimony to overcome our "failure of imagination" in contemplating the fate of distant, suffering people (see Chapter 5).[3] Such documentation can, he asserts, render abstract struggles personal and help make human rights violations "real" to those unlikely to suffer them. Who hasn't gained a deeper understanding of the Holocaust from reading Elie Wiesel's *Night* or *The Diary of Anne Frank*? Fiction, especially, can create empathy and meaning. Novelist Barbara Kingsolver conveys this elegantly:

> The power of fiction is to create empathy. . . . A newspaper could tell you that one hundred people, say, in an airplane, or in Israel, or in Iraq, have died today. And you can think to yourself, "How very sad," then turn the page and see how the Wildcats fared. But a novel could take just one of those hundred lives and show you exactly how it felt to be that person. . . . You could taste that person's breakfast, and love her family, and sort through her worries as your own, and know that a death in that household will be the end of the only life that someone will ever have. As important as yours. As important as mine. (Kingsolver, 1995, p. 231)

If the power of the narrative, and particularly the personal story, can be used to enhance the understanding of large numbers, we should think about how to use this to educate children about numbers. We teach children about the mechanics of operations such as addition, division, and so on, but we do not teach them how to feel the meaning behind numbers that represent real-life entities such as people and endangered species. Research in numerical cognition suggests that we have an "intuitive number sense" (Dehaene, 1997) that allows us to represent and manipulate numerical quantities nonsymbolically (Peters, Slovic, Västfjäll, & Mertz, 2008). This number sense provides the conceptual basis for mapping numerical symbols onto their meaning (Dehaene, 2001) and is present even in infants (Libertus & Brannon, 2009). Yet people fail to assign meaning to large numbers. The number sense initially develops to deal with precise representation of small numbers, while large quantities may be only approximate representations (Feigenson, Dehaene, & Spelke, 2004). The development of a nonverbal number sense, with the ability to approximate larger magnitudes, appears to depend on the input a child receives (Clements & Sarama, 2007). Thus, children have the tools for understanding large numbers but are not given sufficient knowledge on how to apply these tools to appropriately deal with real-world numbers. We believe that development of methods designed to help children feel the meaning of numbers might be an important way to combat psychic numbing. Maybe the intuitive number sense can be more tightly coupled with our moral sensitivities by educating children about the affective meaning of numbers and the need to reflect carefully about their importance.

From Moral Intuition to Moral Judgment

If strategies to educate intuition and overcome psychic numbing are successful, there will be an upsurge of emotion that needs to be channeled into effective action by national governments. Here is where moral intuitions need to be bolstered by moral judgment to design laws and institutions that commit states to respond to mass tragedies rather than being silent witnesses. And if education of intuition proceeds slowly or not at all, maintaining the current level of psychic numbing, the deficiencies of moral intuition point even more strongly to the need for structured decision-aiding procedures and institutionalized mechanisms to protect human rights. The former include sophisticated decision-analytic techniques designed to clarify the relevant objectives and ensure that actions taken are consistent with considered normative values for those objectives (Slovic, Västfjäll, & Gregory, 2012). For lifesaving values, the models in Figures 1.1a and 1.1b might be appropriate. Regarding institutional mechanisms, the Convention on the Prevention and Punishment of the Crime of Genocide (UN, 1948) and the United Nations were supposed to do this, but they have repeatedly failed. Efforts to address this with new treaty provisions such as "responsibility to protect" (UN, 2005) are urgently needed.

Recognizing that international actors will resist laws that precommit them to act to prevent or stop genocide, Slovic, Zionts, Woods, Goodman, and Jinks (2013) have proposed a "softer" solution based on the intrinsic reasonableness of moral judgments applied to the value of human life. Specifically, officials should be required to publicly deliberate and reason about actions to take in response to genocide and other mass atrocities. Just as we expect government to proffer reasons to justify intervention, we should expect and require public justification for decisions not to intervene and attempt to save human lives. This merging of intuition and deliberation may be achieved through the reporting requirements of a deliberation-forcing regime that would likely ramp up pressure on governments to take action.

Conclusion

The stakes are high. Failure to overcome the numbing to which our moral intuitions are susceptible may force us to passively witness another century of genocide and mass abuses of innocent people, as in the previous century. Educating intuitions through the use of images, narratives, and first-person testimony holds promise for infusing numerical data with emotional meaning. Laws and institutions, designed with an understanding of the shortcomings of intuitive response, hold another vital key to meaningful interventions.

REFERENCES

Anderton, C. H. (in press). Datasets and trends of genocide, mass killing, and other civilian atrocities. In C. H. Anderton & J. Brauer (Eds.), *Economic aspects of genocide, mass atrocity, and their prevention*. Oxford, UK: Oxford University Press.

Associated Press. (1994, September 21). 38,000 shoes stand for loss in lethal year. The *Register-Guard*, p. 6A.

Batson, C. D., O'Quin, K., Fultz, J., Vanderplas, M., & Isen, A. (1983). Self-reported distress and empathy and egoistic versus altruistic motivation for helping. *Journal of Personality and Social Psychology, 45*, 706–718.

Blundell, J. E., De Graaf, K., Finlayson, G., Halford, J. C. G., Hetherington, M., King, N. A., et al. (2009). Measuring food intake, hunger, satiety and satiation in the laboratory. In D. B. Allison & M. L. Baskin (Eds.), *Handbook of assessment methods for eating behaviours and weight-related problems: Measures, theory and research* (2nd ed., pp. 283–325). Newbury Park, CA: Sage.

Clements, D. H., & Sarama, J. (2007). Early childhood mathematics learning. In J. F. K. Lester (Ed.), *Second handbook of research on mathematics teaching and learning* (pp. 461–555). New York, NY: Information Age.

Dehaene, S. (1997). *The number sense: How the mind creates mathematics.* New York, NY: Oxford University Press.

Dehaene, S. (2001). Précis of the number sense. *Mind & Language, 16,* 16–36.

Dillard, A. (1999). *For the time being.* New York, NY: Alfred A. Knopf.

Farmer, P. (2005, March). *Never again? Reflections on human values and human rights.* Paper presented at the Tanner Lectures on Human Values, Salt Lake City, Utah. Retrieved from http://tannerlectures.utah.edu/_documents/a-to-z/f/Farmer_2006.pdf.

Feigenson, L., Dehaene, S., & Spelke, E. (2004). Core systems of number. *Trends in Cognitive Sciences, 8,* 307–314.

Fetherstonhaugh, D., Slovic, P., Johnson, S. M., & Friedrich, J. (1997). Insensitivity to the value of human life: A study of psychophysical numbing. *Journal of Risk and Uncertainty, 14,* 283–300.

Grant, A. M., & Schwartz, B. (2011). Too much of a good thing: The challenge and opportunity of the inverted U. *Perspectives on Psychological Science, 6,* 61–76.

Haidt, J. (2001). The emotional dog and its rational tail: A social intuitionist approach to moral judgment. *Psychological Review, 108,* 814–834.

Just, R. (2008, August). The truth will not set you free: Everything we know about Darfur and everything we're not doing about it. *The New Republic, 239,* 36–47.

Kingsolver, B. (1995). *High tide in Tucson.* New York, NY: HarperCollins.

Kogut, T., & Ritov, I. (2005). The "identified victim" effect: An identified group, or just a single individual? *Journal of Behavioral Decision Making, 18,* 157–167.

Kristof, N. D. (2007, May 10). Save the Darfur puppy. *The New York Times.* Retrieved from http://query.nytimes.com/gst/fullpage.html?res=9902EFD61731F933A25756C0A9619C8B63.

Libertus, M. E., & Brannon, E. M. (2009). Behavioral and neural basis for number sense in infancy. *Current Directions in Psychological Science, 18,* 346–351.

Lifton, R. J. (1967). *Death in life: Survivors of Hiroshima.* New York, NY: Random House.

Peters, E., Slovic, P., Västfjäll, D., & Mertz, C. K. (2008). Intuitive numbers guide decisions. *Judgment and Decision Making, 3,* 619–635.

Power, S. (2003). *A problem from hell: America and the age of genocide.* New York, NY: Harper Perennial.

Reutskaja, E., & Hogarth, R. M. (2009). Satisfaction in choice as a function of the number of alternatives: When "goods satiate." *Psychology & Marketing, 26,* 197–203.

Schroeder, P., & Schroeder-Hildebrand, D. (2004). *Six million paper clips: The making of a children's holocaust museum.* Minneapolis, MN: Kar-Ben.

Slovic, P. (2007). "If I look at the mass I will never act": Psychic numbing and genocide. *Judgment and Decision Making, 2,* 79–95.

Slovic, P., Västfjäll, D., & Gregory, R. (2012). Informing decisions to prevent genocide. *SAIS Review, 32,* 33–47.

Slovic, P., Zionts, D., Woods, A. K., Goodman, R., & Jinks, D. (2013). Psychic numbing and mass atrocity. In E. Shafir (Ed.), *The behavioral foundations of public policy* (pp. 126–142). Princeton, NJ: Princeton University Press.

Small, D. A., Loewenstein, G., & Slovic, P. (2007). Sympathy and callousness: The impact of deliberative thought on donations to identifiable and statistical victims. *Organizational Behavior and Human Decision Processes, 102,* 143–153.

Smith, B. D. (1983). Extraversion and electrodermal activity: Arousability and the inverted-U. *Personality and Individual Differences, 4,* 411–419.

Trope, Y., & Liberman, N. (2003). Temporal construal. *Psychological Review, 110,* 403–421.

Ulfelder, J., & Valentino, B. (2008). *Assessing risks of state-sponsored mass killing.* Retrieved from the SSRN website: http://ssrn.com/abstract=1703426.

United Nations (UN) General Assembly. (1948, December). Convention on the prevention and punishment of the crime of genocide. Retrieved from http://www.un.org/millennium/law/iv-1.htm.

United Nations (UN) General Assembly. (2005, October). Resolution adopted by the General Assembly: 60/1. 2005 World Summit outcome. New York. Retrieved from http://unpan1.un.org/intradoc/groups/public/documents/un/unpan021752.pdf.

Västfjäll, D., Slovic, P., Mayorga, M., & Peters, E. (2014). Compassion fade: Affect and charity are greatest for a single child in need. *PLOS ONE, 9* (6), e100115. doi:10.1371/journal.pone.0100115.

Vedantam, S. (2010). *The hidden brain: How our unconscious minds elect presidents, control markets, wage wars, and save our lives.* New York, NY: Spiegel & Grau.

NOTES

1. Full text available at: http://www.un.org/en/documents/udhr/.

2. She struggles to think straight about the great losses that the world ignores: "More than two million children die a year from diarrhea and eight hundred thousand from measles. Do we blink? Stalin starved seven million Ukrainians in one year, Pol Pot killed two million Cambodians" (Dillard, 1999, pp. 130–131).

3. As we corrected the proofs of this book, the world was galvanized by the image of a three-year-old Syrian refugee, Aylan Kurdi, wearing a red T-shirt, dark shorts, black sneakers, and no socks, lying face down, lifeless, on a Turkish beach. Aylan's image brings emotion and meaning to the plight of millions of Syrian refugees who, for years, have been nameless, faceless, and ignored. Just statistics. This photograph has moved world leaders and propelled changes in immigration policy for refugees within days of its publication.

CHAPTER 2

Pseudoinefficacy and the Arithmetic of Compassion

DANIEL VÄSTFJÄLL, PAUL SLOVIC,
AND MARCUS MAYORGA

> Beliefs of personal efficacy constitute the key factor of human agency. If people believe they have no power to produce results, they will not attempt to make things happen.
>
> —ALBERT BANDURA, *Self-Efficacy: The Exercise of Control*

THE INTRODUCTION TO THIS BOOK presented and examined the psychologically complex concept that poet Zbigniew Herbert (1974) called "the arithmetic of compassion." In Chapter 1 we presented research describing two ways that the feeling system performs this arithmetic when valuing lives and serving as our moral compass. When calculating in accord with psychophysical principles, one life plus one life is valued more than one life but less than two lives. When contextual factors induce fading or collapse, one life plus one life may be valued at something even less than one life. In this chapter we introduce yet another cognitive calculus of compassion and valuation that is equally worrisome. In this case, irrelevant external factors may create negative feelings that are inappropriately combined with appropriate feelings, resulting in detrimental fading or collapse of compassion.

To set the stage, recall the famous lifesaving crisis hypothesized in philosopher Peter Singer's "child in the pond" scenario. Singer asks his readers to imagine the moral conundrum of walking by a shallow pond and seeing a child drowning in it. He asserts that getting one's expensive shoes muddy in the process of rescuing the child would be an insignificant sacrifice compared with the moral good of saving the child.

Consider the following addendum to Singer's scenario: "Now suppose, as you see the child go under, you also see, further away, another child begin to drown—one you can't reach. Would you then be less motivated to rescue the child you can reach and perhaps even continue your walk without intervening?" The question strikes us as bizarre, suggesting a change in our values and behavior that is irrational. Unfortunately we have been finding this sort of phenomenon in controlled experiments and observing what seems to be the same sort of behavior in real life, due to a peculiar form of cognitive and affective arithmetic that we call *pseudoinefficacy*. In "Famine, Affluence, and Morality" (1972), Singer argues that "the fact that a person is physically near to us, so that we have personal contact with him, may make it more likely that we *shall* assist him, but this does not show that we *ought* to help him rather than another who happens to be further away" (p. 232).

Specifically, we find that people often feel less good about helping those they can help, and they help less, when their attention is drawn to those they can't help. The demotivation exhibited by these people may be a form of pseudoinefficacy that is nonrational. We should not be deterred from helping whomever we can because there are others we are not able to help.

For those in a position to help, decisions are strongly motivated by perceived efficacy. Inefficacy, real or perceived, shrivels compassion and response, even among those who have the means to protect and improve lives. As Albert Bandura (1989) notes, "People's belief in their capabilities affects how much stress and depression they experience in threatening or taxing situations, as well as their level of motivation" (p. 1177). Thus, perceived rather than actual efficacy is often the determinant of behavior. It is tragic indeed when efficacy goes unrecognized and vital aid that could be provided is withheld due to this illusion of ineffectiveness. Our research has aimed to explore and document the root psychological causes of pseudoinefficacy and develop ways to mitigate its harmful consequences. Although our studies are typically set in the context of humanitarian aid to victims of poverty, food insufficiency, disease, and violence, the problem of pseudoinefficacy is central to a wide range of important personal and societal decisions motivated by perceived efficacy, such as actions to mitigate climate change or other threats to human health and the environment. Indeed, once we become sensitized to this phenomenon, we believe we can see it operating at the highest levels of government in situations of the utmost importance (more about that later).

What Led Us to Pseudoinefficacy?

In reviewing what appeared to be unrelated findings from two of the early studies of lifesaving decisions (described in Chapter 1), we uncovered a curious connection that motivated our subsequent studies of pseudoinefficacy. These prior studies asked people to provide clean water to aid people facing death from disease (Fetherstonhaugh, Slovic, Johnson, & Friedrich, 1997) or to provide money to protect a child from starvation (Small, Loewenstein, & Slovic, 2007). Recall that Fetherstonhaugh et al. found that people were less likely to send clean water that could save forty-five hundred lives in a refugee camp when the number of people in the camp was large (250,000) than when it was small (11,000). Small et al. found that the money donated to a seven-year-old African child facing starvation decreased dramatically when the donor was made aware that the child was one of millions needing food aid.

We recognized that the findings from these two studies may have broad implications for prosocial or humanitarian behavior in light of the insights of Andreoni (1990), who contended that we help others not only because they need our help, but also because we anticipate and experience the warm glow of good feeling associated with giving aid. Subsequent theoretical and empirical studies have supported this contention (e.g., Chilton & Hutchinson, 2000; Costa-Font, Jofre-Bonet, & Yen, 2012; Crumpler & Grossman, 2008; Harbaugh, 1998; Know, 2006; Mayo & Tinsley, 2009; Menges, Schroeder, & Traub, 2005; Null, 2011; Sachdeva, Iliev, & Medin, 2009; Stahl & Haruvy, 2006). We hypothesized that knowledge of those "out of reach" (more people in the large refugee camp and millions of starving people in Africa) may have triggered negative feelings that countered the good feelings anticipated from giving aid, thus demotivating action. A related explanation is that, compared with the large numbers of persons out of reach, the prospective aid created a sense of inefficacy, that is, a "drop-in-the-bucket" feeling (Bartels & Burnett, 2011).

Although the results from these studies by Fetherstonhaugh et al. (1997) and Small et al. (2007) may appear at first glance to reflect inefficacy, this is not really inefficacy, because the donor can actually help some people (from one to forty-five hundred). Instead, it is a form of pseudoinefficacy that is nonrational. We should not be deterred from helping one person, or forty-five hundred, just because there are others we cannot help.

We believe that the demotivating effects shown in these two studies, both of which involved large numbers of unidentified children who could or could not be helped, are one specific form of pseudoinefficacy. Kahneman (2011) summarizes the extensive research documenting the differential effects of fast versus slow thinking (see also Greene, 2013). We propose that the findings of Fetherstonhaugh et al. (1997) and Small et al. (2007) reflect relatively slow or reasoned pseudoinefficacy that arises from more complex thoughts involving calculations of proportions or drop-in-the-bucket imagery, likely causing feelings of despair or hopelessness.

In subsequent research, we have extended these findings to situations involving what we call fast or intuitive pseudoinefficacy, linked to virtually instantaneous dampening of *warm glow* by negative feelings, perhaps of sadness or unhappiness, in situations with small numbers of identified people in need and small numbers unable to be helped.

To test our hypothesis that, even when the numbers of affected individuals are small, awareness of those not helped reduces warm glow, we employed a paradigm involving donations to one or more starving children identified by name, age, photo, and so on. We systematically varied the number of children who could be helped and the number who could not. For instance, in a between-groups design, those in Group 1 were asked, "How good would you feel about donating to help Child A?" Those in Group 2 were asked, "How good would you feel donating to help Child B?" Those in Group 3 were introduced to both children and were asked, "How good would you feel donating to A or B?" In this case, we predicted and found that the expressed warm glow associated with helping was lowest for those in Group 3, as were donations. Clearly drop-in-the-bucket thinking did not underlie these results, given that one of the two children at risk would be helped.

Additional studies demonstrated that pseudoinefficacy is an affective phenomenon—positive feelings about children one can help are dampened by negative feelings associated with children who one cannot help. Specifically, we found that pictures of the children who cannot be helped induced negative affect that reduced the positive warm glow associated with the child that can be helped. The stronger the negative feelings associated with those not helped, the lower the warm glow anticipated from helping the one who can be helped. We also found that the pseudoinefficacy effect is due not merely to visual distraction resulting from images of children not helped. Warm-glow ratings of a single child who could be helped were not reduced when that child was accompanied by nonaffective visual distractors, as shown in Figure 2.1. In further support of an affect-based explanation, we also found that when other, unrelated, pictures that induced negative feelings accompanied the single child (see Figure 2.2), warm-glow ratings were as low as those in the pseudoinefficacy conditions where children who could not be helped were present (see Figure 2.3). The stronger the rated negative affect toward the unrelated pictures, the lower the warm glow associated with helping the child. These effects on warm glow are important in light of the many studies linking warm glow to prosocial actions (e.g., Chilton & Hutchinson, 2000; Crumpler & Grossman, 2008; Menges et al., 2005; Null, 2011; Stahl & Haruvy, 2006).

Fortunately, not all participants were demotivated by the presence of other children out of reach. We also found that some participants remained motivated after seeing the children who could not be helped and donated considerably more than those who became demotivated. A study by Mayorga (2013) suggests that individual differences in emotion regulation ability might predict who becomes demotivated from seeing other children not helped. Effectively regulating the negative affect of seeing the children who could not be helped by donating might act as a buffer against demotivation.

Returning to our analogy of the arithmetic of compassion, we see that, with the common psychophysical form of numbing described in Chapter 1,

FIGURE 2.1 Child and shapes.

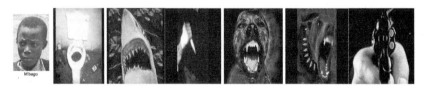

FIGURE 2.2 Child and negative pictures.

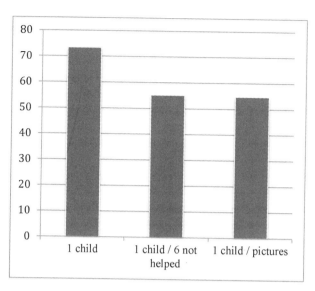

FIGURE 2.3
Mean warm-glow ratings in the picture study. Accompanying the child's image with pictures of other children not able to be helped or with unrelated negative pictures lowered warm glow.

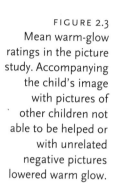

the value attached to saving lives increases with each additional life, but at a decreasing rate, consistent with prospect theory (Kahneman & Tversky, 1979). With pseudoinefficacy, this increase can cease abruptly when one or more lives appear that are beyond help. Our studies find that warm glow increases steadily with one, two, and then six children helped in the context of one child who cannot be helped. But the anticipated warm glow from helping a single child, alone, was far greater than the glow of helping one, two, or even six children in the presence of one out of reach, illustrating a version of what Markowitz, Slovic, Västfjäll, and Hodges (2013) have termed "compassion fade" (see also Västfjäll, Slovic, Mayorga, & Peters, 2014; and Figure 1.1d in Chapter 1).

Overcoming Pseudoinefficacy

It is typically the case that even our best efforts cannot help everyone in need. Thus it would be unfortunate indeed if we let this incompleteness deter us from accomplishing what is within our grasp.

But countering, or at least minimizing, pseudoinefficacy might not be easy. Kahneman (2011) summarizes a vast amount of research demonstrating that the human mind processes information in two ways: fast and slow. Fast thinking, akin to what Haidt (2001) calls "moral intuition," is like perception. Moral feelings arise quickly, without reflection, and appear true to us (Haidt, 2001), much like visual perceptions. But just as the human eye, as accurate as it is, can be deceived by certain patterns creating visual illusions, certain contextual information, such as children who cannot be helped, may create "moral illusions" of inefficacy. And just as visual illusions may persist even when we know them to be false, pseudoinefficacy may be similarly hard to dispel.

Hsee (1998) and Fetherstonhaugh et al. (1997) found that joint (e.g., side-by-side) evaluation reduced valuation biases in lifesaving decisions. But some of our studies have found pseudoinefficacy even in joint evaluation. Just as visual cues cannot be easily ignored, perhaps the affective system cannot ignore affective cues even when they are irrelevant.

One strategy used to debias persistent and deadly visual illusions is to remove the deceptive cues. When pilots in a flight simulator on visual approach to a landing strip were misled by the pattern of runway lights, causing them to land short of the runway, the pattern of lights was quickly and successfully changed (Palmisano & Gillam, 2005). In light of pseudoinefficacy and drop-in-the-bucket thinking, it may be wise to delete or minimize reference to the larger need that the request for aid addresses. One charity solicitation put the statistic "3 million in need" above the picture of a starving child, possibly demotivating many donors.

A more promising strategy may be one used by Schwarz and Clore (1983) to block the intrusion of irrelevant feelings. In their study that found people's assessment of their personal well-being to be influenced by the weather at the time, merely alerting respondents to the possibility of this influence eliminated this bias. In the donation decisions we studied, perhaps alerting participants to the possibility that the source of bad feelings they experienced was the sight of children they could not help would have reduced or eliminated pseudoinefficacy.

The strategy used by Schwarz and Clore worked to alter the immediate feelings associated with fast thinking. Perhaps pseudoinefficacy can be overcome by teaching individuals to be compassionate and helpful through moral arguments—that is, slow thinking. Might the variation of Peter Singer's "child in the pond" scenario described in the introduction to this chapter, with the second child out of reach, be jarring enough to drive home the irrationality of pseudoinefficacy?

Perhaps a lesson in efficacy might also combat pseudoinefficacy. Consider the famous starfish story by American author Loren Eiseley (1969):

The shore grew steeper, the sound of the sea heavier and more menacing, as I rounded a bluff into the full blast of the offshore wind. I was away from the shellers now and strode more rapidly over the wet sand that effaced my footprints. Around the next point there might be a refuge from the wind. The sun behind me was pressing upward at the horizon's rim—an ominous red glare amidst the tumbling blackness of the clouds. Ahead of me, over the projecting point, a gigantic rainbow of incredible perfection had sprung shimmering into existence. Somewhere toward its foot I discerned a human figure standing, as it seemed to me, within the rainbow, though unconscious of his position. He was gazing fixedly at something in the sand.

Eventually he stooped and flung the object beyond the breaking surf. . . .

In a pool of sand and silt a starfish had thrust its arms up stiffly and was holding its body away from the stifling mud.

"It's still alive," I ventured.

"Yes," he said, and with a quick yet gentle movement he picked up another star and spun it over my head and far out into the sea. . . .

"There are not many come this far," I said, groping in a sudden embarrassment for words. "Do you collect?"

"Only like this," he said softly, gesturing amidst the wreckage of the shore. "And only for the living." He stooped again, oblivious of my curiosity, and skipped another star neatly across the water.

"The stars," he said, "throw well. One can help them."

He looked full at me with a faint question kindling in his eyes, which seemed to take on the far depths of the sea.

"I do not collect," I said uncomfortably, wind beating at my garments.
(pp. 70–72)

As Eiseley's "The Star Thrower" proceeds, though, the narrator reflects further on the unique human capacity to make a difference, to choose a cause and contribute something to that cause, even if the precise degree of efficacy is unknown. Our species possesses what Eiseley calls "the awesome freedom to choose" (p. 88). Although the speaker initially thought to himself, "The star thrower was mad, and his particular acts were a folly with which I had not chosen to associate myself" (p. 89), he changes his mind upon reflection and goes looking for the star thrower again on the desolate beach:

On a point of land, as though projecting into a domain beyond us, I found the star thrower. In the sweet, rain-swept morning, that great many-hued rainbow still lurked and wavered tentatively beyond him. Silently I sought and picked up a still-living star, spinning it far out into the waves. I spoke once briefly. "I understand," I said. "Call me another thrower." Only then I allowed myself to think, He is not alone any longer. After us there will be others. (p. 89)

As the narrator flings the starfish into the surf, he imagines to himself, "Perhaps far outward on the rim of space a genuine star was similarly seized and flung. I could feel the movement of my body. It was like a sowing—the sowing of life on an infinitely gigantic scale" (pp. 89–90). The point of Eiseley's seaside parable is that we never quite fathom the true magnitude of our influence on the world, but the slow thinking, or moral reflection, indicated in this story suggests that the potential for positive, life-sustaining impact is in itself motivation to act. The word "perhaps" at the beginning of this final quotation from Eiseley is a clue to the idea that certainty of impact is not necessary—only the imagined possibility of making a difference.

Postscript: Pseudoinefficacy, Strategic Despair, and Humanitarian Intervention

As we write this, Syria is entering the fourth year of the most severe humanitarian crisis since the 1994 genocide in Rwanda. Millions of people are caught in the crossfire of a vicious civil war between rival rebel groups and a government bent on maintaining its power at any cost. A substantial proportion of the population has fled to neighboring countries that are unprepared to accommodate them—one in every four inhabitants of Lebanon, for example, is now a Syrian refugee.

The Obama administration is, in the words of one insider, "constantly reviewing our options" regarding humanitarian intervention, but neither the United States nor the United Nations is taking action. There are, of course, legitimate concerns to weigh against the urgent need to keep millions still in Syria alive until the political dust settles. We could establish a safe zone to provide food, shelter, and medical care, but that would require a military presence that might be construed as a thinly disguised plot to bring down the government. Some would see it as yet another Western attack on a Muslim nation. It would be expensive, and some soldiers and aid workers might be killed.

But in the mix of legitimate risks and benefits are considerations that strike us as ingredients of pseudoinefficacy, introducing negative affect that dampens political will, devoid of compelling logic. Among these are questionable analogies to problematic interventions of the past in Somalia, Iraq, and Afghanistan. Writing in the *Washington Post*, columnist Michael Gerson attributes the lack of American leadership to "strategic despair" arising from arguments that any lifesaving actions would be "inadequate, late, or risky" (Gerson, 2014). Risky, yes. But inadequate and late clearly undermine efficacy, as does the defense for inaction given by an official close to the president who said: "We [the United States] can't fix Syria." Perhaps not. But there are millions of people whose lives we can protect. We should not abandon them.

REFERENCES

Andreoni, J. (1990). Impure altruism and donations to public goods: A theory of warm-glow giving. *The Economic Journal, 100*, 464–477.

Bandura, A. (1989). Human agency in social cognitive theory. *American Psychologist, 44*, 1175–1184.

Bandura, A. (1997). *Self-efficacy: The exercise of control*. New York, NY: W. H. Freeman.

Bartels, D. M., & Burnett, R. C. (2011). A group construal account of drop-in-the-bucket thinking in policy preference and moral judgment. *Journal of Experimental Social Psychology, 47*, 50–57. doi:10.1016/j.jesp.2010.08.003.

Chilton, S. M., & Hutchinson, W. G. (2000). A note on the warm glow of giving and scope sensitivity in contingent valuation studies. *Journal of Economic Psychology, 21*, 343–349.

Costa-Font, J., Jofre-Bonet, M., & Yen, S. T. (2012). Not all incentives wash out the warm glow: The case of blood donation revisited. *Kyklos, 66*, 529–551.

Crumpler, H., & Grossman, P. (2008). An experimental test of warm glow giving. *Journal of Public Economics, 92*, 1011–1021.

Eiseley, L. (1969). The star thrower. *The unexpected universe*. Orlando, FL: Harcourt Brace.

Fetherstonhaugh, D., Slovic, P., Johnson, S. M., & Friedrich, J. (1997). Insensitivity to the value of human life: A study of psychophysical numbing. *Journal of Risk and Uncertainty, 14*, 283–300.

Gerson, M. (2014, February 20). Syria's uncontainable threat. *The Washington Post*. Retrieved from www.washingtonpost.com.

Greene, J. (2013). *Moral tribes: Emotion, reason, and the gap between us and them*. New York, NY: Penguin Press.

Haidt, J. (2001). The emotional dog and its rational tail: A social intuitionist approach to moral judgment. *Psychological Review, 108*, 814–834.

Harbaugh, W. T. (1998). What do donations buy? A model of philanthropy based on prestige and warm glow. *Journal of Public Economics, 67*, 269–284.

Herbert, Z. (1974/1993). Mr Cogito reads the newspaper. *Mr Cogito*. John Carpenter & Bogdana Carpenter (Trans.). Hopewell, NJ: The Ecco Press.

Hsee, C. K. (1998). Less is better: When low-value options are valued more highly than high-value options. *Journal of Behavioral Decision Making, 11*, 107–121.

Kahneman, D. (2011). *Thinking, fast and slow*. New York, NY: Farrar, Straus and Giroux.

Kahneman, D., & Tversky, A. (1979). Prospect theory: An analysis of decision under risk. *Econometrica, 47*, 263–291.

Know, J. (2006). Mixed feelings: Theories and evidence of warm glow and altruism. *MPRA Paper 2727*.

Markowitz, E. M., Slovic, P., Västfjäll, D., & Hodges, S. D. (2013). Compassion fade and the challenge of environmental conservation. *Judgment and Decision Making, 8*, 397–406.

Mayo, J., & Tinsley, C. (2009). Warm glow and charitable giving: Why the wealthy do not give more to charity? *Journal of Economic Psychology, 30*, 490–499.

Mayorga, M. (2013). *Individual differences and feelings of inefficacy in charitable decision making* (master's thesis). Eugene: Department of Psychology, University of Oregon.

Menges, R., Schroeder, C., & Traub, S. (2005). Altruism, warm glow and the willingness-to-donate for green electricity: An artefactual field experiment. *Environmental & Resource Economics, 31*, 431–458.

Null, C. (2011). Warm glow, information, and inefficient charitable giving. *Journal of Public Economics, 95*, 455–465.

Palmisano, S., & Gillam, B. J. (2005). Visual perception of touchdown point during simulated landing. *Journal of Experimental Psychology: Applied, 11*, 19–32.

Sachdeva, S., Iliev, R., & Medin, D. L. (2009). Sinning saints and saintly sinners: The paradox of moral self-regulation. *Psychological Science, 20*, 523–528.

Schwarz, N., & Clore, G. L. (1983). Mood, misattribution, and judgments of well-being: Informative and directive functions of affective states. *Journal of Personality and Social Psychology, 45*, 513–523.

Singer, P. (1972). Famine, affluence, and morality. *Philosophy and Public Affairs, 1*, 229–243. Revised edition retrieved from http://www.utilitarian.net/singer/by/1972----.htm.

Small, D. A., Loewenstein, G., & Slovic, P. (2007). Sympathy and callousness: The impact of deliberative thought on donations to identifiable and statistical victims. *Organizational Behavior and Human Decision Processes, 102*, 143–153.

Stahl, D., & Haruvy, E. (2006). Other-regarding preferences: Egalitarian warm glow, empathy, and group size. *Journal of Economic Behavior & Organization, 61*, 20–41.

Västfjäll, D., Slovic, P., Mayorga, M., & Peters, E. (2014). Compassion fade: Affect and charity are greatest for a single child in need. *PLOS ONE, 9* (6), e100115.

CHAPTER 3

The Prominence Effect

*Confronting the Collapse of Humanitarian Values
in Foreign Policy Decisions*

PAUL SLOVIC

FOR RESEARCHERS, THE END OF A STUDY always leaves further questions to be answered. In the preceding two chapters we have employed emerging knowledge of the psychology of feelings and their integral relationship to the meaning and use of information to search for an answer to the question, "Why do good people and their governments repeatedly turn away from intervening to halt genocides and other mass abuses of human beings?" I began to examine this question when I became aware of the indifference toward the vast scale of atrocities being perpetrated in Darfur, Sudan. I saw a connection between earlier research I had published with David Fetherstonhaugh and colleagues in 1997 and subsequent research with Deborah Small and George Loewenstein (Fetherstonhaugh, Slovic, Johnson, & Friedrich, 1997; Small, Loewenstein, & Slovic, 2007). These studies validated the nonlinear model of valuation proposed by Daniel Kahneman and Amos Tversky (1979) in their landmark paper on prospect theory. Specifically, this work documented the insensitivity to large numbers of lives at risk, which we labeled *psychophysical numbing*. As noted in Chapters 1 and 2, subsequent studies uncovered additional evidence of insensitivity that we have described as *compassion fade* and, in some cases, *compassion collapse*, where valuation actually decreases and may even collapse to zero as the number of lives at stake increases. Further insights led to the discovery of another failing of our "feelings compass," which we've termed *pseudoinefficacy,* as described in Chapter 2.

All of this helps explain why many who care greatly about individual lives lose their enthusiasm and compassion when the numbers get big. In

Chapters 1 and 2, we offered a few suggestions to begin to address this problem, seeking to infuse numbers with emotion and warn readers about potential mistakes in their arithmetic of compassion.

But yet another problem, beyond numbing, has become apparent, one that is inherent in the very foundation of decision making and action. It is all too easy to view inaction on the part of powerful and well-intentioned governments as resulting from a lack of direction or pressure from a numbed public that places little value on saving foreign lives. In her Pulitzer Prize–winning book, Samantha Power (2003) concluded that

> it takes political pressure to put genocide on the map in Washington. . . . Genocide in distant lands has not captivated senators, congressional caucuses . . . lobbyists . . . or individual citizens. The battle to stop genocide has thus been repeatedly lost in the realm of domestic politics. (p. 509)

True enough, and a testimony to numbing, at least on the part of the citizenry.

But as Richard Just points out in the quote in Chapter 1, no genocide has been so thoroughly documented while it was taking place as the one in Darfur, and that documentation has included emotionally jarring testimony and images. Something more must be needed to impel action. Is it a matter of values?

It was easy to blame the Bush administration for being uncaring. Even when Colin Powell returned from Darfur in 2004 and used the "G word" to describe the atrocities there, no action was taken. Then the Obama administration came to power and hopes soared. Surely President Obama cared about humanitarian causes, and he was surrounded by a cadre of aides, including Samantha Power, who certainly placed high value on human lives. In fact, Ambassador Power recalled that, at her first meeting with Obama, he was greatly interested in discussing her book and its documentation of repeated failures of the American government to live up to its ideals (Osnos, 2014). Yet six years into an administration considered most likely to succeed in taking action to mitigate or halt mass atrocities, little seems to have changed—certainly not in Darfur. What's going on?

Perhaps psychology can again provide a possible explanation. Aided by valuable discussions with colleagues Robin Gregory, David Frank, and Daniel Västfjäll, I sought insight from data I began collecting in 1961. That research examined how people made decisions between two options that were equally valuable to them. Consider a gift package made up of two parts—cash and a coupon worth *X* dollars, redeemable at a store you like. There are two such packages. Package A gives you more cash than Package B, but you are able to increase B's advantage in the value of the coupon book to make the two gifts equally attractive to you. But you have to choose. Which one would you take? Naïve theories would predict you will flip a coin, thus being equally likely to choose A or B. That didn't happen. Eighty-eight percent of respondents, each of whom had individually adjusted the packages to make them equally attractive *for them,* made the choice in the same direction. What do you think they did? If you predicted that they chose the package with the greater amount of cash, you are correct.

Similar results occurred with choices among nine other pairs of two-attribute bundles, such as baseball players (described by batting average and number of home-run hits), secretarial applicants (described by typing speed and typing accuracy), and so on. In every case, choices among individually equated pairs were highly predictable, with about 80 percent of respondents adhering to the following rule: choose the option that is better on the attribute or dimension that is inherently more important (e.g., cash, or batting average, or typing accuracy).

Not trusting the adjustment method used to equate the options in each pair, I finally found a way to overcome my methodological concerns and published these findings after more than a decade (Slovic, 1975). Some thirteen years later, Amos Tversky, Shmuel Sattath, and I incorporated this "more important dimension effect" into a new theory of choice (Tversky, Sattath, & Slovic, 1988). The core finding was named "the prominence effect." The essence of this effect is that, although we may have a qualitative sense of the importance of valued attributes, we may not have a sense of the appropriate quantitative trade-offs when these attributes compete with one another. For example, we highly value both affordability and safety in a car, but how much more we should be willing to spend for a specific increment in safety is by no means obvious to us. We struggle with making trade-offs and seek a simple, defensible way to choose among options whose attributes are important but conflicting. Here is where the prominence effect enters. Don't struggle to perform any quantitative calculations to weigh and compare valued objectives. Choose what is best according to the most prominent—that is, the most defensible—attributes. You can't go wrong.

You can well defend your choice to yourself and others. Moreover, it likely "feels" right.

So what does this have to do with genocide, the arithmetic of compassion, or numbers and nerves? A lot. It is well recognized that decisions to save civilian lives by intervening in foreign countries' domestic affairs are among the most difficult and controversial choices facing national decision makers. Although each situation is unique, such decisions typically involve trade-offs that pit the value of human lives against other important objectives. And on rare occasions we do decide to intervene. In 2011, the United States supported military action to protect the lives of civilians living in Libya, and more recently the American military intervened aggressively to protect a threatened population of Yazidi people in Iraq. On the other hand, the United States has done little to intervene in the genocide in Darfur or to halt the barrel bombings and other government-led atrocities in Syria that have led to hundreds of thousands of deaths and millions of displaced people.

The inconsistencies are striking. Why intervene in some situations and not in others that, by the numbers, seem far worse? And how do we reconcile the immense value our society places on an individual life with our failure to respond to the plight of millions? What are our true values when it comes to saving human lives? Should we accept these inconsistencies? Are we oblivious to them? Are other objectives really important enough to outweigh millions of lives? Why can't sheer numbers, once great enough, tip the scales toward at least some forms of meaningful intervention, if not outright troops on the ground?

The light bulb switched on for me in 2014 while at a conference in Jerusalem, listening to a presentation by social psychologist Nurit Shnabel and her colleagues Ilanit SimanTov-Nachlieli and Arie Nadler. The title of their talk says it all: "Sensitivity to Moral Threats Increases When Safety Needs Are Satisfied: Evidence of Hierarchical Organization of Psychological Needs." Their conclusion jumped out at me: consistent with Maslow's (1943) hierarchy of needs, the basic need for security must be satisfied before people will respond to higher-order needs. In other words, when security is tenuous, moral action to help others is unlikely.

Immediately I thought of the prominence effect, where determiners of choice are found to be hierarchical (we called it "lexicographical"), which means choosing to achieve the most important attributes with little or no compensation allowed for lesser attributes. That is, prominent attributes trump less prominent factors. Prominence is driven by the need to justify and defend one's decisions and actions in a way not called for when simply stating one's values. And what is the most prominent set of values in today's foreign policy world? National security interests! Could the unquestioned importance of national security explain, at least in part, the disconnect between the lofty expressed values of our government for protecting distant lives and the minimal valuation of those lives revealed by government inaction when millions are threatened?

The rhetoric of the two most recent American presidents leaves no doubt that, in terms of expressed values, national security and humanitarian lifesaving are both vital objectives. Speaking on CNN in January 2009, George Bush remarked, "The most important job I have had—and the most important job the next president is going to have—is to protect the American public from another [terrorist] attack." Barack Obama echoed this sentiment, saying, "I have a solemn responsibility to keep the American people safe: That's my most important obligation as President and Commander in Chief" (Remnick, 2014). Yet both leaders expressed equally high valuation for lifesaving. Speaking at the Holocaust Museum in Washington, DC, President Obama stated that we need to do everything we can to prevent and end atrocities: "I made it clear that 'preventing mass atrocities and genocide is a core national security interest and a core moral responsibility of the United States of America'" (White House, 2012).

I am drawn to the hypothesis that, because of the prominence effect, lofty humanitarian values are systematically devalued in the decision-making process. When intervention to protect thousands of nameless, faceless lives in a distant land is seen to increase risks to national security, security invariably wins. Decisions in support of security appear vastly more defensible than decisions to protect distant lives. In the few recent situations where the United States has intervened with the stated objective of saving lives, there were presumed security benefits as well, thus no conflict between objectives. We attacked Saddam Hussein not because he was a mass murderer but because we believed he possessed and might use weapons of mass destruction. When Libyan leader Muammar Gaddafi threatened to go door-to-door in Benghazi, killing anyone who opposed his regime, the United States joined a NATO coalition to topple him from power. But he, too, was considered a threat to security, long seen as a loose cannon addicted to violence at home and elsewhere. His menacing visage has adorned the cover of *Time* magazine four times since 1986, when Ronald Reagan referred to him as "this mad dog of the Middle East." When the United States recently decided to come to the rescue of thousands of Yazidis threatened by ISIS in Iraq, we were also protecting American military and diplomatic personnel stationed in nearby Erbil. Without that security objective, would we have aided the Yazidis?

In contrast, humanitarian intervention in Darfur appears to have been blocked by security objectives in addition to the military and domestic political costs. We have long sought to obtain intelligence regarding terrorist operations from the Sudanese government (Albright, 2004). In addition, Sudanese president Omar al-Bashir, who takes a backseat to no one as a murderer, has been protected by the Chinese government, which for many years was the major buyer of Sudanese oil. An action against al-Bashir that strained relations with China would have jeopardized U.S. economic and military interests.

One of the most stunning conclusions by Samantha Power in her book *A Problem From Hell* was that America's repeated refusals to end genocide were not "accidental products of neglect" but rather "they were concrete choices made by the country's most influential decisionmakers after unspoken *and* explicit weighing of costs and benefits" (Power, 2003, p. 508).

But if the prominence effect is indeed infiltrating top-level policy decisions and causing decision makers to systematically devalue humanitarian actions, I doubt that the decision makers are consciously aware of this. The prominence mechanism driving the decision-making process is not consciously expressed as devaluation of distant lives; this would be abhorrent to leaders who truly do value those lives. Rather, I believe that prominent objectives, in particular those offering enhanced security, suck attention away from less prominent goals. All eyes are on options that protect the homeland, and decision makers fixated on the security objectives likely fail to consider adequately the millions of people under siege and left to die. Compensatory weighing of costs and benefits associated with seeking security and saving distant lives is not really occurring.

Thus meaningful action to prevent genocide and mass atrocities faces two psychological obstacles. The prominence effect leads to decisions that favor inaction, even when this violates deeply held values. And decision makers can get away with this because the public is psychologically numbed. As Samantha Power (2003) observed, "No. U.S. president has ever made genocide prevention a priority, and no U.S. president has ever suffered politically for his indifference to its occurrence. It is thus no coincidence that genocide rages on" (p. xxi).

My colleagues and I have been working to design laboratory experiments to test these speculations about the psychological prominence of security in values revealed through decisions. In a recent pilot study, we posed the humanitarian crisis in Syria (prior to the involvement of ISIS) to respondents instructed to play the role of the U.S. president. The objective of protecting one hundred thousand civilian lives by creating a "safe zone" was pitted against the decision to not intervene in order to minimize the political and military risks of intervention. We assumed the latter decision would be prominent. Preliminary results support the hypothesis that an individual's strongly expressed values for intervening to protect lives are often contravened by that same person's decisions in favor of nonintervention for the sake of security.

But amid this sobering view, contrasting our expressed values and our revealed values, the pilot study did offer a ray of hope that needs to be pursued. We found a strong order effect in our data. One group of our respondents was first asked to think about their values for the competing objectives and to quantify them on a 0–100 rating scale of importance. One of the rated objectives was to not intervene in order to protect national interests and national security. The objective of the alternative action—intervention—was characterized by three subgoals:

- Create a no-fly zone to stop Syrian airplanes from attacking citizens.
- Place U.S. troops on the border of the safe zone to protect it.
- Have U.S. troops accompany ground shipments of food and medicine to ensure their delivery to the safe zone.

Those who first decided whether to intervene or not made decisions that conflicted with their subsequent ratings of their goals on the 0–100 scale. As predicted by the prominence hypothesis, choices favored nonintervention to a degree that was not consistent with respondents' stated values, which tended to assign greater importance to objectives linked to intervention.

However, those who first searched their souls and expressed their values quantitatively for the various objectives subsequently made choices that were highly consistent with their expressed values. This suggests that introduction of techniques known as *decision analysis* and *value-focused thinking* (Keeney, 1992; Gregory et al., 2012) may help policy makers act in ways that don't contradict their expressed values: perhaps a triumph of numbers over nerves, of rational analysis over gut response.

Postscript

The current application of the prominence effect as a means of critiquing foreign policy decisions was certainly never envisioned by Tversky et al. in 1988. But the derivation of this principle, based on data from a wide range of social and consumer choices, suggests its far-ranging implications. Consider climate change. Polls show that more and more Americans now attach high value to halting the adverse effects of fossil-fuel use and meeting the moral obligation to preserve the planet for future generations. But consistent and effective actions on the part of citizens and their governments are rare. We express strong commitment to both environmental protection and our obligations to future generations, but these values are likely to be nullified in decisions where the immediate comforts, conveniences, and other direct benefits we gain from climate-destructive actions are prominent. More generally, prominence appears likely to be aligned with immediate and certain benefits to individuals whom we care about. Without incorporating decision analysis and value-focused thinking, it will be hard to defend actions that protect distant, anonymous masses—ranging from today's victims of genocide to future generations imperiled by a degraded planet—in opposition to prominent objectives. I hope that the efforts of writers and artists, such as those described and demonstrated later in this book, will make protecting the environment and threatened human communities more meaningful and more defensible in decision making.

REFERENCES

Albright, M. (2004, March 24). Full text: Madeleine Albright Statement. National Commission on Terrorist Attacks upon the United States. Washington, DC.

Fetherstonhaugh, D., Slovic, P., Johnson, S. M., & Friedrich, J. (1997). Insensitivity to the value of human life: A study of psychophysical numbing. *Journal of Risk and Uncertainty, 14,* 283–300.

Gregory, R., Failing, L., Harstone, M., Long, G., McDaniels, T., & Ohlson, D. (2012). *Structured decision making: A practical guide to environmental management choices.* Chichester, West Sussex, UK: Wiley-Blackwell.

Kahneman, D., & Tversky, A. (1979). Prospect theory: An analysis of decision under risk. *Econometrica, 47*, 263–291.

Keeney, R. L. (1992). *Value-focused thinking: A path to creative decisionmaking.* Cambridge, MA: Harvard University Press.

Maslow, A. (1943). A theory of human motivation. *Psychological Review, 50*, 370–396.

Osnos, E. (2014, December 22). In the land of the possible: Samantha Power has the president's ear. To what end? *The New Yorker.*

Power, S. (2003). *A problem from hell: America and the age of genocide.* New York, NY: Harper Perennial.

Reagan, Ronald. (1986, April 9). "The President's News Conference." Online by Gerhard Peters and John T. Woolley, *The American Presidency Project.* http://www.presidency.ucsb.edu/ws/?pid=37105.

Remnick, D. (2014, January 27). Going the distance: On and off the road with Barack Obama. *The New Yorker.* Retrieved from http://www.newyorker.com/magazine/2014/01/27/going-the-distance-2.

Slovic, P. (1975). Choice between equally valued alternatives. *Journal of Experimental Psychology: Human Perception and Performance, 1*, 280–287.

Small, D. A., Loewenstein, G., & Slovic, P. (2007). Sympathy and callousness: The impact of deliberative thought on donations to identifiable and statistical victims. *Organizational Behavior and Human Decision Processes, 102*, 143–153.

Tversky, A., Sattath, S., & Slovic, P. (1988). Contingent weighting in judgment and choice. *Psychological Review, 95*, 371–384.

The White House. Office of the Press Secretary. (2012, April 23). Remarks by the president at the United States Holocaust Memorial Museum. Retrieved from http://www.whitehouse.gov/the-press-office/2012/04/23/remarks-president-united-states-holocaust-memorial-museum.

CHAPTER 4

The Age of Numbing

ROBERT JAY LIFTON AND GREG MITCHELL

L IKE THE SURVIVORS OF THE ATOMIC BOMBINGS, Americans have
sought to distance themselves from the consequences of Hiroshima
and Nagasaki—with devastating effects. An important, but largely unexamined, dimension of Hiroshima is the lasting psychological, ethical, and
political impact on those who used the first nuclear weapons and continued
to develop them. The cumulative influence of Hiroshima is much greater
than most Americans suspect. Indeed, one may speak of the bomb's contamination not only of Japanese victims and survivors, but of the American
mind as well.

From the time of Hiroshima, Americans have assigned themselves the
task of finding virtue in the first use of the most murderous device ever created. These efforts have taken us to the far reaches of moral argument. We
have felt the need to avoid at any cost a sense of moral culpability for the
act. And there has indeed been a cost, one much greater than we wish to
recognize.

"Psychic numbing" can be defined as a diminished capacity or inclination to feel. Hiroshima survivors remember witnessing at the time of the
bomb terrible scenes of suffering—nothing less than a sea of death around
them—but found very quickly that they simply ceased to feel. They spoke
of "a paralysis of the mind," of becoming "insensitive to human death," of
being "temporarily without feeling." This useful defense mechanism prevents the mind from being overwhelmed and perhaps destroyed by the
dreadful and unmanageable images confronting it.

But psychic numbing extends further, to those who created the weapon,
made the decision to use it, or carried out the atomic bombing. While the

tendency toward numbing in relation to Hiroshima is universal, it is bound to be greatest in Americans, where it serves the additional purpose of warding off potential feelings of guilt. As in the very different case of German attitudes toward Auschwitz, we have not wished to permit Hiroshima to enter our psyches in ways that could affect our feelings. Hence we construct around Hiroshima what the American philosopher Edith Wyschogrod calls a *cordon sanitaire,* a barrier designed to prevent the spread of a contagious illness—the illness in this case being the awareness of what we did there. Indeed, the establishment of a *cordon sanitaire* has been the official policy of the American government.

From the start, Americans were not shown the human impact of the bomb. Government and military officials sought to hide its grotesque effects and so to deny the weapon's revolutionary significance. The visual record of the atomic bombings was largely restricted to shots of rubble.

Though the U.S. government officially ended wartime censorship at home on August 15, 1945, articles and photographs documenting the use of the atomic bomb remained under strict review. In Japan, censorship continued throughout the Occupation: American military officials destroyed or withheld all photographs taken by Japanese citizens following the bombings and banned all filming at the two sites.

The first photographs of the ruins shown in the United States were taken from the air at the end of August 1945. Though stark, they hardly did justice to the catastrophe; Hiroshima looked much like the incinerated section of Tokyo, except that the rubble was more pulverized. There was no way of knowing that much of Tokyo remained standing, while nearly all of Hiroshima had been destroyed. A few days later, magazines began to publish photographs taken from the ground. The photographs in *Life* magazine, for instance, showed a "still stinking junk-pile," as one caption put it: factory ruins, charred trees and telephones, the skeleton of a bus. There were no injured Japanese in these photographs, no doctors and nurses treating the ill and wounded, no funeral pyres, no one mourning.

It wasn't that *Life* was squeamish. In August it had published a gruesome series of photos of a Japanese soldier in Borneo set on fire by a flamethrower. But in that instance, only one person died; he was a combatant, not a civilian; and the wielder of the weapon was Australian, not American.

Shortly after the bombings, the U.S. Strategic Bombing Survey did hire a Japanese film crew, supervised by Lieutenant Daniel McGovern, to shoot a three-hour black-and-white documentary chronicling the effects of the bomb. But the film was declared top secret, locked away, and never shown to the American public. In early 1946, an American crew, also supervised by McGovern, filmed the only color footage taken in Hiroshima and Nagasaki. It too was stamped top secret and remained hidden for more than three decades, despite strenuous efforts by one of the filmmakers to win its release. McGovern later recalled, "The AEC (Atomic Energy Commission), the Pentagon, and the Manhattan Project people . . . were fearful because of the horror it contained. They didn't want that material shown, because it showed effects on men, women, and children."

The federal government established a similar pattern of obscuring the truth about radiation. Fallout was absent from every account of the immediate aftermath of the Hiroshima bomb. Although the effects of radiation were well known, atomic scientists and military officials publicly dismissed as hoaxes and propaganda Japanese reports of a soaring death toll and "ghost parades" of the living doomed to die. A research team sent to Hiroshima in September 1945 by General Leslie Groves, the military head of the Manhattan Project, was told, in the words of one member, that "our mission was to prove that there was not radioactivity from the bomb."

Of all the aspects of the bomb considered too sensitive for public consumption, radiation was perhaps the most sensitive. The effects of radiation symbolized the bomb's radical discontinuity with previous weapons, its special character as a destroyer of human beings not only at the moment of impact but throughout survivors' lives and across generations. Our government's need to deny the most disturbing aspect of these weapons has extended to situations that endanger its own people—workers in the nuclear weapons industry, residents of communities adjoining nuclear facilities and test sites, soldiers exposed to radioactive fallout, and the hundreds of Americans subjected to radiation experiments, often without their consent.

No wonder, then, that the American people have come to feel deceived by the bomb and its caretakers. We sense that ominous truths have been withheld from us. Hiroshima was the mother of all cover-ups; it spawned patterns of distortion, manipulation, and concealment that have contaminated American life ever since—from Vietnam to Watergate to the Iran-Contra affair. We have to ask ourselves how much of our rising mistrust of politicians and officials of all kinds—the angry cynicism so evident in our public life—emanates from the Hiroshima and post-Hiroshima nuclear deceptions.

Over time, the boundaries of numbing can blur. By closing ourselves off from the human costs of our devastating weapon, we are more able to do the same when confronted with other instances of collective suffering—the 1994 genocides in Bosnia and Rwanda, for example. We all become increasingly insensitive to the physical violence around us, as well as the institutionalized violence of poverty and homelessness. The tendency toward numbing can even extend to everyday forms of human interaction. As a character in an Alice Walker novel puts it, "The trouble with numbness . . . is that it spreads to all your organs, mainly the heart. Pretty soon after I don't hear the white folks crying for help, I don't hear the black."

If we can speak of an age of numbing, especially for Americans, much of it begins with Hiroshima. But confronting Hiroshima can be a powerful source of renewal. It can enable us to emerge from nuclear entrapment and rediscover our imaginative capacities on behalf of human good. We can break out of our individual and cultural habits of numbing. We can cease to justify weapons or actions of mass killing. And we can end our national self-betrayal by freeing our society from patterns of concealment.

CHAPTER 5

Epidemic Disease as Structural Violence

An Excerpt from Never Again?
Reflections on Human Values and Human Rights

PAUL FARMER

IT WAS THE PHILOSOPHER EMMANUEL LEVINAS who observed—and I'm just paraphrasing here—that ethics precedes epistemology.[1] Our responsibility to each other precedes and grounds our duty to discover the truth. But where does ethics start? What makes a problem an ethical problem, as opposed to a merely technical or public-relations one?[2] Can ethical thinking assume the willingness to act ethically? Do theory and rhetoric lead to action? Since these questions too have been argued for ages, I will start in what is, for me, an uncontentious arena: the medical and public health challenges before us right now.

The control of epidemic disease may seem an unlikely place to start in discussing human values, but the numbers are telling. Even if we consider only the big three infectious killers—AIDS, tuberculosis, and malaria—we are faced with tens of millions of preventable deaths slated to occur during our lifetimes. A recent document from the United Nations suggests, for example, that more than eighty million Africans might die from AIDS alone by 2025.[3] A similar toll will be taken, on that continent, by tuberculosis and malaria. Adding other infectious killers to the list, the butcher's bill totals hundreds of millions of premature deaths over the next century.

But these numbers have lost their ability to shock or even move us. What are the human values in question when we hear, and fail to react to, the news that each day thousands die of these maladies unattended? Where, in the midst of all of these numbers, is the human face of suffering? Can the reader discern the human faces in these reports? A failure of imagination

66

is one of the greatest failures registered in contemplating the fate of the world's poorest. Can photographs and personal narratives play a role, even as rhetorical tools, in promoting those human values that might lessen the magnitude of these disasters?

The strategy of countering a failure of imagination by having readers see the face of suffering is an old one in human rights struggles, as old at least as the eighteenth-century antislavery movement. Images, stories, and first-person testimony—rhetorical strategies or documentation or both?—remain the most relied-upon means of rendering these abstract struggles personal. Personalizing human suffering can help to make rights violations "real" to those unlikely to suffer them. Sometimes the challenge is to use narrative and imagery to shift the issue from "preserving my rights" to "defending the rights of the other person."

Susan Sontag has written compellingly of the minefields one must traverse to use vivid images relating the pain and suffering of others. Writing of famine, genocide, and AIDS in Africa, she warns that the photographs "carry a double message. They show a suffering that is outrageous, unjust, and should be repaired. They confirm that this is the sort of thing which happens in that place. The ubiquity of those photographs, and those horrors, cannot help but nourish belief in the inevitability of tragedy in the benighted or backward—that is, poor—parts of the world."[4] The same critique has been leveled at the use of personal narratives.

In this lecture, as noted, the ethics of responding to the large-scale misery still rife in the modern world will precede the epistemological issues. And to prevent us from assuming that these tragedies are inevitable, we turn to the experience of a young Haitian man who lay dying of AIDS and tuberculosis only a year or two ago. The story of his illness, and also of his failure to die, offers us a chance to consider the role human values play in confronting what is surely one of the greatest moral challenges of our times: addressing, through medicine and public health, inequalities of risk and outcome that have grown as steadily as has the gap between the richest and the poorest.[5]

On the afternoon of March 17, 2003, four men appeared at the public clinic in Lascahobas, a town in central Haiti; each carried one corner of a makeshift stretcher. On the stretcher lay a young man, eyes closed and seemingly unaware of the five-mile journey he had just taken on the shoulders of his neighbors. When they reached the clinic after the four-hour trip, the men placed their neighbor, Joseph, on an examination table. The

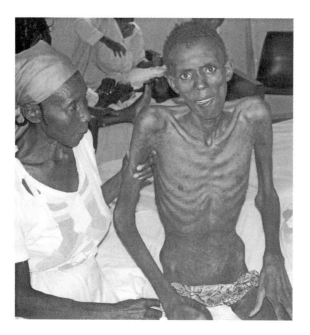

FIGURE 5.1
Joseph shortly
after his diagnosis
of AIDS and
disseminated
tuberculosis and
prior to therapy.
Photo by
David Walton.

FIGURE 5.2
Joseph after six months
of AIDS and tuberculosis
therapy. Photo by
David Walton.

physician tried to interview him, but Joseph was already stuporous. His brother recounted the dying man's story.

Joseph, twenty-six years old, had been sick for months. His illness had started with intermittent fevers, followed by a cough, weight loss, weakness, and diarrhea. His family, too poor, they thought, to take him to a hospital, brought Joseph to a traditional healer. Joseph would later explain: "My father sold nearly all that he had—our crops, our land, and our livestock—to pay the healer, but I kept getting worse. My family barely had enough to eat, but they sold everything to try to save me."

Joseph was bed-bound two months after the onset of his symptoms. He became increasingly emaciated and soon lost all interest in food. As he later recalled, "My mother, who was caring for me, was taking care of skin and bones."

Faced with what they saw as Joseph's imminent death, his family purchased a coffin. Several days later a community health worker, employed by Partners In Health, visited their hut. The health worker was trained to recognize the signs and symptoms of tuberculosis and HIV and immediately suspected that the barely responsive Joseph might have one or both of these diseases. Hearing that their son might have one last chance for survival, Joseph's parents pleaded with their neighbors to help carry him to the clinic, since he was too sick to travel on a donkey and too poor to afford a ride in a vehicle.

At the clinic, Joseph was indeed diagnosed with advanced AIDS and disseminated tuberculosis. He was hospitalized and treated with both antiretrovirals and antituberculous medications. Like his family, however, Joseph too had almost lost faith in the possibility of recovery. He remembers telling his physicians, early in the course of his treatment, "I'm dead already, and these medications can't save me." Contemplating a photograph taken by Dr. David Walton as Joseph began his treatment (Figure 5.1), one can understand readily why he had given up hope.

Despite his doubts, Joseph dutifully took his medications each day, and he slowly began to improve. Several weeks later, he was able to walk. His fevers subsided, and his appetite returned. After discharge from the hospital, he received what is termed "directly observed therapy" for both AIDS and tuberculosis, visited each day by a neighbor serving as an *accompagnateur*.[6] After several months of therapy, Joseph had gained more than thirty pounds (Figure 5.2).

A couple of years later, Joseph frequently speaks in front of large audiences about his experience. "When I was sick," he has said, "I couldn't farm the land, I couldn't get up to use the latrine; I couldn't even walk. Now I can do any sort of work. I can walk to the clinic just like anyone else. I care as much about my medications as I do about myself. There may be other illnesses that can break you, but AIDS isn't one of them. If you take these pills this disease doesn't have to break you."

What sort of human values might be necessary to save a young man's life? Compassion, pity, mercy, solidarity, and empathy come immediately to mind. But we also must have hope and imagination in order to make sure that proper medical care reaches the destitute sick. Naysayers still argue that it is simply not possible, or even wise, to deliver complex medical services in settings as poor as rural Haiti, where prevention should be the sole focus.[7] Joseph's story answers their misgivings, I feel, both in terms of fact (you can successfully treat advanced AIDS in this setting, and because good treatment serves to strengthen prevention programs) and in terms of value (it is worthwhile to try to do so). Certainly Joseph and his family would agree, as would thousands of other Haitians who have benefited from these services.

But is the story over? Are the human values of compassion, pity, mercy, solidarity, and empathy all there is to it? How might the notion of *rights* reframe a question often put as a matter of charity or compassion? Conversely, what happens when other human values come to play in settings of epidemic disease? What happens when the human values in question are selfishness, greed, callousness, resignation, or just plain lack of imagination?

We know at least one answer to these questions. The director of Partners In Health and I were in Kenya in January 2004 and visited, along the shores of Lake Victoria, a number of communities seemingly bereft of young adults. We had not met any poor Kenyans receiving antiretroviral therapy—to date the only effective means of treating AIDS—and were anxious to learn more about efforts to introduce it to the Lake Victoria region. This is one of the epicenters of the AIDS pandemic, and surveys of young adults over the past two decades indicate rates of infection that range upward of 30 percent.[8] Many of those people infected are dead or dying—even now, well over a decade after the introduction of effective antiretroviral therapy. In some areas, kinship networks have been nearly overwhelmed: in certain villages, children of those who die of AIDS are placed in orphanages almost as often as they are placed among their extended families. These days we hear a lot about the need for compassion for AIDS orphans, who number in the millions in Africa alone, but what arrangements might have prevented their orphaning?

The medications that saved Joseph's life are commodities available throughout the global economy to those who can pay for them, and this is no less true in Kenya than in any other place. The people who have died without a single dose of effective therapy over the past decade are, almost without exception, people who lived and died in poverty. In order to make sure that poor people dying from AIDS stop dying, it will be necessary to move beyond what Sontag referred to as the "unstable emotions" of compassion or pity,[9] to more stable arrangements for all those afflicted with this and other treatable diseases. Translating compassion, pity, mercy, solidarity, or empathy into policy or rights is a difficult task.

But it is not an impossible task. How might we draw on certain human values to promote the notion of a right to health care and spark the imagination? A subsequent visit to Kenya, a year after the first one and again in the company of the director of Partners In Health, reminded us of the power of photographs. This time, we were traveling with the head of mission of a large charity that had recently received a significant amount of funding for AIDS relief. "Treatment is important," he remarked after a day of home visits, adding that he'd recently seen a before-and-after-treatment photograph of a man who he assumed was Kenyan, since these images appeared in a Kenyan newspaper. "The difference between the two photographs was extraordinary," he added. It was clear that he'd been moved and it seemed, too, that he was in a position to do something about it—to translate his reaction to the photograph, however "unstable," into interventions designed to save the lives of those already sick. The photographs, it turns out, were the same ones you see above. Joseph's images had made it across the world from Haiti to Kenya.

Do the destitute sick of Haiti or Kenya ask for our pity and compassion? Often they do. But can't we offer something better? The human values required to save one person's life, or to prevent children in a single family from losing their parents, surely include pity and compassion, and those sentiments are not to be scorned. Often it is possible to save a life, to save a family. But "scaling up" such efforts requires a modicum of stability and the cooperation of policy makers and funders, themselves unlikely to suffer the indignities of structural violence. Partners In Health has worked for a long time in a small number of settings, seeking to make common cause with local partners to establish long-term medical projects that strengthen, rather than weaken, public health. This means strengthening what is termed "the public sector" rather than, say, other nongovernmental organizations like ours or private clinics and hospitals. Nongovernmental organizations themselves can and should strengthen the faltering public sector.[10] We proceed in this manner because we've learned that the public sector, however weak in these places, is often the sole guarantor of the *right* of the poor to health care. Our own efforts take seriously the notion of the right to health care and also to freedom from hunger, homelessness, illiteracy, and other problems encountered in settings of great poverty. Others involved in nongovernmental organizations are also learning these lessons when they seek to inspire projects by social justice and a rights framework rather than by what Rony Brauman of Médecins Sans Frontières has termed "the politics of pity."[11]

To move from pity and compassion for a sufferer like Joseph—a young man with a story, a face, and a name—to the values inherent in notions of human rights is a long leap. For many, especially those far removed from conditions such as those faced in rural Haiti or rural Kenya, the struggle for basic rights lacks immediacy. But sometimes we can entrap ourselves into becoming decent and humane people by advancing sound policies and laws. The road from unstable emotions to genuine entitlements—rights—is one we must travel if we are to transform humane values into meaningful and effective programs that will serve precisely those who need our empathy and solidarity most. In other words, we are not opposed to pity, but we're anxious to press for policies that would protect vulnerable populations from structural violence and advance the cause of social and economic rights.

Social and economic rights, which include the right to health care, have been termed the "neglected stepchildren" of the human rights movements and held up in opposition to the political and civil rights now embraced, at least on paper, by many of the world's most powerful governments. So striking is this division within the rights movements that some have come to refer to social and economic rights as "the rights of the poor." Certain African voices, at least, have argued that human rights language is not widely used on that continent because so little attention is paid, by the mainstream human rights organizations, to health care, clean water, primary education, and other basic entitlements. This means that little attention is paid to the voices of those who do not enjoy these rights.[12] The language of political rights has become meaningless to many people living in the worst imaginable poverty. Conversely, the language of economic rights is sometimes viewed as excessive, menacing, and irresponsible in the eyes of people living in the midst of plenty. This growing rift, I would argue, is the most pressing human rights problem of our times. As long as mainstream human rights organizations do not understand how poverty and inequality are also human rights violations, rather than simply distracting background considerations, there is little hope of advancing the case for social and economic rights. Any doctor or public health specialist concerned with the health of the poor should agree, certainly. As long as certain fruits of modernity—in speaking of AIDS, certain diagnostic tests and medications—are considered commodities rather than rights, such sentiments as pity and compassion are not likely to be translated into meaningful changes for the millions who now need these resources to survive.

NOTES

P. Farmer, (2006), *Never Again? Reflections on Human Values and Human Rights*, in G. B. Petersen (Ed.), The Tanner Lectures on Human Values (vol. 25, pp. 137–188), Salt Lake City: University of Utah Press, 2006. The Tanner Lectures on Human Values, delivered at University of Utah, March 30, 2005.

1. Theologian Wayne Cavalier writes,

> Because it is the primordial encounter with the other upon which our subjective being is predicated, we therefore owe our being to the other. Therefore, our moral indebtedness to the other is prior to our being, and it is the being as subject who "knows." . . . Another way to put it: the encounter with the other gives rise to the subject; therefore, our indebtedness to the other is at the very root of being. Epistemologically, this encounter and its consequences are the foundations of knowing. This radically changes the understanding of knowing from a process of absorbing the unknown into the subject to the fact of becoming through the primordial encounter with the other. This changes the understanding of knowledge, understood from the prior ethical or moral indebtedness that brings the subject (usually understood as the knower) into being as a coming near, an encounter with extreme ethical consequences. (Personal communication, July 22, 2005)

2. Elsewhere we have argued that contemporary medical ethics focuses on certain challenges (defining brain death, say, or the ethics of stem cell research) while ignoring others (lack of access to care for those living in poverty). See Paul

Farmer and Nicole Gastineau Campos (2004), "Rethinking Medical Ethics: A View from Below," *Developing World Bioethics*, 4, 17–41.

3. Joint United Nations Program on HIV/AIDS (2005), *AIDS in Africa: Three Scenarios to 2025*, Geneva, Switzerland: UNAIDS. One hopes and expects, of course, that the toll will be much lower. But the report outlines three plausible scenarios of the African HIV/AIDS epidemic over the next twenty years based on the current actions of the global and African communities; all three scenarios— a "best-case situation," a "middle-case" condition, and a "doomsday scenario"— warn that "the worst . . . is still to come" (p. 20).

4. Susan Sontag (2003), *Regarding the Pain of Others* (New York, NY: Picador/ Farrar, Straus and Giroux), p. 71.

5. I have explored the growing gap between rich and poor and its relationship to epidemic disease and violence in *Infections and Inequalities* (Berkeley: University of California Press, 1999) and *Pathologies of Power* (Berkeley: University of California Press, 2003). A new book by Jeffrey Sachs (2005), *The End of Poverty* (New York, NY: Penguin), offers an economist's view of this gap and its growth over the past three centuries; he also engages current debates among development economists. See also Jim Yong Kim, Joyce V. Millen, Alec Irwin, and John Gershman, eds. (2000), *Dying for Growth: Global Inequality and the Health of the Poor* (Monroe, ME: Common Courage Press).

6. *Accompagnateurs* are almost always neighbors of patients—some of them patients themselves—who accept responsibility for supervising daily care and support for people suffering from AIDS or tuberculosis; they are trained by Partners In Health staff and are the cornerstones of our projects in Haiti, Peru, Boston, Rwanda, and elsewhere. This strategy for treating AIDS in what are now termed "resource-poor settings" is described in a number of papers in the medical literature. See, for example, Paul Farmer, Fernet Léandre, Joia Mukherjee, et al. (2001), "Community-Based Approaches to HIV Treatment in Resource-Poor Settings," *Lancet, 358*, 404–409; Paul Farmer, Fernet Léandre, Joia Mukherjee, et al. (2001), "Community-Based Treatment of Advanced HIV Disease: Introducing DOT-HAART (Directly Observed Therapy with Highly Active Antiretroviral Therapy)," *Bulletin of the World Health Organization, 79*, 1145–1151; and Heidi L. Behforouz, Paul E. Farmer, and Joia S. Mukherjee (2004), "From Directly Observed Therapy to *Accompagnateurs*: Enhancing AIDS Treatment Outcomes in Haiti and in Boston," *Clinical Infectious Diseases, 38*, S429–436.

7. These debates continue. See, to cite but one very recent example, the assertions by Harvard-trained economist Emily Oster, who seems to argue against the provision of antiretroviral therapy to patients such as Joseph, claiming that "antiretroviral treatment is around 100 times as expensive in preventing AIDS deaths as treating other sexually transmitted infections and around 25 times as expensive as education" ("Treating HIV Doesn't Pay," July 25, 2005, *Forbes* online). But these inputs are changing rapidly with time: over the past few years, we have

seen an over 90 percent decline in the cost of antiretrovirals, and there is little agreement about the efficacy of current prevention methods and of educational campaigns among the very poor—the victims of structural violence. While noting that "it may be that we have an objective other than maximizing the efficiency of dollars spent," Oster nevertheless hews to static cost-effectiveness analyses, given these changes and debates: "In my work I have assumed that our goal in the face of the epidemic is to maximize life. In other words, to save the most years of life with the funding available." But why is funding the constant in this life-or-death equation when funding and the cost of inputs are poorly studied and rapidly changing? Nor is her analysis epidemiologically sound: while citing the importance of treating sexually transmitted infections in order to prevent HIV transmission, she fails to link the critical importance of treating HIV infection (itself a sexually transmitted infection in most parts of the world) in order to prevent HIV transmission. Our experience in rural Haiti has shown that demand for HIV screening, a cornerstone of prevention efforts, is low as long as effective care remains unavailable. For more on the debate, see Paul Farmer (2000), "Prevention without Treatment Is Not Sustainable," *National AIDS Bulletin* (Australia), *13*, 6–9, 40; my exchange with Edward Green explores some of these complexities (Edward C. Green, "New Challenges to the AIDS Prevention Paradigm," and Paul Farmer, "AIDS: A Biosocial Problem with Social Solutions," both in *Anthropology News, 44* [2003], 5–7), as do Helen Epstein's recent essays in the *New York Review of Books* ("God and the Fight Against AIDS" [April 28, 2005], *52* (7), 47–51; and "The Lost Children of AIDS" [November 3, 2005], *52* (17), 41–46).

8. Joint United Nations Program on HIV/AIDS (2004), *Epidemiological Fact Sheets on HIV/AIDS and Sexually Transmitted Infections: Kenya, 2004* (Geneva, Switzerland: World Health Organization). Available at www.unaids.org/EN/ Geographical+Area/by+country/kenya.asp.

9. Sontag, *Regarding the Pain of Others*, p. 101.

10. David A. Walton, Paul E. Farmer, Wesler Lambert, et al. (2004), "Integrated HIV Prevention and Care Strengthens Primary Health Care: Lessons from Rural Haiti," *Journal of Public Health Policy, 25*, 137–158.

11. See Rony Brauman (1996), "L'Assistance Humanitaire Internationale," in *Dictionnaire de Philosophie Morale et Politique*, Monique Canto-Sperber, ed., Paris, France: Presses Universitaires de France, pp. 96–101. Reflecting on his experience during the convoluted Cambodian refugee crisis of the late 1970s and early 1980s, Brauman (1998) notes that, for aid workers, "the choice was . . . not between a political position and a neutral position, but between two political positions: one active and the other by default" (Rony Brauman, "Refugee Camps, Population Transfers, and NGOs," in *Hard Choices: Moral Dilemmas in Humanitarian Intervention*, ed. Jonathan Moore, pp. 177–194, Oxford: Rowman and Littlefield).

12. Chidi Anselm Odinkalu (2000), in critiquing conventional human rights work in Africa, hazards a guess as to why so many human rights groups mirror

the inequalities of our world: "Local human rights groups exist to please the inter-national agencies that fund or support them. Local problems are only defined as potential pots of project cash, not as human experiences to be resolved in just terms, thereby delegitimizing human rights language and robbing its ideas of popular appeal" (Chidi Anselm Odinkalu, "Why More Africans Don't Use Human Rights Language," *Human Rights Dialogue: Human Rights for All? The Problem of the Human Rights Box 2*, 3–4, available at www.cceia.org/viewMedia.php/prm TemplateID/8/prmID/602).

PART II

Narrative, Analytical, and Visual Strategies for Prompting Sensitivity and Meaning

Introduction

SCOTT SLOVIC AND PAUL SLOVIC

T HE ARTICLES, BOOK CHAPTERS, AND LECTURE TRANSCRIPTS in this
section aim to describe and demonstrate particular strategies that can
help readers, listeners, and observers become more sensitive to the meaning of elusive, numerically abstract phenomena. Scholars of environmental
and socially relevant communication have traditionally written about the use
of language in order to persuade audiences toward particular ideological
stances. In her 2006 study, *Communicating Nature: How We Create and
Understand Environmental Messages*, Julia B. Corbett highlights the wide
spectrum of environmental ideologies, ranging from "unrestrained instru-
mentalism" (nature exists for human use) at one extreme to "transformative
ideologies" (belief systems aiming to replace anthropocentrism with ecocen-
tric relationships) at the other. She suggests that environmental communication is fundamentally related to public relations—a matter of pitching
news stories and spinning information in order to compel listeners and
readers to come into line (see her chapter titled "Battle for Spin: The Public
Relations Industry"). Other scholars, such as J. Robert Cox, use concepts
such as "narrative framing" to emphasize the role of story in "build[ing]
interesting environmental coverage" (Katherine McComas qtd. in Cox, 2013,
p. 164), aiding audiences' "understanding," and affecting their "relationships to the phenomena being represented" (p. 164). Cox also emphasizes

J. Shanahan's notion that "cultivation analysis" is "a theory of story-telling, which assumes that repeated exposure to a set of messages is likely to produce agreement in an audience with opinions expressed in . . . those messages" (Shanahan qtd. in Cox, p. 165), describing this as a "process of gradual influence or cumulative effect" (p. 165). This line of thinking echoes Scott Slovic's discussion of Robert Zajonc's work on the "mere-exposure effect" in the 1992 book *Seeking Awareness in American Nature Writing*, tracing the "attitudinal effects" of repeated exposure to particular ideas about the natural world.

For Corbett, environmental communication is principally a matter of rhetorical impact or persuasion, a steering of audiences toward agreement with whoever might be seeking to communicate a "message." Corbett describes message formation as a process of making "tactical communication choices," suggesting that subject matter can be deliberately shaped and specific audiences "targeted" in order to maximize message impact (p. 291). While the writers who have contributed their work to this section of the book are certainly interested in spurring readers to think in new ways, these professional communicators are also doing something slightly different than what the above-mentioned communication scholars have outlined. In the selections below, there is a sense that certain kinds of numerically based phenomena are exceedingly difficult for people not only to comprehend, but to *apprehend*—we can scarcely begin to grasp the concept of multiple lives lost (in instances of genocide) or, for that matter, the excessive proliferation of lives (in the case of overpopulation). In a sense, the writers of the following selections, and the other writers and artists interviewed in Part III, are asking about the meaning of "meaning." How does information register on the human mind? What kinds of representations of information prompt us to "care" and, sometimes, to act? And when does information pass over our heads or in one ear and out the other? At issue here is not just how to make a winning argument, but how to use language to navigate the capacities and limitations of human sensitivity, of human thinking.

In his two *New York Times* columns collected in this book, Nicholas D. Kristof explicitly reflects on the rhetorical techniques that might be needed to "galvanize," or *move*, national leaders (and, implicitly, the general public) to respond to humanitarian crises, ranging from the genocide in western Sudan to war and poverty in eastern Congo. In "Save the Darfur Puppy,"

Kristof repeatedly uses the visual image of a puppy with "big eyes and floppy ears" to emphasize the importance of concrete imagery of a single individual in evoking compassion and spurring action on the part of audiences. While this article is ostensibly a plea for the international community to become engaged in the Darfur crisis, the meta-argument in the column is that there is something profoundly and perhaps tragically ironic about human nature that enables the imagined visage of a single puppy to tweak our heartstrings more effectively than the news of "the slaughter of hundreds of thousands of fellow humans."

A month later, Kristof published a second column (also included here) titled "A Student, a Teacher and a Glimpse of War," in which he likewise explored how the psychological power of the individual "glimpse" (the single example or experience) may work to compel concern far exceeding the rational magnitude of the case itself. In the second piece, the journalist points out the irony that "instead of spending a few hundred dollars trying to save [a single victim], who might die anyway, we could spend that money buying vaccines or mosquito nets to save a far larger number of children in other villages." He recognizes the moral and emotional difficulty of coming to such a rational decision, however, when he immediately continues by stating: "And yet—how can you walk away from a human being who will surely die if you do so?" Kristof's columns employ several fascinating communication strategies that both deepen our understanding of the psychological aspects of numbers and nerves and, at the same time, move readers to care about the social issues that concern him. First, by juxtaposing the individual, emotionally compelling dog or hawk or person to the large-scale phenomena that, from a rational perspective, ought to compel more concern than they do, Kristof helps graft audience engagement from the small, evocative phenomena to the large, emotionally numbing phenomena. Second, by noting the irony of human reactions to small- and large-scale phenomena without being caustically accusatory, Kristof coaxes readers toward an extension of their concern to the large-scale rather than simply entrenching them in their narrow scope of caring. And third, by offering the meta-discussion of the paradox of human psychology—our greater concern for minutiae than for vast crises—the author supplies readers with a cognitive foundation for changing our responses to future situations, or at least he provides us with information about our psychological tendencies that may enable us to correct or modify the extremity of such tendencies.

Kenneth Helphand, a distinguished historian of gardens and landscape architecture, asks us to think about the challenges and possibilities of communicating quantitative information not only by way of words, but also through visual and other modes of sensory experience. His article offers a series of examples of installations and visual displays that encourage "combination[s] of participatory actions," such as looking, reading, moving, contemplating, and touching. Much as photographer Chris Jordan's compositions invite observers to participate in the images as a way of connecting the viewing self to the collective human behaviors captured in the art, the works presented in Helphand's essay call for audience engagement in a more active sense than is typically the case for readers of literature. Often "audiences" for memorial installations are standing in the locations where dreadful events have occurred, such as the abduction of Holocaust victims. Essential to the meaningful experience of information presented in these projects is the capacity of viewers to identify with individuals whose lives were directly affected by the memorialized events—in other words, "the fate of too many is best understood through identification with the singular." Helphand's essay anticipates some of the strategies for helping viewers apprehend the relationship between the individual and the collective that Chris Jordan explores in his interview in Part III.

Annie Dillard, one of the leading American authors of the late twentieth century (winner of the Pulitzer Prize for nonfiction in 1974), guides readers through a fundamental consideration of what numbers mean and how they accrue meaning in her essay "The Wreck of Time." At first glance her piece seems to be a concatenation of unrelated images, bits of information, and fragmentary stories, but as the essay develops it is possible to see the author's particular interest in numbers. As the collage of examples proceeds, it further becomes clear that the point of this display is to tease out the distinction between genuine emotional attachment (one kind of meaning) and more abstract appreciation of the opacity of data (also a kind of meaning, but not one that could be described as compassion or caring). In the fourth section of the essay, Dillard exposes what may be the core of her free-form argument about the psychology of human responses to fragmentary data in general and to numbers in particular when she asks, "Do you not suffer this sense? How about what journalists call 'compassion fatigue'? Reality fatigue? At what limit for you do other individuals blur? Vanish?" As we know from some of the psychological studies offered in Part I, human experimental subjects may begin to experience "compassion fatigue" when an individual becomes a pair of individuals—when we jump from one to two. When the numbers rise to a hundred or a thousand or into the millions, the inability to focus our concern becomes utterly overwhelming.

Lest we respond to Dillard's poignant evocation of the slippery slope toward numbness by assuming that stories of individual experience serve uniformly well as introductions to vast, abstract phenomena, Scott Slovic's study of two novels about climate change—Michael Crichton's *State of Fear* and Susan M. Gaines's *Carbon Dreams*—calls into question the potential use of narrowly ideological narratives that undermine public appreciation of complex ideas. Into the mix of our discussion of conveying technical information about social and environmental phenomena to the general public comes the question of trust. Psychologists have observed that trust is "asymmetrical"—difficult to create, relatively easy to erode. In *State of Fear*, the skilled popular novelist Crichton offers a realistic, highly credible, and yet ideologically driven critique of climate change science as a hoax invented by self-interested radical environmentalists, concerned only with fomenting public fear and thus raising money for their organizations. By contrast, Gaines's novel tells the story of a young climate scientist who collects data, questions its meaning, and resists communicating the implications of her work to the public until she is forced to respond to a fellow scientist who misrepresents the meaning of various data. Garrett Hardin (1985) once criticized the use of scientific data (including numerical information) by "the merely eloquent," by which he meant writers and artists. Juxtaposing the examples of these two novels, it's possible to see precisely what can happen when a talented storyteller like Crichton uses narrative not to explore important questions about human nature or the physical world but to distort the complexity and uncertainty of climate science and impugn its practitioners.

Terry Tempest Williams is widely known as one of the major voices of contemporary American environmental literature, a gifted teller of poetic stories in volumes of nonfiction such as *Refuge: An Unnatural History of Family & Place*. "Healing Rwanda" first appeared as an article in *Orion* magazine and later was included as a section of the book *Finding Beauty in a Broken World*. It is not so much a story of environmental experience (like much of Williams's work) but rather a commentary on a social phenomenon. The central stylistic trope of this book is the mosaic, the piecing together of shards of ceramic to form a meaningful, beautiful composite, particularly when viewed from afar. In her piece on Rwanda, Williams recounts her experience in accompanying an American visual artist to Rwanda in the years following the genocide of the mid-1990s in the hope of memorializing the victims of the genocide and helping the survivors tell their stories, heal their feelings, and move forward with their lives. This is an article about the *aftermath* of a terrible human tragedy, not about the tragedy itself—but its vivid evocation of places and characters, its use of local voices to produce a sense of Rwanda today, shows a mosaic-like use of tiny pieces of verbal detail to attach emotion to a large-scale social phenomenon. This piece of writing steadfastly sidesteps the use of quantitative information in order to develop a human picture of genocide.

We sometimes refer to the movement back and forth between abstract, technical information and intimate, personal narrative as a "telescoping." The result of this technique is a combination of the "big picture" of a particular topic and detailed, vivid examples that show the meaning of the topic, its specific implications and connections with recognizable places, with individual human lives. Ideally, this telescoping technique, when it moves from big picture to intimate example, will bring to life a large, subtle topic without distorting or obscuring the general subject. Much of journalist Bill McKibben's work, ranging from his 1989 clarion call about global warming, *The End of Nature*, to his 1998 meditation on population issues, *Maybe One*, operates by way of this alternation of intimate personal narratives and more detached analysis of the social and environmental topics he's addressing. In recent years, McKibben has become especially active with the anti-global-warming group called 350.org, and his essay in this collection addresses the challenge and the virtue of relying on something as abstract as the number 350 to help the public understand the atmospheric processes of climate change and motivate readers to take personal and collective action. Other writers, such as Diane DiPrima (2011), in her poem "350," have also struggled with the challenge of "how to make the 'fact' 350 is named for come alive in the reader's mind" (p. 245)—she, for instance, came up with a unique, numerically based poetic form consisting of ten stanzas, five lines each, with seven words per line, totaling 350 words. McKibben, too, seems to be suggesting that numbers can outweigh words—images, stories, explanations—in the public imagination. Of course, the upshot of his literary discussion of the number 350 in this essay is that words do not "fail" entirely—indeed, words are necessary in tandem with the number itself. This approach essentially corroborates Edward Tufte's argument, mentioned in the Introduction to this book, that multidimensionality is typically the most effective way of conveying quantitative information.

Finally, we have included Rick Bass's "The Blood Root of Art" in this section of the book in order to show one of the leading contemporary American environmental authors explicitly wrestling with the different capacities of numerical and nonnumerical language. Bass's essay confronts directly the different kinds of meaning that attach themselves to numbers and images. The goal of his essay is to be both informative (about the current state of resource extraction, particularly logging, in the remote Yaak Valley of northwest Montana) and persuasive, urging lawmakers to restrict logging access to this ecologically delicate and significant region.

In the Introduction, we cite historian Alfred Crosby's study of quantification in Western culture, in which he traces the process by which numbers have come to be the essential "measure of reality." Perhaps the ultimate example of this devotion to numbers is evident in the monetization of every possible phenomenon, as if worth is determined by how much someone or some group would be willing to pay if the place or species or object were available for purchase. This expression of worth in terms of monetary amount is widespread, and yet many find themselves viscerally resisting this idea. Australian essayist William J. Lines, for instance, in a 2001 piece called "Money," writes that "people exploit what has a price or what they conclude to be merely of value; they defend what they love. Love cannot be priced." In order to know what we love and then fight to protect what we love, Lines says, "we need a particularizing language, for we love what we particularly know" (p. 26). Bass recognizes that numbers will speak to certain kinds of audiences, and he states, in fact, that he had "meant for this whole essay to be numbers: a landslide of numbers." But he admits that he "cannot tolerate them, at present," that "there is a space in me, this short winter day, that cries out for words." This passage in Bass's essay eloquently evokes the larger conundrum for all of us living in societies of quantification, so to speak. Our cultures have come to rely on numbers, economic and otherwise, to describe reality, to measure its worth and establish priorities, and to determine many aspects of our behavior. And yet we yearn to understand and express our attachments, our emotional relationships, with other modes of discourse. Bass's essay, like many of the other examples offered in this section of the book, shows the interesting process of balancing, if not truly synthesizing, quantitative and qualitative discourse in order to articulate our understanding of a wide range of important phenomena, from genocide to deforestation, from global climate change to overpopulation and extinction.

REFERENCES

Corbett, J. B. (2006). *Communicating nature: How we create and understand environmental messages.* Washington, DC: Island Press.

Cox, R. J. (2013). *Environmental communication and the public sphere* (3rd ed.). Los Angeles, CA: Sage.

DiPrima, D. (2011). 350. *Interim: The eco issue, 29,* 1 and 2, 244–245.

Hardin, G. (1985). *Filters against folly: How to survive despite economists, ecologists, and the merely eloquent.* New York, NY: Penguin Books.

Killingsworth, M. J., & Palmer, J. S. (1991). *Ecospeak: Rhetoric and environmental politics in America.* Carbondale: Southern Illinois University Press.

Lines, W. J. (2001). *Open air: Essays.* Sydney, Australia: New Holland Publishers.

Slovic, S. (1992). *Seeking awareness in American nature writing.* Salt Lake City: University of Utah Press.

CHAPTER 6

The Power of One

NICHOLAS D. KRISTOF

Save the Darfur Puppy

Finally, we're beginning to understand what it would take to galvanize President Bush, other leaders and the American public to respond to the genocide in Sudan: a suffering puppy with big eyes and floppy ears.

That's the implication of a series of studies by psychologists trying to understand why people—good, conscientious people—aren't moved by genocide or famines. Time and again, we've seen that the human conscience just isn't pricked by mass suffering, while an individual child (or puppy) in distress causes our hearts to flutter.

In one experiment, psychologists asked ordinary citizens to contribute $5 to alleviate hunger abroad. In one version, the money would go to a particular girl, Rokia, a 7-year-old in Mali; in another, to 21 million hungry Africans; in a third, to Rokia—but she was presented as a victim of a larger tapestry of global hunger.

Not surprisingly, people were less likely to give to anonymous millions than to Rokia. But they were also less willing to give in the third scenario, in which Rokia's suffering was presented as part of a broader pattern.

Evidence is overwhelming that humans respond to the suffering of individuals rather than groups. Think of the toddler Jessica McClure falling down a well in 1987, or the Lindbergh baby kidnapping in 1932 (which Mencken described as the "the biggest story since the Resurrection").

Even the right animal evokes a similar sympathy. A dog stranded on a ship aroused so much pity that $48,000 in private money was spent trying to rescue it—and that was before the Coast Guard stepped in. And after I began visiting Darfur in 2004, I was flummoxed by the public's passion to save a red-tailed hawk, Pale Male, that had been evicted from his nest on Fifth Avenue in New York City. A single homeless hawk aroused more indignation than two million homeless Sudanese.

Advocates for the poor often note that 30,000 children die daily of the consequences of poverty—presuming that this number will shock people into action. But the opposite is true: the more victims, the less compassion.

In one experiment, people in one group could donate to a $300,000 fund for medical treatments that would save the life of one child—or, in another group, the lives of eight children. People donated more than twice as much money to help save one child as to help save eight.

Likewise, remember how people were asked to save Rokia from starvation? A follow-up allowed students to donate to Rokia or to a hungry boy named Moussa. Both Rokia and Moussa attracted donations in the same proportions. Then another group was asked to donate to Rokia and Moussa together. But donors felt less good about supporting two children, and contributions dropped off.

"Our capacity to feel is limited," Paul Slovic of the University of Oregon writes in a new journal article, "Psychic Numbing and Genocide," which discusses these experiments. Professor Slovic argues that we cannot depend on the innate morality even of good people. Instead, he believes, we need to develop legal or political mechanisms to force our hands to confront genocide.

So, yes, we should develop early-warning systems for genocide, prepare an African Union, UN and NATO rapid-response capability, and polish the "responsibility to protect" as a legal basis to stop atrocities. (The Genocide Intervention Network and the Enough Project are working on these things.)

But, frankly, after four years of watching the UN Security Council, the International Criminal Court and the Genocide Convention accomplish little in Darfur, I'm skeptical that either human rationality or international law can achieve much unless backed by a public outcry.

One experiment underscored the limits of rationality. People prepared to donate to the needy were first asked either to talk about babies (to prime the emotions) or to perform math calculations (to prime their rational side). Those who did math donated less.

So maybe what we need isn't better laws but more troubled consciences—pricked, perhaps, by a Darfur puppy with big eyes and floppy ears. Once we find such a soulful dog in peril, we should call ABC News.

ABC's news judgment can be assessed by the 11 minutes of evening news coverage it gave to Darfur's genocide during all of last year—compared with 23 minutes for the false confession in the JonBenet Ramsey case.

If President Bush and the global public alike are unmoved by the slaughter of hundreds of thousands of fellow humans, maybe our last, best hope is that we can be galvanized by a puppy in distress.

A Student, a Teacher and a Glimpse of War

I'm taking a student, Leana Wen, and a teacher, Will Okun, along with me on this trip to Africa. Here in this thatch-roofed village in the hills of eastern Congo, we had a glimpse of war, and Leana suddenly found herself called to perform.

Villagers took what looked like a bundle of rags out of one thatch-roof hut and laid it on the ground. Only it wasn't a bunch of rags; it was a woman dying of starvation.

The woman, Yohanita Nyiahabimama, 41, weighed perhaps 60 pounds. She was conscious and stared at us with bright eyes, whispering answers to a few questions. When she was moved, she screamed in pain, for her buttocks were covered with ulcerating bedsores.

Leana, who had just graduated from medical school at Washington University, quickly examined Yohanita.

"If we don't get her to a hospital very soon, she will die," Leana said bluntly. "We have to get her to a hospital."

There was nothing special about Yohanita except that she was in front of us. In villages throughout the region, people just like her are dying by the thousands—of a deadly mixture of war and poverty.

Instead of spending a few hundred dollars trying to save Yohanita, who might die anyway, we could spend that money buying vaccines or mosquito nets to save a far larger number of children in other villages.

And yet—how can you walk away from a human being who will surely die if you do so?

So we spoke to Simona Pari of the Norwegian Refugee Council, which has built a school in the village and helped people here survive as conflict has raged around them. Simona immediately agreed to use her vehicle to transport Yohanita to a hospital.

The village found a teenage girl who could go with Yohanita and help look after her, and the family agreed that it would be best to have her taken not to the local public hospital but to the fine hospital in Goma run by Heal Africa, an outstanding aid group with strong American connections (www .healafrica.org).

Now, nearly four days later, Yohanita is on the road to recovery, lying on a clean bed in the Heal Africa Hospital. Leana saved one of her first patients.

What almost killed Yohanita was starvation in a narrow sense, but more broadly she is one more victim of the warfare that has already claimed four million lives in Congo since 1998. Even 21st-century wars like Congo's—the most lethal conflict since World War II—kill the old-fashioned way, by starving people or exposing them to disease.

That's what makes wars in the developing world so deadly, for they kill not only with guns and machetes but also in much greater numbers with diarrhea, malaria, AIDS and malnutrition.

The people here in Malehe were driven out of their village by rampaging soldiers in December. Yohanita's family returned to their home a few months later, but their crops and livestock had been taken. Then Yohanita had a miscarriage and the family spent all its money saving her—which meant that they ran out of food.

"We used to have plenty to eat, but now we have nothing," Yohanita's mother, Anastasie, told us. "We've had nothing to eat but bananas since the beginning of May." (To see video of our visit and read blogs by Leana and Will, go to nytimes.com/twofortheroad.)

I'm under no delusion that our intervention makes a difference to Congo (though it did make quite a difference to Yohanita). The way to help Congo isn't to take individual starving people to the hospital but to work to end the war—yet instead the war is heating up again here, in part because Congo is off the world's radar.

One measure of the international indifference is the shortage of aid groups here: Neighboring Rwanda, which is booming economically, is full of aid workers. But this area of eastern Congo is far needier and yet is home to hardly any aid groups. World Vision is one of the very few American groups active here in the North Kivu area.

Just imagine that four million Americans or Europeans had been killed in a war, and that white families were starving to death as a result of that war. The victims in isolated villages here in Congo, like Yohanita, may be black and poor and anonymous, but that should make this war in Congo no less an international priority.

CHAPTER 7

From One to Too Many

KENNETH HELPHAND

CREATIVE GRAPHIC DESIGN can address the display of complex information. For example, projects and installations created by artists and others can take information out of books, newspapers, or conversations and place it directly in the landscape to be physically experienced. These spatial projects can be experienced in three and four dimensions.

The designs and techniques of spatial projects vary in terms of scale, duration, location, and how they are created. Spatially they may be vast in scale or minute, they may extend to the horizon or be found beneath your feet. They can be temporary installations or designed for "eternity." They may be found near or at the exact site of events or a distant locale. They may be located in the most prominent places (i.e., the Mall in Washington, DC) or be "discovered" on the most ordinary street. They may be permanent or transportable. They can be created by individuals or as the product of collective action.

These projects all have a goal. They aspire to reach individuals both rationally and emotionally, to connect the numbers with the nerves. They want to make anonymity personal, to have you feel for strangers. This may happen through a variety of means. It can be visual experience—just looking—but more often it is through a combination of participatory actions: looking, reading, moving, and contemplating. A walk could be past thousands of graves or along a painted graph that goes down a street for blocks. Some projects have a tactile dimension, asking to be touched—and in the act the touchers are touched. These projects emphasize the representation of numbers in ways that are viscerally meaningful to all who create, install, and experience these environments. Words are often present but are not always necessary, as the "explanation" happens in the experience of the place and the "facts" may not be needed in the moment. The experience of any of these will vary depending whether one is alone, in a small group, or among many others. These places often suggest or imply a silence in their presence, but the silence may paradoxically enrich the shared experience. The story they tell may be about an individual—the "one"—or about collective experience, but often the fate of "too many" is best understood through identification with the singular. These projects use a range of design strategies, employing numbers, names, faces, bodies, artifacts, and places to stimulate a response. The effect is unpredictable, but for at least some who encounter such creative designs and installations, the experience may lead to greater understanding, a glimpse into the horrific, and even to action.

The Stolpersteine Project, Europe

The Stolpersteine project was conceived by the German artist Günter Demnig (born in Berlin in 1947). The Stolpersteine (Stumbling Blocks) are brass blocks, the size of the granite stones that pave European streets and

FIGURE 7.1 Stolpersteine (Stumbling Blocks) 1933–1945. On a Berlin sidewalk the shiny brass Stolpersteine stand out amongst the black stone pavers. Photo by Kenneth Helphand.

sidewalks. The blocks are located at the last known addresses of Holocaust victims. The addresses cannot be places they were forced to move to by the Nazis. The project began as a guerilla action and a conceptual art project in 1996 and has since expanded, with procedures for permission from local authorities, to which there has been occasional resistance from occupants of nearby structures and some communities who do not wish to be reminded of their local history. By 2014 more than 43,500 stones had been placed in over a thousand locations in Germany, Austria, Hungary, Belgium, Czech Republic, Netherlands, Croatia, France, Poland, Slovenia, Switzerland, Luxembourg, Russia, and Ukraine.

Each stone has an inscription, "Hier Wohnte" (here lived, or also here worked, practiced, studied, taught), followed by the person's name, year of birth, year and place of deportation, and her or his fate—most often *ermödet* (murdered)—and its location.

Originally created by the artist, stones can now be purchased. Demnig or members of his team individually install each stone, and when possible a surviving family member is present at the occasion.

Along a city sidewalk, no indicators or guidebooks point to the locations of the stones. Thus, each is stumbled upon, "discovered," even with a bit of guilt for having stepped atop what is manifestly a memorial. After looking at your feet your eyes are inevitably drawn upward to a building. It may be the same structure that was there seventy years ago, or it may have been replaced. The location is "ordinary," not a killing field or a concentration camp. This amplifies the impact. Your imagination attaches to the place, the name, and the victim's fate, and perhaps there is an unconscious feeling that this could have been you, for you are walking the same streets. The pervasiveness of the stones suggests the extent of the crime, the surrounding gray blocks devoid of names suggest the willful ignorance or complicity of the victim's neighbors.

Cambridge historian Joseph Pearson (2010) argues, "It is not what is written [on the Stolpersteine] which intrigues, because the inscription is insufficient to conjure a person. It is the emptiness, void, lack of information, the maw of the forgotten, which gives the monuments their power and lifts them from the banality of a statistic." Günter Demnig himself said, "If you read the name of one person, calculate his age, look at his old home and wonder behind which window he used to live, then the horror has a face to it" (Grieshaber, 2003).

World War I Cemeteries, United Kingdom

Cemeteries are sacred gardens. Before modern warfare most soldiers' bodies were brought home for burial in their community. The vast casualties of the American Civil War, followed by the incomprehensible enumeration of World War I, catalyzed the development of military cemeteries, interring soldiers on the battlefield where they fell. In Britain the architects Sir Edwin Luytens, Sir Herbert Baker, and Sir Reginald Bloomfield were chosen to design cemeteries for the Imperial War Graves Commission (now the Commonwealth War Graves Commission). Their design set the pattern and standard for British Military Cemeteries around the world. One million seven hundred thousand dead are buried in 153 countries from both world wars. There are over a thousand along the western front, the border between France and Belgium. Uniform white tombstones are aligned in perfect formation, undifferentiated by rank, representing "equality in death." Each cemetery bears a Cross of Sacrifice designed by Bloomfield, the sword of war sheathed by the cross. There is also the sarcophagus-like Stone of

FIGURE 7.2 One of hundreds of war grave cemeteries along the western front between Belgium and France where millions of soldiers died. Photo by Kenneth Helphand.

Remembrance, inscribed "Their Name Liveth for Evermore." The quotation from Ecclesiastes was chosen by Rudyard Kipling, whose son fell at the second Battle of Loos.

These memorials are still visited a century later, the incomprehensibly vast carnage of the war manifest in ranks of thousands of stones. Down row after row, individual names identify the soldier's name, rank, age, and date and place of death, along with the appropriate religious symbol (cross, Crescent, Star of David, and even Sikh, Hindu, Buddhist, and Confucian symbols). Families were permitted a short epitaph, such as "Oh why are we dead, we youth, all ye that pass by, forget not" and "Some day, Some time, We'll Understand." The graves of those who fell at the Battle of Kohima are inscribed, "When you go home, tell them of us and say 'For your to-morrows these gave their to-day.'"

The graves are a catalogue of the British Commonwealth, but the most common inscription is one Kipling wrote: "A Soldier of the Great War/ Known Unto God."

These cemeteries are found mostly in fields, as battlefields were restored to their immemorial productivity. They vary in size from a few score of graves to tens of thousands. The actual experience of the land, its fields and hills, its dimension, and the resonance of its spirit can bring visitors closer to a realization of what the war was like in this place. Smaller cemeteries are particularly poignant. There is a walk along a pathway between furrows of grain to a meticulously maintained low-walled compound. You are aware that the soldiers buried here fell within sight of where you are standing. This happened "here" is an extraordinarily powerful emotional catalyst.

The western front also has memorials; the grandest is the Thiepval Memorial, where a great arched structure overlooks graves and former battlefields. On its walls are the names of over seventy-two thousand of the "missing" of the Somme, bodies not recovered or identified. One can't help reading and notice the repetitions of Abbotts, Smiths, Joneses, Turners, Youngs. In every village and town in Britain there is a war memorial, inscribed with the names of the dead, located in their communities. Even in small hamlets the lists are long, leading to a conscious calibration of the war's devastating impact across the country.

Kigali Memorial Centre, Rwanda

During the 1994 Rwandan genocide some eight hundred thousand people were murdered in about one hundred days. The brutality, ferocity, and

FIGURE 7.3 The individual photographs in the Kigali Memorial Centre portray only a fraction of the over 250,000 people entombed in the mass graves under slabs of concrete on a hillside overlooking Kigali. Photo by Radu Sigheti.

rapidity of the killing among a population that had previously lived together peacefully is still shocking. Eighty-five percent of the Tutsi population was killed. In tallies of large numbers of victims, their individual identities are lost. Individuality can be retained or brought to consciousness in several ways. Words can do it, in telling the stories of each person. For example, the stories in "Portraits of Grief," which the *New York Times* produced for the victims of 9/11, provided personal glimpses into the lives of those who died at the World Trade Center. Readers identified with poignant tales of the ordinary lives and personal quirks of husbands, fathers, mothers, brothers and sisters, friends and colleagues that transcended the traditional obituary recitation of accomplishments and biographical facts.

Individual lives are also preserved in photographs. Only since the invention of photography fewer than two hundred years ago do we know what our ancestors looked like.

The Kigali Memorial Centre in Rwanda is located where over two hundred thousand victims are buried in mass graves. The memorial includes a documentation center and a gallery of victims' photos. The photos read as a collective Rwandan community album. Surviving Rwandans can identify relatives and friends. Others look into the eyes of the dead and imagine their fate and the brutality of their murder. The photographs are hung in lines, and look much like a bookstore, with each image suggesting a story captured in each "book." The pictures are of persons young and old, men and women, children and their parents, formal portraits and snapshots. When a house is burning, the first artifacts that are salvaged are photo albums. These are all family photographs that have been recovered; sometimes they are the only remnants left of these lives. All photographs frame, freeze, and capture a moment that is never to be repeated: the image as an act of preservation. These are relicts, records of moments lost, and, especially for survivors and relatives or friends, they act as mnemonic devices to recall the dead. One area, the "Children's Room," contains large portraits. Reporting in "How Rwandans Cope with the Horror of 1994," Lauren Wolfe (2014) wrote, "[The portraits hang] above descriptions of their favorite foods, what they loved in the world, and how they were murdered. Reading about Ariane, 4, she was a 'neat little girl' who loved cake. She was fatally 'stabbed in her eyes and head.' Her parents said she enjoyed singing and dancing." Wolfe understandably had to leave the building to recover.

Graph of U.S. Federal Budget, Eugene, Oregon

A group of students at the University of Oregon painted a bar graph of portions of the federal budget onto Thirteenth Street. The street is a pedestrian way that cuts through the middle of the campus; thus the graph was seen by the entire university community. The graph comprised color-coded columns, signifying such categories as veterans' services, justice, health, the environment, and the Pentagon. The scale of the graph was 1 foot = $1 billion.

Unlike a conventional graph, this one was at grand scale and on the ground. It begged to be walked along. Material presented on the ground is experienced differently than on a wall or miniaturized on a page. Looking down to read a text or numerical data catches and focuses our attention. The physical experience of marching along the lines, even counting steps, dramatized the budget in a visceral way. Most striking was that after all the other budget items had been exhausted, the military line just kept going and going, for another thousand feet, far beyond the other expenditures, even for entitlements such as social security.

FIGURE 7.4 The multicolored bar graph running through the center of the
University of Oregon campus, Eugene, 1985. Photo by Kenneth Helphand.

Flags Representing Iraq War Dead, Eugene, Oregon

In the winter of 2007, four years after the start of the war in Iraq, wavy
lines of small flags filled the main quadrangle of the University of Oregon.
The grass fronting the library had been planted with thousands of flags that
appeared overnight. They were the tiny surveyor's flags used to mark territory, but they staked out a different kind of survey: a statistical demonstra-
tion dramatizing the costs of war. This was the Iraq Body Count Exhibit
sponsored by various peace and veterans groups. Several things were striking about the installation. The flags filled the spaces and were impossible
to count, even if one attempted to do so. The pathways between the buildings were kept open, making an encounter with the installation inevitable.
The long rows and uniformity of the flags echoed the pattern of a military
cemetery, seen even more dramatically when viewed from the upper floors
of adjacent buildings. The flags were in two colors: red flags represented
American soldiers who had been killed, white represented Iraqis. Even
though the number of Iraqi dead, largely civilians, is debated, the disparity

FIGURE 7.5 Iraq Body Count Exhibit. Red flags for American soldiers, white for Iraqi war dead. University of Oregon, 2005. Photo by Kenneth Helphand.

between the two colors was overwhelming, and even more so with the realization that each white flag stood for five Iraqis. Contemplating the mathematics of the ratio was chilling, irrespective of whether one supported or protested the war.

The project, initiated at the University of Colorado at Boulder by a student named Juan Stewart Alvarez, was first displayed there. Alvarez said, "Looking around me, especially on a college campus, and seeing the apathy and complacency . . . it seemed like no one cared. I can't just sit here and see how things are going fine here and understand how hundreds of thousands of people are dying so people here can have a good life" (*Daily Emerald* archives, 2007). The project traveled to other universities and public places, and was always installed in a central location. At Portland State University it filled much of the South Park Blocks that run through the center of that campus. In Sacramento it filled five blocks of the Capitol Mall. At the University of Oregon the space of the quadrangle was insufficient to contain the flags. They bled off into the surrounding open spaces and even down sidewalk planting strips. This amoeba-like phenomenon suggested that the war was spreading like a cancer that could not be contained, that more flags would be needed. The war continued during the installation, and flags could have been added for casualties even during the time one was looking at and walking through it.

One Million Bones, Washington, DC

In 2009, the artist Naomi Natale conceived the One Million Bones project. Four years later, one million handcrafted white bones were carefully carpeted across the green grass of the Washington, DC, National Mall by thousands of white-clad individuals. The project's aim was to call attention

FIGURE 7.6 A million clay human bones fill the National Mall, June 8, 2013. Photo by Naomi Natale.

to the persistence of genocide in the contemporary world, in Somalia, Sudan, Burma, the Democratic Republic of the Congo, and Syria.

It took three years to collect the bones, handcrafted in communites across the United States and in thirty countries by 150,000 individuals. In 2011, as a prelude, fifty thousand bones were displayed in Albuquerque, and the next year thirty-five cities followed suit. Most of the bones were created by thirteen hundred teams of schoolchildren, for it was a multipronged assault on the question of genocide. Bone-making was tied to a school curriculum, and educators were provided with a teacher toolkit available for grades kindergarten through high school. The toolkit offered information on the materials needed to make the bones, including drawings of the entire human skeleton and images of bones to copy: spines, hands, skulls, jaws, femurs.

While One Million Bones was an activist art project, curricular lessons were also provided for classes in English, social studies, science, and math. Project leaders and teachers emphasized respect, peace, and hope during the creation of the bones and discussions of their meaning. One key exercise asked students of all ages to address the meaning of the expression, "I feel it in my bones."

In this multiple-stage project, materials were gathered, groups assembled, and bone-making was a group activity, as portions of skeletons made of clay or plaster gauze were carefully shaped and lessons given. Refugees were participants in bone-making: Burmese refugee Myra Dahgaypaw said that it was a way to "pull out the pain and put it into this bone" (Skibitzke, Donnell, & Hudock, 2013). Finished bones were fired, and boxes of bones were transported to Washington and ultimately displayed on the National Mall. Throughout the process, event leaders were encouraged to post photographs of the project and share the images, for a continued life online.

The impact of the project was different for those who created bones and those who witnessed the events or have seen images. Bones are potent symbols, and the teacher toolkit explicitly adddessed that aspect. The idea of a bone as relic is an ancient concept, that a fragment of a body embodies the characteristics or spirit of an individual. The bones suggest the value of every human life. Displayed en masse, they emphasize a connection between the individual and the collective. The Mall display was as if an ossuary had been emptied. The extent of the blanket of bones was critical to the experience, as was the number one million and the Mall location, the site of previous demonstrations and the 1987 display of the AIDS quilt. Artist Naomi

Natale described it as a "symbolic mass grave and visible petition to these atrocities." She said, "People see themselves in it, they see other people in it" (Skibitzke et al., 2013).

One Million Bones will have an afterlife. The Bones of the Balkans project will take one hundred thousand bones from the original project and employ them for a permanent installation in Bosnia twenty years after the massacre of Bosnians at Srebrenica in July 1995. The one hundred thousand bones will be supplemented by eight thousand additional bones made in Bosnia, the total number of those killed.

"Street Folk," Detroit, Michigan

For thirty years, the Detroit artist-activist Tyree Guyton has transformed derelict buildings into canvases for public artworks. He highlighted the area's blight by painting the walls of buildings as well as using the structures and the adjacent, often vacant, lots as a sculptural tableaux of artifacts and debris collected from the area. Known as the Heidelberg Project, his

FIGURE 7.7 Tyree Guyton's installation to highlight the plight of the city's homeless population, April 2011. Photo by Kenneth Helphand.

work has received international attention. Sadly, portions have been torn down, and in 2014 other sections burned to the ground.

In 2011 Guyton created "Street Folk." From sidewalk to sidewalk, he arranged ten thousand donated and discarded shoes of all sizes, kinds, and colors; some were even donated from abroad. There were children's and adult's shoes, men's and women's, high heels and high-tops, sandals and slippers, boots and brogues. It was a field of shoes walking in every direction. Guyton painted and ornamented the shoes and also arrayed them in patterns, some seemingly random, in other places a spiral, a mandala, and piles, a cairn of shoes. The arrangements and the artistry invited engagement, encouraging lingering over the display.

The intent was to dramatize the plight of the city's homeless and transient population. Guyton said, "I live around the corner here, and so I see every day this church behind me, feeding people every Wednesday, and I knew I wanted to say something," he said. "And it came to me to talk about the plight of the people right here. . . . I find shoes to be interesting—fascinating—because life is a journey. . . . [A shoe is] a tool that helps us to go from one point to the next," he continued. Guyton was clear in his desire:

> The shoes are a reflection of people, all going in different directions and yet they are all in the streets. The streets have no closing hours; they are open 7 days a week, 24 hours a day, all year long. You have night people living in the streets and you have day people living in the streets but we're all living in the streets chasing whatever your life calls for. In some cases you don't know what your life is calling for. In the end, we are all Street Folk. (Art X Detroit, 2011)

Some donated shoes were accompanied by notes. One fireman wrote, "These boots have seen both the best and worst of what can happen in our lives . . . and tell the tales of house fires and births of babies." Another note read, "I had 30 touchdowns with these shoes in football" (Householder, 2011). There were signs explaining the project, but there was also an implicit message: each pair of shoes represents a life. Tied to the fence along with a drawing of the shoes, "Dear Tyree, These shoes represent my MOM. Please hold them in your hands and feel what a *good person* she was." The variety of shoes stood for the diversity of the community and, implicitly, society. They asked a question: What is it like to walk in another's shoes, to project yourself into their experience?[1]

The Valley of the Communities, Jerusalem, Israel

The Valley of the Communities is the final memorial, the last station, the termination of a sacred progression at Yad Vashem, Israel's memorial to the Holocaust (the Shoah). From an upper terrace, visitors peer into a miniature canyon. Exiting the world above, the green of pine trees, the level terrain of the earth, you enter the world below. Massive walls of limestone blocks ten meters high envelop you into a procession through zigzag passageways. Inscriptions filling entire walls periodically punctuate the passage. Moving closer, you read names of places, towns, and villages. You recognize many—Paris, Berlin, Vilna, Kracow, Strasbourg—a litany of places you may have visited, enjoyed, that were filled with pleasure. You read on to unfamiliar and strange names in foreign tongues: Domazlice, Butla, Vercelli, Thann, Bistra. This is a gazetteer of destruction, a list of destroyed communities.

We know the number—six million—but those millions lived in thousands of places; from the shtetl to the metropolis there was no refuge. As each person has a name and a history, so too do places. As much as individuals were exterminated so were places, and we are compelled to remember their names—both people and places.

The walls are a horrific enumeration, a sacred catalogue of communities from which the Jewish population was exterminated, or where the lucky, resourceful or prescient few escaped in time. In most of these five thousand communities, no Jews remain. The memorial stands for these communities and to their ways of life, languages, the mundane and profound that made up the character of a civilization that was deliberately destroyed. Each place-name is a world obliterated, a catalogue of the Shoah, a Yizkor book carved in stone.[2]

The genius of the labyrinthine walk through the valley emerges through the associations it conjures up and its ability to act as a grand mnemonic device. The experience is simultaneously instructive and visceral, of mind and body. There is no escape. The valley's extent is a reminder of the Holocaust's vast reach, its insidious quality of reaching to the far corners of countries, including the great cities but also the small towns, the hidden valleys, the caves and attics where people hoped they would be safe. Subtly you become aware of the geography, that this wall and its list encompass Germany, another Poland, another France, another Netherlands. The valley

FIGURE 7.8 One wall of the names of over 5,000 communities destroyed during the Holocaust. Photo by Kenneth Helphand.

is a geography of destruction, a three-dimensional atlas of 107 pages, an abstracted map of Europe and North Africa.

This is a construction that is about destruction. It is a memorial and a ruin. The stone walls speak symbolically and as markers, echoing the Kotel (the Western Wall or the Wailing Wall, a sacred place in Jewish culture), ancient quarries, headstones, catacombs, sacred tablets, and the ruins of a city. The valley is like a vast columbarium or mausoleum, but instead of bones lovingly and ritually placed, decaying behind the walls, visitors know that the inhabitants are ashes in the air we breathe. The names of over five thousand communities have a biblical resonance. They are the opposite of the "begats," the litany in Genesis of the generations. These are the reverse, an *erasure* from history.

The valley has the capacity to transport one across space and time. You are not "there," of course, at the actual site of horrific events, but it is like hearing the sounds of a deep echo, the rippling waves of the experience transmitted through time. Even in its brief lifespan, the memorial's stones have begun to register change. The action of the harsh sun bleaches the stone. Water from rain and irrigation seeps through cracks where a few plants tenaciously volunteer. At times it appears as if the names are weeping. The walls speak.

Remembrance Day, 888,246 Ceramic Poppies, London, England

The Great War, World War I, ended on the eleventh hour of the eleventh day of the eleventh month. On November 11, 2014, Remembrance Day, the final red ceramic poppies were "planted" in the moat surrounding the Tower of London, making a total of 888,246—one poppy for each British or Commonwealth soldier who had died in World War I. The poppy was the obvious symbol, inspired by the scene of red poppies growing near the gravesite of the Canadian physician, Lieutenant Colonel John McCrae, who witnessed the horrors of battle at Ypres and composed the iconic poem "In Flanders Fields." The practice of wearing a red poppy on Remembrance Day began shortly after the war ended, as did the practice of placing poppies at memorials and gravesites. On July 1, 1916, the first day of the Battle of the Somme, a British mine exploded, creating the seventy-foot-deep Lochnagar Crater. Each year, on the anniversary of the explosion, poppies fill the crater bottom. They slowly decay, only to be replenished the following year.

Ceramic artist Paul Cummins and stage designer Tom Piper entitled their Tower of London installation "Blood Swept Lands and Seas of Red."

The title was inspired by a line from the will of a soldier who perished in Flanders. The ceramic flowers were made from a common template, but each was handmade and individualized before the red blossom was placed on a metal spike for planting. Installation of the poppies began on July 17, 2014. The poppies first spilled over the walls of the Tower through a "weeping window." The installation grew during the summer, aided by nineteen thousand volunteer planters. Like blood seeping from a wounded soldier, the red mass slowly crept across and gradually filled the Tower's sixteen-acre moat. A nightly ritual consisted of planting poppies as names of the dead were read before the playing of "Last Post."

Few observers realized that during World War I the moat, which now presents this red mass of memorial poppies, was the site of victory gardens. The mass of flowers is simultaneously a river of blood, a sea of remembrance, and a garden of memory. In 2014, the poppies encircled one of England's most sacred sites; from an aerial perspective, they looked much like the poppy wreaths placed at war memorials. In the days following November 11, the poppies were harvested, carefully boxed, and sent to the

FIGURE 7.9 888,246 red ceramic poppies in the Tower of London moat representing commonwealth soldiers who died in World War I. Photo by Kenneth Helphand.

six hundred thousand people who each gave £24 to charities benefiting veterans and soldiers.

By the end of the installation, four million individuals had visited the site in person and millions more had seen it in newspapers, magazines, and on television, and it has an afterlife on the Internet. In the final days, thousands slowly and respectfully circumnavigated the installation; there was an all-night floodlit vigil to see the poppies. London's mayor Boris Johnson said, "For the first time in 100 years an artist had managed to express what had hitherto been inexpressible: the sheer extent of the slaughter in the First World War."

REFERENCES

Art X Detroit. (2011). *Street folk.* Retrieved from http://www.artxdetroit.com/past -exhibitions/tyree-guyton/.

Daily Emerald archives. (2007, January 26). Anti-war rally in EMU amphitheater. *Daily Emerald.* Retrieved from http://dailyemerald.com/2007/01/26/anti-war -rally-in-emu-amphitheater/.

Grieshaber, K. (2003, November 29). Plaques for Nazi victims offer a personal impact. *The New York Times.* Retrieved from http://www.nytimes.com/2003/ 11/29/arts/design/29HAMB.html.

Householder, M. (2011, April 8). Detroit artist uses 10,000 shoes to bring together community, raise homelessness awareness. *The Huffington Post.* Retrieved from http://www.huffingtonpost.com/2011/04/08/detroit-artist-enlists-vo_n_84 6951.html#s262829.

Pearson, J. (2010). Nazi victims and stumbling blocks to memory. Retrieved from http://needleberlin.com/2010/08/23/nazi-victims-and-stumbling-blocks -to-memory/.

Skibitzke, S., Donnell, B., & L. Hudock. (2013). (Writers and Producer). *One million bones* [Film trailer].

Wolfe, L. (2014). How Rwandans cope with the horror of 1994. *The Atlantic.* Retrieved from http://www.theatlantic.com/international/archive/2014/04/how -rwandans-cope-with-the-horror-of-1994/360204/.

NOTES

1. A time-lapse video of the project is available at http://www.freep.com/ VideoNetwork/889006341001/-Street-Folk-at-Art-X-Detroit.

2. Yizkor books were compilations of the history and life of communities destroyed by the Holocaust. Most often they were written by survivors as a concrete manifestation of Yizkor, the memorial prayer recited at four Jewish holidays, especially on Yom Kippur. While usually said for family members in many congregations, the prayer is now recited for the six million.

CHAPTER 8

The Wreck of Time

ANNIE DILLARD

TED BUNDY, THE SERIAL KILLER, after his arrest, could not fathom the fuss. What was the big deal? David Von Drehle quotes an exasperated Bundy in *Among the Lowest of the Dead:* "I mean, there are *so* many people."

One R. Houwink, of Amsterdam, uncovered this unnerving fact: The human population of earth, arranged tidily, would just fit into Lake Windermere, in England's Lake District.

Recently in the Peruvian Amazon a man asked the writer Alex Shoumatoff, "Isn't it true that the whole population of the United States can be fitted into their cars?"

How are we doing in numbers, we who have been alive for this most recent installment of human life? How many people have lived and died?

"The dead outnumber the living, in a ratio that could be as high as 20 to 1," a demographer, Nathan Keyfitz, wrote in a 1991 letter to the historian Justin Kaplan. "Credible estimates of the number of people who have ever lived on the earth run from 70 billion to 100 billion." Averaging those figures puts the total persons ever born at about 85 billion. We living people now number 5.8 billion. By these moderate figures, the dead outnumber us about fourteen to one. The dead will always outnumber the living.

Dead Americans, however, if all proceeds, will not outnumber living Americans until the year 2030, because the nation is young. Some of us will be among the dead then. Will we know or care, we who once owned the still bones under the quick ones, we who spin inside the planet with our heels in the air? The living might well seem foolishly self-important to us, and overexcited.

e who are here now make up about 6.8 percent of all people who have
?ared to date. This is not a meaningful figure. These our times are, one
might say, ordinary times, a slice of life like any other. Who can bear to
hear this, or who will consider it? Are we not especially significant because
our century is—our century and its nuclear bombs, its unique and unprec-
edented Holocaust, its serial exterminations and refugee populations, our
century and its warming, its silicon chips, men on the moon, and spliced
genes? No, we are not and it is not.

Since about half of all the dead are babies and children, we will be among
the longest-boned dead and among the dead who grew the most teeth—for
what those distinctions might be worth among beings notoriously indifferent to appearance and all else.

In Juan Rulfo's novel *Pedro Páramo,* a dead woman says to her dead son,
"Just think about pleasant things, because we're going to be buried for a
long time."

II

On April 30, 1991—on that one day—138,000 people drowned in Bangla-
desh. At dinner I mentioned to my daughter, who was then seven years old,
that it was hard to imagine 138,000 people drowning. "No, it's easy," she
said. "Lots and lots of dots, in blue water."

The paleontologist Pierre Teilhard de Chardin, now dead, sent a dispatch
from a dig. "In the middle of the tamarisk bush you find a red-brick town,
partially exposed. . . . More than 3,000 years before our era, people were
living there who played with dice like our own, fished with hooks like ours,
and wrote in characters we can't yet read."

Who were these individuals who lived under the tamarisk bush? Who
were the people Ted Bundy killed? Who was the statistician who reckoned
that everybody would fit into Lake Windermere? The Trojans likely thought
well of themselves, one by one; their last settlement died out by 1,100 B.C.E.
Who were the people Stalin killed, or any of the 79.2 billion of us now dead,
and who are the 5.8 billion of us now alive?

"God speaks succinctly," said the rabbis.

Is it important if you have yet died your death, or I? Your father? Your
child? It is only a matter of time, after all. Why do we find it supremely
pertinent, during any moment of any century on earth, which among us is

topsides? Why do we concern ourselves over which side of the membrane of topsoil our feet poke?

"A single death is a tragedy, a million deaths is a statistic." Joseph Stalin, that connoisseur, gave words to this disquieting and possibly universal sentiment.

How can an individual count? Do we individuals count only to us other suckers, who love and grieve like elephants, bless their hearts? Of Allah, the Koran says, "Not so much as the weight of an ant in earth or heaven escapes from the Lord." That is touching, that Allah, God, and their ilk care when one ant dismembers another, or note when a sparrow falls, but I strain to see the use of it.

Ten years ago we thought there were two galaxies for each of us alive. Lately, since we loosed the Hubble Space Telescope, we have revised our figures. There are nine galaxies for each of us. Each galaxy harbors an average of 100 billion suns. In our galaxy, the Milky Way, there are sixty-nine suns for each person alive. The Hubble shows, says a report, that the universe "is at least 15 billion years old." Two galaxies, nine galaxies . . . sixty-nine suns, 100 billion suns—

These astronomers are nickel-and-diming us to death.

III

What were you doing on April 30, 1991, when a series of waves drowned 138,000 people? Where were you when you first heard the astounding, heart-breaking news? Who told you? What, seriatim, were your sensations? Who did you tell? Did you weep? Did your anguish last days or weeks?

All my life I have loved this sight: a standing wave in a boat's wake, shaped like a thorn. I have seen it rise from many oceans, and I saw it rise from the Sea of Galilee. It was a peak about a foot high. The standing wave broke at its peak, and foam slid down its glossy hollow. I watched the foaming wave on the port side. At every instant we were bringing this boat's motor, this motion, into new water. The stir, as if of life, impelled each patch of water to pinch and inhabit this same crest. Each crest tumbled upon itself and released a slide of white foam. The foam's bubbles popped and dropped into the general sea while they were still sliding down the dark wave. They trailed away always, and always new waters peaked, broke, foamed, and replenished.

What I saw was the constant intersection of two wave systems. Lord Kelvin first described them. Transverse waves rise abaft the stern and stream away perpendicular to the boat's direction of travel. Diverging waves course on in a V shape behind the boat. Where the waves converge, two lines of standing crests persist at an unchanging angle to the direction of the boat's motion. We think of these as the boat's wake. I was studying the highest standing wave, the one nearest the boat. It rose from the trough behind the stern and spilled foam. The curled wave crested over clear water and tumbled down. All its bubbles broke, thousands a second, unendingly. I could watch the present; I could see time and how it works.

On a shore, 8,000 waves break a day. James Trefil, a professor of physics, provides these facts. At any one time, the foam from breaking waves covers between 3 and 4 percent of the earth's surface. This acreage of foam is equal to the entire continent of North America. By coincidence, the U.S. population bears nearly the same relation to the world population: 4.6 percent. The U.S. population, in other words, although it is the third largest population among nations, is as small a portion of the earth's people as breaking waves' white foam is of the sea.

"God rises up out of the sea like a treasure in the waves," wrote Thomas Merton.

We see generations of waves rise from the sea that made them, billions of individuals at a time; we see them dwindle and vanish. If this does not astound you, what will? Or what will move you to pity?

IV

One-tenth of the land on earth is tundra. At any time, it is raining on only 5 percent of the planet's surface. Lightning strikes the planet about a hundred times every second. The insects outweigh us. Our chickens outnumber us four to one.

One-fifth of us are Muslims. One-fifth of us live in China. And every seventh person is a Chinese peasant. Almost one-tenth of us live within range of an active volcano. More than 2 percent of us are mentally retarded. We humans drink tea—over a billion cups a day. Among us we speak 10,000 languages.

We are civilized generation number 500 or so, counting from 10,000 years ago, when we settled down. We are *Homo sapiens* generation number 7,500, counting from 150,000 years ago, when our species presumably arose; and we are human generation number 125,000, counting from the earliest forms of *Homo.*

Every 110 hours a million more humans arrive on the planet than die into the planet. A hundred million of us are children who live on the streets. Over a hundred million of us live in countries where we hold no citizenship. Twenty-three million of us are refugees. Sixteen million of us live in Cairo. Twelve million fish for a living from small boats. Seven and a half million of us are Uygurs. One million of us crew on freezer trawlers. Nearly a thousand of us a day commit suicide.

Head-Spinning Numbers Cause Mind to Go Slack, the *Hartford Courant* says. But our minds must not go slack. How can we think straight if our minds go slack? We agree that we want to think straight.

Anyone's close world of family and friends composes a group smaller than almost all sampling errors, smaller than almost all rounding errors, a group invisible, at whose loss the world will not blink. Two million children die a year from diarrhea, and 800,000 from measles. Do we blink? Stalin starved 7 million Ukrainians in one year, Pol Pot killed 1 million Cambodians, the flu epidemic of 1918 killed 21 or 22 million people . . . shall this go on? Or do you suffer, as Teilhard de Chardin did, the sense of being "an atom lost in the universe"? Or do you not suffer this sense? How about what journalists call "compassion fatigue"? Reality fatigue? At what limit for you do other individuals blur? Vanish? How old are you?

V

Los Angeles airport has 25,000 parking spaces. This is about one space for every person who died in 1985 in Colombia when a volcano erupted. This is one space for each of the corpses of more than two years' worth of accidental killings from leftover land mines of recent wars. At five to a car, almost all the Inuit in the world could park at LAX. Similarly, if you propped up or stacked four bodies to a car, you could fit into the airport parking lot all the corpses from the firestorm bombing of Tokyo in March 1945, or the corpses of Londoners who died in the plague, or the corpses of Burundians killed in civil war since 1993. But you could not fit America's homeless there, not even at twenty to a car.

Since sand and dirt pile up on everything, why does the world look fresh for each new crowd? As natural and human debris raises the continents, vegetation grows on the piles. It is all a stage—we know this—a temporary stage on top of many layers of stages, but every year a new crop of sand, grass, and tree leaves freshens the set and perfects the illusion that ours is the new and urgent world now. When Keats was in Rome, I read once, he saw pomegranate trees overhead; they bloomed in dirt blown onto the Colosseum's broken walls. How can we doubt our own time, in which each bright instant probes the future? In every arable soil in the world we grow grain over tombs—sure, we know this. But do not the dead generations seem to us dark and still as mummies, and their times always faded like scenes painted on walls at Pompeii?

How can we see ourselves as only a new, temporary cast for a long-running show when a new batch of birds flies around singing and new clouds move? Living things from hyenas to bacteria whisk the dead away like stagehands hustling between scenes. To help a living space last while we live on it, we brush or haul away the blowing sand and hack or burn the greenery. We are mowing the grass at the cutting edge.

VI

In northeast Japan, a seismic sea wave killed 27,000 people on June 15, 1896. Do not fail to distinguish this infamous wave from the April 30, 1991, waves that drowned 138,000 Bangladeshi. You were not tempted to confuse, conflate, forget or ignore those deaths, were you?

On the dry Laetoli plain of northern Tanzania, Mary Leakey found a trail of hominid footprints. The three barefoot people—likely a short man and woman and child *Australopithecus afarensis*—walked closely together. They walked on moist volcanic tuff and ash. We have a record of those few seconds from a day about 3.6 million years ago—before hominids even chipped stone tools. More ash covered their footprints and hardened. Ash also preserved the pockmarks of the raindrops that fell beside the three who walked; it was a rainy day. We have almost ninety feet of the three's steady footprints intact. We do not know where they were going or why. We do not know why the woman paused and turned left, briefly, before continuing. "A remote ancestor," Leakey said, "experienced a moment of doubt." Possibly they watched the Sadiman volcano erupt, or they took a last look back before they left. We do know we cannot make anything so lasting as these three barefoot ones did.

After archaeologists studied this long strip of record for several years, they buried it again to save it. Along one preserved portion, however, new tree roots are already cracking the footprints, and in another place winds threaten to sand them flat; the preservers did not cover them deeply enough. Now they are burying them again.

Jeremiah, walking toward Jerusalem, saw the smoke from the Temple's blaze. He wept; he saw the blood of the slain. "He put his face close to the ground and saw the footprints of sucklings and infants who were walking into captivity" in Babylon. He kissed the footprints.

Who were these individuals? Who were the three who walked together and left footprints in the rain? Who was that eighteenth-century Ukrainian peasant the Baal Shem Tov, the founder of modern Hasidism, who taught, danced, and dug clay? He was among the generations of children of Babylonian exiles whose footprints on the bare earth Jeremiah kissed. Centuries later the Emperor Hadrian destroyed another such son of exile in Rome, Rabbi Akiba. Russian Christians and European Christians tried, and Hitler tried, to wipe all those survivors of children of exile from the ground of the earth as a man wipes a plate—survivors of exiles whose footprints on the ground I kiss, and whose feet.

Who and of what import were the men whose bones bulk the Great Wall, the 30 million Mao starved, or the 11 million children under five who die each year now? Why, they are the insignificant others, of course; living or dead, they are just some of the plentiful others. And you?

Is it not late? A late time to be living? Are not our current generations the important ones? We have changed the world. Are not our heightened times the important ones, the ones since Hiroshima? Perhaps we are the last generation—there is a comfort. Take the bomb threat away and what are we? We are ordinary beads on a never-ending string. Our time is a routine twist of an improbable yarn.

We have no chance of being here when the sun burns out. There must be something ultimately heroic about our time, something that sets it above all those other times. Hitler, Stalin, Mao, and Pol Pot made strides in obliterating whole peoples, but this has been the human effort all along, and we have only enlarged the means, as have people in every century in history. (That genocides recur does not mean that they are similar. Each instance of human evil and each victim's death possesses its unique history and form. To generalize, as Cynthia Ozick points out, is to "befog" evil's specificity.)

Dire things are happening. Plague? Funny weather? Why are we watching the news, reading the news, keeping up with the news? Only to enforce our fancy—probably a necessary lie—that these are crucial times, and we are in on them. Newly revealed, and I am in the know: crazy people, bunches of them! New diseases, sways in power, floods! Can the news from dynastic Egypt have been any different?

As I write this, I am still alive, but of course I might well have died before you read it. Most of the archaeologists who reburied hominid footprints have likely not yet died their deaths; the paleontologist Teilhard is pushing up daisies.

Chinese soldiers who breathed air posing for 7,000 individual clay portraits—twenty-two centuries ago—must have thought it a wonderful difference that workers buried only their simulacra then so that their sons could bury their flesh a bit later. One wonders what they did in the months or years they gained. One wonders what one is, oneself, up to these days.

VII

Was it wisdom Mao Tse-tung attained when—like Ted Bundy—he awakened to the long view?

"The atom bomb is nothing to be afraid of," Mao told Nehru. "China has many people. . . . The deaths of ten or twenty million people is nothing to be afraid of." A witness said Nehru showed shock. Later, speaking in Moscow, Mao displayed yet more generosity: he boasted that he was willing to lose 300 million people, half of China's population.

Does Mao's reckoning shock me really? If sanctioning the death of strangers could save my daughter's life, would I do it? Probably. How many others' lives would I be willing to sacrifice? Three? Three hundred million?

An English journalist, observing the Sisters of Charity in Calcutta, reasoned: "Either life is always and in all circumstances sacred, or intrinsically of no account; it is inconceivable that it should be in some cases the one, and in some the other."

One small town's soup kitchen, St. Mary's, serves 115 men a night. Why feed 115 individuals? Surely so few people elude most demographics and achieve statistical insignificance. After all, there are 265 million Americans, 15 million people who live in Mexico City, 16 million in greater New York, 26 million in greater Tokyo. Every day 1.5 million people walk through Times Square in New York; every day almost as many people—1.4 million—board a U.S. passenger plane. And so forth. We who breathe air now will join the already dead layers of us who breathed air once. We arise from dirt and dwindle to dirt, and the might of the universe is arrayed against us.

CHAPTER 9

Science, Eloquence, and the Asymmetry of Trust

What's at Stake in Climate Change Fiction

SCOTT SLOVIC

My country is extremely attentive to the slightest increase in a risk from terror, and that's appropriate. . . . But why should we be so tolerant of risk where the future habitability of our planet is concerned?

> —AL GORE, quoted in Mattias Karen,
> "Gore: I Don't Plan to Run for President," *Truthout*

The United States is the most disproportionate producer of global warming, governed by the most disregardful administration. This country often seems like a train heading for a crash, with a gullible, apolitical, easily distracted population bloating itself on television's political distortions and repellent vision of human life, runaway rates of consumption, violent interventions around the world, burgeoning prison and impoverished and crazy populations, the malignancy of domestic fundamentalism, the decay of democracy, and on and on. It's hard to see radical change in the United States, and easy to see how necessary it is. I spend a lot of time looking at my country in horror.

> —REBECCA SOLNIT, *Hope in the Dark: Untold Histories,*
> *Wild Possibilities*

Prediction and Precaution in Environmental Science

In his 1997 essay "Why Do Scientists Argue?" American biologist John Janovy explains that "argument," in the context of scientific discovery, is how knowledge progresses—through observation, interpretation, counterinterpretation, replicated observation with refined tools, further interpretation and counterinterpretation, and so forth. The subtext of Janovy's discussion—

in his book explicitly written for "busy people" like lawyers and business people—is that the public needs to understand not only the *ideas* of science but also something about how science *operates* in order to appreciate the recommendations of science in the context of public policy. Realizing that many of his hoped-for readers might disagree with his perspectives on issues such as human population growth and the implications of global climate change, Janovy downplays the specific cases of scientific argument that were making headlines in the mid-1990s when he was drafting his book, although the one specific example he uses is climate science. One of the major stories of that time (a story that continues to be powerfully relevant today) comes from a 1995 report of the United Nations and World Meteorological Organization's Intergovernmental Panel on Climate Change (known as the IPCC). Of particular interest is the much-discussed (and somewhat disputed) Chapter 8 of the report, which tried to reach some conclusions, based on the state of scientific knowledge in the mid-1990s, about the impact of human behavior on climate. In examining this controversy, Janovy's gentle conclusion is that argument (even disagreement) is a normal part of science, and scientists "don't usually make controversial predictions without some reason"—he makes this point to counteract the layperson's assumption that scientists might weigh in on controversial topics pertaining to their research without careful consideration. In light of scientists' typical reluctance to make casual claims regarding the predictive validity of their experimental results, says Janovy, "it's not always a good idea to completely ignore scientists' predictions just because these hypotheses 'have not been proved'" (p. 103).

What the biologist is hinting at in his discussion of why scientists occasionally hazard predictions and how decision makers and the general public should respond to such predictions is that it might be a good idea for Americans to consider embracing the "precautionary principle" that was endorsed in 1987 by European environmental ministers, who were at that time reacting to concerns about the deterioration of the North Sea. In her well-known book about industrial waste and cancer clusters, *Living Downstream: A Scientist's Personal Investigation of Cancer and the Environment* (which appeared, like Janovy's book, in 1997), Sandra Steingraber defines the precautionary principle as "the idea that public and private interests should act to prevent harm before it occurs." She continues: "It dictates that indication of harm, rather than proof of harm, should be the trigger for action—especially if delay may cause irreparable damage" (p. 270). Although Steingraber discusses this widely known (and widely applied) concept in the specific context of water pollution and human health, the principle applies equally well to many other social and environmental situations, including the issue of climate change. Whether we (humans around the world) respond to current assessments of climate change and predictions that Earth is in the process of becoming a "different planet" with precautionary behavior or continue with business as usual depends on how we understand the work of environmental science and on our adherence to principles of precaution or heedlessness.

In this chapter, which seeks to offer a historical discussion of the turn-of-the-century stalemate in public responses to climate change science, I consider why it was so easy for a small number of "contrarian" scientists and writers to stir up enough skepticism to stall progress (at least within the United States) on the development of a climate change policy that could have brought this country more quickly in line with the preponderance of scientific evidence and the preponderance of international public opinion on this matter. My goal is to offer a kind of answer to Al Gore's question, "Why should we be so tolerant of risk where the future habitability of our planet is concerned?"

The first three chapters of this book describe a variety of psychological mechanisms pertinent to this question. The consequences of climate change are multiple, diffuse, statistical, seemingly distant from us in time and location, and, accordingly, hard to imagine. Much like genocide and mass atrocities, climate change is real but doesn't "feel real" to a public whose senses are dulled by psychic numbing and who are prey to feelings of inefficacy. Moreover, even when educational efforts effectively raise concerns and a desire to act before it's too late, the prominence effect described in Chapter 3 raises yet another possible psychological impediment to action. Climate-friendly actions, even when highly valued, often conflict with near-term comforts, convenience, and lower immediate costs associated with "doing the wrong thing," and these other objectives are likely to be prominent in determining behavior.

Activist and author George Marshall, in his book *Don't Even Think About It: Why Our Brains Are Wired to Ignore Climate Change* (2014), has sought to elucidate a variety of psychological processes and conditions that limit human ability to comprehend and respond to climate change. Along with chapters addressing "The Power of the Mob," "Uncertain Long-Term Costs," and various other phenomena, Marshall offers a chapter titled "Communicator Trust: Why the Messenger Is More Important Than the Message." "If words are frames and stories are the medium," he writes, "then the person who communicates them becomes the most important and potentially the weakest link in the chain between scientific information and personal conviction. This sense of trustworthiness is a powerful bias and is entirely driven by the emotional brain and our intuitive ability to separate friends and foes" (pp. 116–117).

In this chapter, I address another important aspect of the psychology of trust that is central to answering Al Gore's question: specifically, the role *asymmetry of trust* plays in a democratic society and in policy formation pertaining to technological issues. I'm particularly interested in how writers—journalists and even novelists, such as Michael Crichton and Susan M. Gaines—have contributed to or undermined public trust in the mainstream science of climate change. In responding to phenomena like climate change, which are vast and essentially indiscernible to human senses, the general public and government decision makers must rely on data compiled by experts and on stories and images developed by communicators (journalists, literary writers, and artists). This topic is thus a matter of "information management," much like the examples presented elsewhere in this book.

Trust, Scientific Uncertainty, and Words of Warning

The politics and technical details of climate science and policy have been discussed at length by journalists in recent decades—well-known examples of this include Ross Gelbspan's 1998 *The Heat Is On* and his follow-up, *Boiling Point*, in 2004; Chris Mooney's 2005 *The Republican War on Science*; and Elizabeth Kolbert's 2006 *Field Notes From a Catastrophe: Man, Nature, and Climate Change*. Mooney's chapter "The Greatest Hoax" focuses on Oklahoma senator James Inhofe's notorious efforts, as chairman of the Senate Committee on Environment and Public Works, to obfuscate and stagnate any efforts by United States legislators to pass a national policy to mitigate anthropogenic climate change (Inhofe further embraced this extreme perspective when he published *The Greatest Hoax: How the Global Warming Conspiracy Threatens Your Future* in 2012). In light of the widespread public acknowledgment of the seriousness of climate change in 2015, such efforts seem like something out of the Dark Ages, but Inhofe's

2005 invitation to novelist Michael Crichton to testify before the United States Senate on the subject of climate change is an important moment in the history of managing information about this phenomenon. Crichton was, at the time, a hugely successful sower of climate change doubt by way of his novel *State of Fear*, which I'll discuss in more detail below. His Senate testimony, presented on September 28, 2005, is more measured with regard to climate change than the story offered in his novel, which appeared a year earlier. Crichton's testimony is primarily critical of science that has not been, or cannot be, "independently verified." He accuses American climate scientist Michael Mann and his colleagues, whose work contributed to the 2001 report of the IPCC, of calculation errors, repeated use of the same data, and predetermined analysis of the data. Although he concludes his testimony by stating that "nothing in [his] remarks should be taken to imply that we can ignore our environment, or that we should not take climate change seriously," Crichton's statement clearly aims to puncture any trust lawmakers may have had in the scientific validity of the IPCC report. When he states, in his final lines, "In an information society, public safety depends on the integrity of public information," he seems unaware of the role his own critique may play in undermining the broader "integrity" and validity of the preponderance of climate change data already available in 2005.

Regarding Inhofe's own twelve-thousand-word speech on the Senate floor on July 28, 2003, which attacked the IPCC findings that "the balance of evidence suggests that there is a discernible human influence on global climate" (Stevens, 1999, p. 229), Chris Mooney (2005) remarks, "And so the cacophony began. If Inhofe's goal was to create confusion and hence the appearance of scientific uncertainty, he succeeded brilliantly" (p. 87). Mooney explains that Senator Inhofe and his aides, when responding to journalists' written questions, misrepresented the National Academy of Sciences' report prepared in response to the IPCC's most recent publications. "Much of the misrepresentation," says Mooney, "exploits a classic strategy for abusing science: magnifying uncertainty" (p. 91). He concludes his discussion of the political abuse of climate change science by stating,

To be sure, it remains up to policymakers to decide whether the economic costs of such preventive measures outweigh the benefits. But that key question isn't even being properly debated. Instead, climate change has become an issue on which conservatives have elected to fight over science at least as much as over economics, relying on stunning distortions and a shocking disregard for both expertise and the most reputable sources of scientific assessment and analysis.

If this situation is maddening, it is also tragic. There may be no other issue today where a corruption of the necessary relationship between science and political decision-making has more potentially disastrous consequences. . . . Not only do [Senator Inhofe and his conservative colleagues] prevent the public from understanding the gravity of the climate situation, but in sowing confusion and uncertainty, they help prevent us from doing anything about it. (p. 101)

In other words, the consequences of sowing confusion about science and technology—including about such issues as climate change—are enormous, potentially catastrophic. Ironically, many of the world's leading climate scientists, including Benjamin Santer (one of the principal authors of the 1995 IPCC report), hail from the United States, the principal contributor to global warming (along with China) and the most visible non-signatory to the Kyoto Protocol and other international treaties on this issue.

What Inhofe and other conservative politicians and contrarian scientists (many of them funded by ExxonMobil, the world's largest nongovernmental petroleum company[1]) realize—and what the mainstream scientific community has yet to appreciate effectively—is that all you have to do to obstruct science-based policy is plant the seeds of doubt in the public imagination, particularly in societies that have not embraced the precautionary principle, as discussed above. This sowing of doubt is really quite easy to do. Psychologists have conducted empirical studies of "trust," powerfully revealing the asymmetry of this psychological phenomenon: the difficulty of building trust and the ease with which trust can be fractured. In a chapter titled "Perceived Risk, Trust and Democracy," from his 2000 book *The Perception of Risk*, Paul Slovic surveys the current state of research on the importance of trust in technological risk perception and points out the striking polarization between fears of certain risks among members of the public and the fears and concerns of scientists and industrialists. The four central findings of the psychological community are: "1. Negative (trust-destroying) events are more visible than positive (trust-building) events. . . . 2. When events do come to our attention, negative (trust-destroying) events carry much greater weight than positive events. . . . 3. Adding fuel to the fire of asymmetry is yet another idiosyncrasy of human psychology—sources of bad (trust-destroying) news tend to be seen as more credible than sources of good news. . . . 4. Another important psychological tendency is that distrust, once initiated, tends to reinforce and perpetuate distrust" (pp. 320–323). These findings imply that, in the arenas of environmental science and policy, the corporate official or politician—or the corporate-funded scientist—who wishes to stop environmental legislation in its tracks need only cast a broad shadow of "uncertainty" over the claims of cautious scientists and tree-hugging environmentalists. One might ask whether the environmentalist who deploys catastrophist rhetoric could similarly undermine the certainty of industrial progress and economic growth (driving forces behind anthropogenic climate change); however, because capitalism is the foundation of comfortable living standards in many of the countries with deep carbon footprints (and this includes mainland China), catastrophic pronouncements work against (or *seem* to work against) the grain of audiences' lifestyles and worldviews.

In other words, it is generally more difficult for environmentalists to undermine trust in business-as-usual than it is for the anti-environmentalist to undermine trust in environmental science. The critic of science need not have any scientific credentials or understanding. The mere statement that "scientists don't agree with each other" about the finding in question is usually enough to sow dismay and disinterest in the passive public—people think to themselves, "Well, we should at least wait until the experts can get their story straight." But, of course, the experts will *never* achieve unanimity—for science is built on the scaffolding of disagreement, contention, and the earnest search for better data and better explanations. A public that cannot appreciate the difference between mainstream science and outlier science and between fundamental nonacceptance of a scientific claim among fellow scientists and uncertainties regarding specific nuances of that claim is ill-equipped to communicate with public officials about the formation of policy.

This has particular implications for the issue of climate change, where assessment and prediction are extraordinarily complex and uncertain. During the American climate debates of the late 1990s and early 2000s '
was the public supposed to parse a statement like Benjamin S
response to IPCC critics? "Uncertainties," he wrote,

are a fundamental part of any branch of science, not just climate science, not just climate change science. Although we will never have complete certainty about the exact size of the past, present and future human effect on climate, we do know—beyond any reasonable doubt—that the burning of fossil fuels has modified the chemical composition of the atmosphere.

The question is not whether, but to what extent such changes in atmospheric composition have already influenced the climate of the past century and will continue to influence the climate of the twenty-first century. (Qtd. in Stevens, 1999, p. 235)

We can always know more about how the world works and the implications of our own behavior, but in the instance of climate change science, the so-called greenhouse fingerprint has been thoroughly studied and is unmistakably human. For a risk-sensitive society, as Al Gore points out in this chapter's first epigraph, to ignore the risk of planetary uninhabitability (or at least the potentially grave effects of shifting climate on the ability to provide enough food and water for our rapidly growing population) seems fundamentally illogical. And yet the general public, during the early phases of scientific and government debate about complex social and environmental issues, is likely to hear a statement like this and think, "When you can tell me the extent and severity of these changes—what they really mean for my life and that of my children—then come back and tell me what to do." This was especially true just after the turn of the century when apparently authoritative treatments of climate issues for the general public, such as the World Meteorological Organization's *Climate Into the 21st Century* (Burroughs, 2003), stated, "The fact that we may face greater climate variability in the future is only another form of the challenges that have been faced throughout human history. We have adapted to a wide range of climates around the world, so accommodating climate change could be a viable option" (p. 214). Of course, by the time predictive science can become descriptive science, assessing what's already happened or is incontrovertibly in the midst of happening, it may well be too late for meaningful behavioral and policy changes—sometimes it's "too late" even when initial *predictions* are being developed. I should mention, too, that the essential goal of predictive environmental science is, in many cases, to be proven wrong. Alan AtKisson, in a 1999 book, refers to the "issuing [of] unpopular warnings of avoidable dangers" as "Cassandra's Dilemma," calling this a "no-win situation" and continuing, "Failure to convey the message effectively results in catastrophe. Success in being understood means ultimately being proven wrong" (pp. 22–23).

So, is it better, in a democratic society where we want to prove our Cassandras wrong, to have a trusting public or a skeptical, question-asking public? Both, I would say. What's needed is a public that realizes when to trust and when to question—that realizes the need to ask questions in pursuit of public policies that might help us to achieve a society that seems to match our view of the world. How can this happen, though, in a diverse and democratic society, where you have a wide range of interests, beliefs, and concerns? This is, of course, one of the basic sticking points of democracy—the achievement of workable consensus among diverse groups and individuals. It would be impossible and presumptuous to attempt to state, in brief, an overarching worldview to which the majority of Americans—let alone a majority of people throughout the world—might subscribe, so as to develop a climate change policy in keeping with that worldview. I certainly realize that there tends to be a significant difference between most Americans and Europeans when it comes to technological developments such as biotechnology, the Europeans being more likely to adhere to the precautionary principle in forming laws and policies to guide the application of such technologies. And still, as Al Gore (who surely has access to the most detailed information about the views of the American public) suggests, it's quite a challenge to figure out where most Americans are willing to draw the line when it comes to accepting risk. We'll go to dramatic (and expensive) lengths to mitigate the risks of terrorism, but we're dragging our feet when it comes to forestalling the effects of climate change.[2]

For better or worse, the role of communicating important social and environmental issues to general audiences, ranging from gunrunning to extinction, has been tacitly delegated to entertainment media, such as movies and popular literature. These media have also taken on the task of illuminating how scientific processes work and how science is used in supporting political action and policy development.

Environmental Fiction and the Science of Climate Change

I explore the implications of climate communication by focusing on two specific novels—Susan M. Gaines's 2001 *Carbon Dreams* and Michael Crichton's 2004 *State of Fear*—that appeared in the midst of turn-of-the-century debates about climate change and demonstrate the pros and cons of having literary artists weigh in on important environmental issues. In his 1985 book *Filters Against Folly: How to Survive Despite Ecologists, Economists, and the Merely Eloquent,* Garrett Hardin castigated environmental writers who masked scientific ignorance beneath what he called a "patina of poetic language"—in particular, Hardin was critiquing John Muir's famous (and oft-quoted) line about everything in the universe being "hitched to everything else." The literature of climate change can sometimes *help* readers formulate their own understanding of the science and politics of this issue, but other times a vivid fictional narrative (coupled with pseudoscientific apparatus) can *diminish* the public's capacity to process information about this subtle and complex phenomenon.

Michael Crichton's best-selling[3] novel *State of Fear* presents a startling caricature of environmentalists as fearmongers who will go to almost any lengths to frighten the public and secure funding to support their activist agendas. Crichton's activists use paramilitary tactics in their attempts to fracture the continental ice in Antarctica, seed vicious storms in the American Southwest, and instigate tsunami-causing undersea rockslides in Southeast Asia—all in the name of public relations and in defiance of scientific findings that discount the theory of global warming. One of the central characters in the novel, Nicholas Drake, the villainous leader of NERF (the National Environmental Resource Fund), declares out of frustration,

> I *hate* global warming. . . . It's a goddamn disaster. . . . It *doesn't work.* . . . That's my point. You can't raise a dime with it, especially in winter. Every time it snows people forget all about global warming. Or else they decide some warming might be a good thing after all. They're trudging through the snow, *hoping* for a little global warming. (p. 295)

To which Drake's PR adviser, John Henley, responds,

> So what you need . . . is to structure the information so that whatever kind of weather occurs, it always confirms your message. That's the virtue of shifting the focus to abrupt climate change. It enables you to use everything that happens. There will always be floods, and freezing storms, and cyclones, and hurricanes. These events will always get headlines and airtime. And in every instance, you can claim it is an example of abrupt climate

change caused by global warming. So the message gets reinforced. The urgency is increased. (p. 314)

The environmentalists in *State of Fear* come across as self-interested, scientifically ignorant, arrogant, and deceitful, as perpetrators of a vast pseudoscientific hoax (exactly as described by Senator Inhofe to his fellow United States senators). In his "author's message" at the end of the book, Crichton states, "I conclude that most environmental 'principles' (such as sustainable development or the precautionary principle) have the effect of preserving the economic advantages of the West and thus constitute modern imperialism toward the developing world. It is a nice way of saying, 'We got ours and we don't want you to get yours, because you'll cause too much pollution'" (p. 571). Here Crichton seems to echo the line of argumentation in Richard Grove's *Green Imperialism: Colonial Expansion, Tropical Island Edens and the Origins of Environmentalism, 1600–1860* (1996), which suggests that Western environmentalism is deeply (and problematically) associated with colonial devastation of local cultures and physical environments around the world. This is, in other words, a *leftist* critique of environmentalism. It is ironic (in various ways) that Crichton received the 2006 *journalism* award from the American Association of Petroleum Geologists for *State of Fear*—a work of fiction (not journalism), and a work that castigates environmentalists for various sins, including "imperialism toward the developing world" (one might ask what the relationship between the petroleum industry and developing nations has been).

Fictional MIT professor John Kenner, who leads Crichton's band of lawyers and philanthropists in a fight to thwart purported environmental extremism in the novel, calmly cites scientific articles and machine-guns ELF (Environmental Liberation Front) terrorists, while working on behalf of a clandestine U.S. government agency to preserve the American way of life. The association of environmental activists with terrorism is a particularly drastic move on the novelist's part in the wake of September 11, 2001, playing on public fears and the apparently bolstering efforts of the Bush administration to portray itself as a strong and decent defender of "homeland security." In light of the novel's violent melodrama, it is jarringly peculiar that Crichton actually provides footnotes throughout the narrative, citing articles from such periodicals as the *Journal of Glaciology* and the *Bulletin of the American Meteorological Society*, suggesting that when his characters—

usually Kenner—contradict the theories of global warming and climate change, this information is derived from actual science. Unable to rebut the professor's scientific claims, several of the moderate environmentalists in the novel actually convert to Kenner's side and help him to stop the ELF extremists. And even some of the author's comments in his author's message seem so neutral—and, in a way, liberal—as to lure progressive readers to appreciate his narrative debunking of global warming. This is, in many ways, a rhetorically impressive work.

The actual model for Crichton's fictional hero, John Kenner, seems to be, in part, MIT professor Richard Lindzen, whose work is cited several times (more than any other individual author) in the novel's extensive bibliography (yes, the novel's bibliography).[4] Journalist Ross Gelbspan provides a rather detailed portrayal of Lindzen in his 1998 treatment of climate issues, *The Heat Is On*, in which he recounts visiting the professor at his home in 1995: "Both he and his wife are exceedingly gracious and hospitable people. In contrast to his often-tortured scientific pronouncements, I found his social and political expressions to be lucid, succinct, and unambiguous. Indeed, I found him to be one of the most ideologically extreme individuals I have ever interviewed" (p. 52). Just as journalist Gelbspan sees through Richard Lindzen's gracious hospitality and ascertains the role of his ideological extremism in his contributions to national climate policy,[5] I believe it's important for readers of Crichton's novel—and any other fictional or nonfictional writings about climate issues—to realize that an engaging and lucid story does not represent the final word on this complex, elusive, and still-unfolding phenomenon. In fact, this seemingly authoritative narrative flies in the face of the views and writings of the vast majority of climate change scientists. Yet in America today, one need not have knowledge to express a point of view—indeed, as mentioned above, in September 2005, Senator Inhofe paraded novelist Michael Crichton into the United States Senate to testify against climate change legislation. Where were our "filters against folly" on that occasion? In his 2005 testimony before the United States Senate Committee on Environment and Public Works, Crichton said that "a focused effort on climate science, aimed at securing sound, independently verified answers to policy questions, is so important now." But even in calling for good climate science, he implicitly belittles and negates the existing science. In a 2005 article called "Michael Crichton and Global Warming," David Sandalow of the Brookings Institution, who says *State of Fear* is "notable mainly for its nuttiness," concludes that "Crichton should hold himself to a higher standard with regard to all the arguments in the book" and "if he has something serious to say on the science of climate change, he should say so in a work of nonfiction and submit his work for peer review."

In his testimony before the U.S. Senate, delivered one year after *State of Fear* appeared, Crichton expresses grave concern about the "integrity of public information" and takes individual scientists vividly to task for their misuse of information, which he repeatedly calls "unverifiable" (he uses such words as "valid," "invalid," "verification," and "unverifiable" nineteen times in his brief speech). Although he is concerned about the integrity of information in specific scientific texts, his own testimony stops far short of acknowledging the credibility and significance of the vast majority of scientific studies of climate change at that time. In any case, as I have indicated above, the psychology of information management suggests that it is much easier to puncture trust than to bolster understanding and acceptance of information about new and controversial phenomena. In addition to eroding lawmakers' trust in climate science by way of his Senate testimony, Crichton caricatures environmental scientists and activists in *State of Fear*, a work that had an initial print run of 1.7 million, was the number-one bestseller on Amazon.com, and reached number two on the *New York Times* bestseller list in January 2005. In light of the psychology of trust, it's clear that all it takes is one articulate naysayer to sink lawmakers' (and the public's) trust in science, while a chorus of actual experts can scarcely outweigh the "negative event," as psychologists would describe it.[6] But it is not my intention to disparage environmental fiction altogether, including works of fiction that seek to explore matters pertinent to climate change. What is particularly egregious about Crichton's novel is how it trespasses on the territory of scientific discourse (even referring to technical scientific articles in footnotes to the story and providing a concluding author's note that takes actual climate science to task)—and yet this work has not itself been subject to peer review prior to publication. While the book demonstrates Crichton's skill as a storyteller, from a scientific perspective it is "demonstrably garbage," as Stanford climatologist Stephen H. Schneider put it when interviewed by Cordelia Dean (2006) for the *New York Times* after the novel received the "journalism award" from the national organization for petroleum geologists.

A somewhat different approach to the issue of trustworthiness in telling the story of climate change—and a more legitimate one, I believe—is offered in Susan M. Gaines's 2001 novel *Carbon Dreams*. What I particularly appreciate about this book is how it prompts readers to ponder the proper role of science in society rather than simply advocating a particular viewpoint on the climate change controversy—this seems like a much more suitable role (getting readers to think) for environmental literature. The novel tells the story of a young female Latin American scientist, whose research in the field of paleoclimatology (the study of ancient climates through the gathering of core samples from the ocean floor) leads her unintentionally into the current controversy regarding global warming and climate change. The novel is not simply an indirect way of espousing the politically loaded idea of global warming. It also explores the predicament of a scientist who merely wishes to understand the planet's natural history and tries to avoid extrapolating from her findings in statements about today's environmental issues. But other scientists get wind of her findings and, she believes, misinterpret the data in support of their own political goals, so she is forced to become involved in the public discussion, despite her wishes. Gaines's novel explores the role of science in contemporary society and, in a sense, tells the story of climate change by showing how none of us, scientists and nonscientists alike, can simply sit back passively and ignore the political implications of our actions or inaction. Fictional paleoclimatologist Dr. Cristina Teresa Arenas is all the more credible for her *reluctance* to join the fray of scientists scrambling for power, publicity, and money ("funding") by insisting on the relevance of arcane research to headline topics of the day. Arenas, while she seems initially to overstate the neutrality of science, is an admirable character because of her cautious attitude and her commitment to being careful with ideas:

> The science doesn't take sides. The science just is whatever it is, and if I'm going to communicate with the press then *that* is what I have to communicate. I can't say I know, when I don't. I can't make knowledge absolute, when it isn't. It doesn't matter what I might imagine or dream or even feel is true. I can only repeat what the data says, what the science is. (pp. 334–335)

Many would argue that even scientists choose research topics (and interpret data) according to conscious or unconscious ideologies. But when aware of the power of ideology, scientists may be better able to withstand politics and personal leanings in explaining how the world works. Susan M. Gaines's protagonist, despite her reluctance, gradually comes to realize that the public and the press hunger to understand what's going on with the earth's atmosphere, and that her research on ancient core samples from the ocean floor might hold certain subtle clues to the relationship between carbon dioxide and climate. But her authority and persuasiveness are earned through faithful empiricism and cautious conclusions, not through rhetorical games, flamboyant leaps of logic, or the dramatic polarizing of villains and heroes. Gaines tells a scientific story that shows how careful empirical research combined with critical thinking can support a humanistic science informed by the political but not merely a tool of politics.

In conclusion, let me ask again, "Why should we be so tolerant of risk where the future habitability of our planet is concerned?" And what's more, why should it be necessary for so many of us in the United States—like activist and writer Rebecca Solnit—to spend so much time "looking at [our] country in horror"? I believe we are overly tolerant of the risk of climate change because, in part, we—the general public in the United States and elsewhere in the world—seem not to appreciate the nature of scientific argument and scientific uncertainty. Vested interests (namely, politicians and scientists beholden to particular industries and literary artists with deeply held ideological stances) are able to exaggerate and distort reasonable forms of uncertainty as a means of casting doubt on an overwhelming body of scientific evidence, undermining appropriate public trust in this evidence. While vested interests may be found across the political spectrum, scientists dedicated to determining the processes and implications of climate change are less likely to be compromised than those who draw their research funding from industries that stand to gain from downplaying the dangers of climate change and from libertarian think tanks. Al Gore asks why we're so tolerant of the risks posed by global warming, and Solnit asserts that she views American complacency with "horror"—by contrast, Michael Crichton looks in horror at how "Western societies have become panic-stricken and hysterically risk averse" (p. 589) and claims that "we spend far too much time soothing false or minor fears" (p. 601).[8]

Failing to appreciate how trust works (or perhaps intuiting the psychology of trust and actively seeking to undermine public trust in climate science), Crichton was able, through his popular novel *State of Fear*, to accentuate

public distrust toward cautionary science on the issue of global warming—
and he brought this distrust explicitly into the lawmaking arena by testifying
before the Senate. In doing so, Crichton became the darling of turn-of-the-
century anti-environmental brownlashers[7] such as Joseph Bast (the author of
a book called *Eco-Sanity: A Common-Sense Guide to Environmentalism*), who
crowed in the 2005 article "State of Fear: Michael Crichton and the End of
Radical Environmentalism" (published in the online *Capitalism Magazine*),

> Public support for [radical environmentalism] was already shrinking as its
> Chicken Little predictions failed to come true and its obsolete big-government
> ideology put it far outside the political mainstream. But Crichton's remark-
> able book may mark the end of the beginning, and the start of a "new envi-
> ronmental movement" that puts science ahead of ideology—and considers
> the legitimate interests of the everyone rather than the careers of a few.

Despite efforts by writers like Susan M. Gaines to offer a more realistic
picture of how scientists conduct and think about their work, and how they
cautiously develop predictive models based on quantitative data, I'm afraid
that American fiction writers, until the recent wave of significant climate
fiction (or "cli-fi") by Barbara Kingsolver, Kim Stanley Robinson, Nathaniel
Rich, and others, have a rather mixed track record on the topic of climate
change.

In *Bringing the Biosphere Home: Learning to Perceive Global Environmental
Change*, Mitchell Thomashow argues that understanding biospheric phenomena, such as climate change, "is such a profound conceptual challenge
because it entails stunning juxtapositions of scale—moving from a fifteen-
minute thunderstorm to a million-year climatological trend, shifting from
tending your garden soil to observing the patterns and trends of biodiversity." (p. 106). Climate fiction—and other media, such as film and digital
art, as discussed in the interview with Chris Jordan later in this volume—
has the capacity to expand our imaginative apprehension of natural processes regardless of scale and our understanding of how data are collected,
analyzed, and communicated. The arts can enhance our appreciation of scientific information and methodologies without simply cultivating uncritical
trust in scientists. We must also apply a critical eye to the misrepresenta-
tions of socially relevant science that sometimes occur in literature and
other media.

REFERENCES

AtKisson, A. (1999). *Believing Cassandra: An optimist looks at a pessimist's world.* White River Junction, VT: Chelsea Green.

Bailey, R. (1993). *Eco-scam: The false prophets of ecological apocalypse.* New York, NY: St. Martin's Press.

Bast, J. L. (2005, January 1). State of fear: Michael Crichton and the end of radical environmentalism. The Heartland Institute. http://heartland.org/policy-docu ments/michael-crichton-and-end-radical-environmentalism?artId=16252.

Bloom, D. (2014, July 30). Movies like "Snowpiercer" can sound the alarm. *The New York Times.* http://www.nytimes.com/roomfordebate/2014/07/29/will -fiction-influence-how-we-react-to-climate-change/movies-like-snowpiercer -can-sound-the-alarm.

Burroughs, W. J. (2003). *Climate: Into the 21st century.* Cambridge, UK: Cambridge University Press.

Christianson, G. E. (2000). *Greenhouse: The 200-year story of global warming.* New York, NY: Penguin Books.

Crichton, M. (2004). *State of fear.* New York, NY: HarperCollins.

Crichton, M. (2005, September 28). Statement of Michael Crichton, M.D. U.S. Senate Committee on Environment & Public Works. http://www.epw.senate .gov/hearing_statements.cfm?id=246766.

Dean, C. (2006, February 9). Truth? Fiction? Journalism? Award Goes to . . . Retrieved from http://www.nytimes.com/2006/02/09/national/09prize.html ?_r=0.

Easterbrook, G. (1995). *A moment on the Earth: The coming age of environmental optimism.* New York, NY: Viking.

Ehrlich, P. R., & Ehrlich, A. H. (1996). *Betrayal of science and reason.* Washington, DC: Island.

Gaines, S. M. (2001). *Carbon dreams.* Berkeley, CA: Creative Arts.

Gelbspan, R. (1998). *The heat is on: The climate crisis, the cover-up, the prescription.* Reading, MA: Perseus Books.

Gelbspan, R. (2004). *Boiling point: How politicians, big oil and coal, journalists, and activists have fueled the climate crisis—and what we can do to avert disaster.* New York, NY: Basic Books.

Grove, R. H. (1996). *Green imperialism: Colonial expansion, tropical island Edens and the origins of environmentalism, 1600–1860.* New York, NY: Cambridge University Press.

Hardin, G. (1985). *Filters against folly: How to survive despite economists, ecologists, and the merely eloquent.* New York, NY: Penguin Books.

Inhofe, J. (2012). *The greatest hoax: How the global warming conspiracy threatens your future.* Long Beach, CA: WND Books.

Janovy, J., Jr. (1997). *Ten minute ecologist: 20 answered questions for busy people facing environmental issues.* New York, NY: St. Martin's.

Karen, M. (2005, October 12). Gore: I don't plan to run for president. *Truthout*.

Kolbert, E. (2006). *Field notes from a catastrophe: Man, nature, and climate change*. New York, NY: Bloomsbury.

Leiserowitz, A. (2004). Before and after *The Day After Tomorrow*: A U.S. study of climate change risk perception. *Environment, 46*, 22–37.

Lomborg, B. (2001). *The skeptical environmentalist: Measuring the real state of the world*. New York, NY: Cambridge University Press.

Lomborg, B. (2007). *Cool it: The skeptical environmentalist's guide to global warming*. New York, NY: Knopf.

Maduro, R., & Schauerhammer, R. (1992). *The holes in the ozone scare: The scientific evidence that the sky isn't falling*. Washington, DC: 21st Century Science Associates.

Marshall, G. (2014). *Don't even think about it: Why our brains are wired to ignore climate change*. New York, NY: Bloomsbury.

Meadows, D. (2008, May 4). How the ozone story became a volcano story. Retrieved from http://www.sustainer.org/dhm_archive/index.php?display_a.

Mooney, C. (2005). *The republican war on science*. New York, NY: Basic Books.

Oreskes, N., & Conway, E. M. (2010). *Merchants of doubt: How a handful of scientists obscured the truth on issues from tobacco smoke to global warming*. New York, NY: Bloomsbury.

Pilkey, O. H., & Pilkey-Jarvis, L. (2007). *Useless arithmetic: Why environmental scientists can't predict the future*. New York, NY: Columbia University Press.

Ray, D. L., & Guzzo, L. (1990). *Trashing the planet*. Washington, DC: Regnery Gateway.

Ray, D. L., & Guzzo, L. (1993). *Environmental overkill: Whatever happened to common sense?* New York, NY: Perennial.

Sandalow, D. B. (2005, January 28). Michael Crichton and global warming. Retrieved from http://www.brookings.edu/research/opinions/2005/01/28energy-sandalow.

Slovic, P. (Ed.). (2000). *The perception of risk*. London, England: Earthscan.

Solnit, R. (2004). Doubt. In *Hope in the dark: Untold histories, wild possibilities* (pp. 133–134). New York: Nation Books.

Steingraber, S. (1997). *Living downstream: A scientist's personal investigation of cancer and the environment*. New York, NY: Vintage.

Stevens, W. K. (1999). *The change in the weather: People, weather, and the science of climate*. New York, NY: Delacorte.

Thomashow, M. (2002). *Bringing the biosphere home: Learning to perceive global environmental change*. Cambridge, MA: MIT Press.

Wyatt, E. (2005, February 9). Analyzing sales of Wolfe's new book. *The New York Times*, http://www.nytimes.com/2005/02/09/books/09wolf.html?pagewanted=print&position=&_r=0.

NOTES

When I presented an earlier version of this essay as a paper at the November 2005 conference on The Endangered Planet in Literature at Dogus University in Istanbul, Turkey, I realized I would run out of time before reading the whole manuscript, so I offered my conclusion right at the beginning: a little bit of environmental knowledge and a lot of literary eloquence can be dangerous. This is not such a new concept, as we learn from the mere title of Garrett Hardin's 1985 book *Filters Against Folly: How to Survive Despite Economists, Ecologists, and the Merely Eloquent.* But in the context of contemporary literature on the subject of climate change, the eloquent—or at least vivid—misuse of science has ominous implications, especially because of the ease with which public trust in the scientific community can be eroded. I have spent the past thirty years celebrating and defending environmental literature and ecocriticism—at this time, I feel compelled to point out not only the power of this work, but also its potential danger.

1. Paul and Anne Ehrlich (1996) directly address the issue of corporate-funded science in *Betrayal of Science and Reason* when they ask, "Why would a qualified scientist help disseminate brownlash ideas? We can think of only two reasons. He or she believes that the scientific consensus is in error (a perfectly valid position, provided it is well reasoned and supported by evidence) and/or enjoys financial support from anti-environmental elements (not so valid)" (p. 36).

2. Scholars such as Anthony Leiserowitz have led the way in exploring how public attitudes toward climate change have been affected by the mainstream media. For instance, for the 2004 article "Before and After *The Day After Tomorrow*," Leiserowitz surveyed viewers of the Hollywood film to determine whether or not the fictional movie (with a clear catastrophist message) had an effect on their concerns about global warming. Forty-nine percent of respondents stated that watching the movie made them somewhat more worried or much more worried about global warming, while 42 percent said their views of global warming were unchanged by the film, and only 1 percent said they felt less worried as a result of watching the film. More recent studies indicate that public concerns about climate change have nearly doubled in the past decade. Blogger and cli-fi activist Dan Bloom has triggered an international discussion of the specific role of climate fiction in galvanizing public attention to the significance of climate change; in his July 30, 2014, piece titled "Movies Like 'Snowpiercer' Can Sound the Alarm," he writes, "'Cli-fi' movies and novels have the power to change minds. That's their mission."

3. According to a February 2005 *New York Times* article by Edward Wyatt, Crichton's book sold 516,000 hardcover copies for HarperCollins during its first year in print. A month earlier, Joseph L. Bast reported that Crichton's book had an initial print run of 1.7 million copies. By contrast, Susan M. Gaines's publisher, Creative Arts Book Company, went out of business in 2003, and sales figures for *Carbon Dreams* are not available.

4. One could write an entire article about the rhetorical function of Crichton's eclectic, annotated bibliography in *State of Fear*. The mere inclusion of such a document in a work of fiction—on top of the footnotes sprinkled throughout the narrative—suggests the author's goal of convincing readers that his imagined narrative is actually founded on accurate and fair assessment of climate science and other relevant studies. Closer inspection of the bibliography shows Crichton to be profoundly anti-precautionary, as he harshly criticizes scientists and journalists ranging from Rachel Carson to the authors of *The Limits to Growth* to Ross Gelbspan for "urgent overstatement bordering on hysteria" (p. 597), while applauding Richard Lindzen's climate research (considered highly suspect by the scientific community) and clearly allying himself with the "crisp, calm, clean" tone and clearheaded deconstruction of environmentalist and scientific dogma (p. 595) that he finds in the writings of Alston Chase and Bjorn Lomborg, two high-profile brownlashers.

5. William K. Stevens (1999) notes, in *The Change in the Weather: People, Weather, and the Science of Climate*, that Lindzen "has gone so far as to liken the [climate change] models to Ouija boards" (p. 215).

6. By disseminating "junk science" and distorting the politics of climate activism in *State of Fear*, Michael Crichton has not simply raised questions about particular claims made by environmental scientists or about the rhetorical stridency of specific scientists and journalists—his comments have had the effect of impugning the entire discipline of environmental science in the public imagination. This is reminiscent of Dixy Lee Ray and Lou Guzzo's reliance on the scientific distortions in Rogelio Maduro's and Ralf Schauerhammer's *The Holes in the Ozone Scare: The Scientific Evidence That the Sky Isn't Falling* in writing such books as *Trashing the Planet: How Science Can Help Us Deal with Acid Rain, Depletion of the Ozone, and Nuclear Waste (Among Other Things)* (1990) and *Environmental Overkill: Whatever Happened to Common Sense?* (1993), infamous works of brownlashing that have been principal sources of misinformation for the likes of Rush Limbaugh and Fox News in their attacks on climate and ozone science. Regarding the damage to scientific credibility caused by the garbling of ozone science in Ray and Guzzo's *Trashing the Planet*, Nobel laureate and atmospheric chemist Sherwood Rowland has stated that "it will be difficult for my message to catch up with their misstatements" (quoted by Donella Meadows, 2008). Naomi Oreskes and Erik Conway probe the processes and rationale for the undermining of scientific credibility in their book *Merchants of Doubt: How a Handful of Scientists Obscured the Truth on Issues From Tobacco Smoke to Global Warming* (2010).

7. The term "brownlash" comes from *Betrayal of Science and Reason: How Anti-Environmental Rhetoric Threatens Our Future*, by Paul and Anne Ehrlich. The Ehrlichs define the term as follows: "The brownlash has been generated by a diverse group of individuals and organizations, doubtless often with differing motives and backgrounds. We classify them as brownlashers by what they say, not by who they are. With strong and appealing messages, they have successfully sowed seeds of

doubt among journalists, policy makers, and the public at large about the reality and importance of such phenomena as overpopulation, global climate change, ozone depletion, and losses of biodiversity" (p. 1). In addition to the works of Dixy Lee Ray and Lou Guzzo (mentioned above) and Michael Crichton's *State of Fear*, other well-known works of brownlashing include Ronald Bailey's *Eco-Scam: The False Prophets of Ecological Apocalypse* (1993), Gregg Easterbrook's *A Moment on the Earth: The Coming Age of Environmental Optimism* (1995), and Bjorn Lomborg's *The Skeptical Environmentalist: Measuring the Real State of the World* (2001) and *Cool It: The Skeptical Environmentalist's Guide to Global Warming* (2007).

8. Another explanation for the failure to act aggressively to stem climate change, even among those who have come to accept the verdict of science, is the prominence effect. See the postscript to Chapter 3.

CHAPTER 10

Healing Rwanda

TERRY TEMPEST WILLIAMS

Twibuke: Beauty and Healing Amid the Shards of Rwanda

A woman stands at the opening of a descending staircase. Her eyes—her red-streaked eyes—see inside me as she puts her arm through mine. We kiss each other on either side of our cheeks, one-two-three, Rwandan style. Her eyes. She directs me down to the basement, where there is a pyramid-shaped glass case of bones rising from a floor of white square tiles. The bones—skulls, femurs, ribs, vertebrae—are organized in rows, columns, piles.

You can look through the glass floor of the bone pyramid to another floor below where a single coffin rests. We are told that inside is the body of a mother holding a child. "I saw this woman," a man interrupts. "I knew her. For years, her skeleton was exposed for everyone to see." As we listened to what happened to this woman, what was done to her, the repeated rapes and a violence impaled with a gun, I didn't want to hear it. And now that I had, I couldn't get this image out of my mind.

Rwanda: I didn't want to come here. I didn't want to be in a place so familiar with death. I had seen enough in my own family. I was also scared. The only thing I knew of Rwanda was genocide, the weight of that word. Nineteen ninety-four, the year we Americans turned our backs. No. I would not go to Rwanda.

I said no. And then I said yes. I said yes to Lily Yeh, a Chinese-American artist who understands mosaic as taking that which is broken and creating something whole. She helped to create The Village of Arts and Humanities in Philadelphia from the poorest of neighborhoods. She stood in the center of an empty lot littered with glass, picked up a stick, and drew a circle around herself. One by one, a curious community came to see who this tiny Chinese woman was and what she was doing. She invited them to pick up shards of glass and together they began making art. Mosaics. A Tree of Life was constructed on the only standing wall of a building otherwise destroyed. It was the first of many mosaics to restore beauty to a place of violence and abuse.

"Barefoot Artists," she said as she began to describe the Rwandan project. She had been asked by a member of the Red Cross to help design a genocide memorial in the village of Rugerero, very near the town of Gisenyi, on the border of the Congo. "Will you be part of our team? I need you as our scribe." I said no. And then I said yes. I knew in my heart that my own spiritual evolution depended on it.

There are four of us: Lily Yeh; Alan Jacobson, an environmental designer; Meghan Morris, a graduate student whose work focuses on the effects of war on adolescents; and myself. Rukirande Musana Jean Bosco is our sponsor from the Red Cross, the man who invited Lily to come work with him on this project. He is accompanied by Damas Ndebwohe, a tall, impressive young man with a broad smile. We are traveling on a red dirt road outside Kigali, the capital city of Rwanda, on our way to see two churches that are now memorials to the 1994 genocide. Large expanses of wetlands are on either side of us. "This is where many Tutsi hid," Jean Bosco tells us. "It is also where many were hunted and butchered by the Hutu militia known as the Interahamwe." We cross a bridge. "There was a time when this river was choked with bodies," Jean Bosco says.

Inside the church at Nyamata, my eyes are drawn to the ceiling. Holes from grenades appear as stars. Light is streaming down onto the empty pews. There are rooms full of bones. Bags of bones, bulging, closed. Sacks of skulls. Piles of faded clothing. The altar cloth, once white, is brown with blood. Ten thousand people were murdered here.

Belyse, a young woman, twenty-one years old, is the witness here at Nyamata who tells the story. She shows us where the door was kicked down. She shows us an identity card. Hutu. Tutsi. "It came down to this," she says. She tells of those murdered, bodies piled over one another on pews. She tells of how the Virgin survived and points to a statue on a shelf, the Blessed Mother perfectly intact.

Beautiful in her ethereal presence, Belyse is barely here. She inhabits the past, hunkered in the grasses, nine years old, listening, waiting. Her parents told her to hide in the fields. She remembers the screams, the silences, looking for her parents, searching for her parents, and then the years of wandering. She has come back. This church is now her home. Her parents' home. Their bones are in the church. Purple fabric covers coffins. Flowers now dried are draped over the wooden boxes.

Damas is standing in front of an alcove inside the church. The brick wall is stained with blood. Wild with grief, he tells me about babies pulled out of their mothers' arms and thrown against the wall by the killers. "In that moment," Damas says to me, "the devil came into the churches and murdered every Tutsi."

My eyes follow the birds flying inside, swallows banking before stained-glass windows—red drops of blood, rendered in glass, below a window of deliverance, blue, yellow.

Outside, the sun is blinding. I can breathe again. I look back at the church with its red bricks of sandstone. Swallows circle the white cross. Purple ribbon is strewn through the wrought-iron fence like crepe paper woven through the spokes of bicycles.

We descend into what looks like a root cellar. There is just enough light to see that it is filled with coffins covered with purple cloth. Some of the coffins are open. "That is not one person—but many persons," says Belyse. "Each coffin contains many people." She pauses. "Whole families."

This is a hell of our own making—those who killed and those of us who looked away. No surgical strikes, computerized by military minds and carried out by top-gun pilots, the eyes of these killers were on the eyes of those they killed. By hand. Nearly one million Tutsis murdered by hand in one hundred days, murdered by their neighbors with farm tools, machetes, and hoes. Hundreds of skulls, shelves of skulls—ten thousand bodies—are here at Nyamata.

We are walking inside a mass grave, genocidal tourists. I am sick to my stomach. All I can see are the whites of Belyse's eyes in darkness. I cannot walk any farther down this narrow, damp hallway of bones, shelves and boxes of bones. Damas calls me back. "Here, look, the skin has not separated from the bones . . . " From the corner of my eye, I see a flesh-fallen hand, disembodied. Below, a large, amber cockroach scurries across the cement floor. *Inyezi.* Cockroach. The Hutu name for Tutsi.

Back outside, I sit in the garden and take a picture of white blossoms against red sand. Damas sits down next to me. Lily, Alan, and Meghan are still underground.

"It is impossible to imagine—" I say to Damas.

"It is impossible to accept," he replies. "When I see those skulls, I see me."

∽

We arrive in Gisenyi at dusk. Smoke. Shadows. Figures caught in headlights. Lake Kivu is a long reflective mirror. I am reminded of scenes captured in a ring I once had as a child; inside a plastic orb were the silhouettes of palms against a twilight sky made of iridescent butterfly wings, turquoise blue. We are surrounded by enormous mountains, a crown of peaks, snow-tipped and jagged. And then, suddenly, an eerie red glow is emanating from the Congo. An active volcano.

Jean Bosco refers to the volcano as a woman, Nyiragongo. He tells us that three years ago when she erupted, Gisenyi needed no electricity at night, the sky was so bright. Louis Gakumba, a young man of twenty-two years, tells of carrying his mother on his back across the smoldering lava, how they fled their home, carrying mattresses to the hillside where they watched as Gisenyi burned.

"Louis will be our translator," Jean Bosco says. Louis shakes our hands. He is elegant and poised. His eyes are almond-shaped, brown with curled lashes. And when he smiles, we relax, believing joy can cohabit with hardship.

Louis tells us that he taught himself English through books and by watching American movies. "It was a competition with my brother," he says. "I wanted to speak English better than he did." His native language is Kinyarwanda, spoken by both Tutsi and Hutu. He also speaks French, Swahili, and two Congolese dialects. "This is his first experience as an interpreter," says Jean Bosco. Louis's formal education was truncated by war. "I was nine years old when the genocide began," he says. I notice a long centipedelike scar on his left hand. "Yeah, we all have stories."

A deep silence takes hold of us on the porch of the house where we will be staying for a month. In candlelight, Lily says, "The results of the violence we witnessed today is not just outside us but within us, capable of erupting at any moment."

∽

On my first morning in Gisenyi, I take a brisk walk through the town to orient myself. As I head toward the market, groups of men, young and old, begin to heckle me, jeering and laughing. I look straight ahead only to be approached by a man with a crutch who is missing his left leg from the knee down. He speaks to me. I don't understand. He holds out his hand.

Now I do, and give him the Rwandan francs that I have in my pocket. It isn't enough. He grows impatient, shakes his head, and moves on. Women pass with baskets of bananas on their heads and smile. I smile back. Four small boys follow me, practicing their English, tugging at my shirt. *Hello, madame, how are you? Muzungu! Muzungu!* they shout, using the word for white person.

Bicycles flash by, their drivers ringing bells to tell me that I am in their way; trucks and motorbikes speed by too close for comfort. Dust envelops me, and I cover my mouth with my scarf. The chaos grows as the crowds grow. All roads lead to the market, where the pulse of Gisenyi intensifies. Western Union is on my left. An Internet café with wooden benches outside is on my right. There is a bank with people openly making deals for the best exchange rate. A barbershop. A bike repair shop. A hardware store with men next door shining shoes. Six women are crouched down around a blue plastic tub outside what appears to be a clinic. Looking sideways, I see a baby with its eyes closed and legs folded. I think the baby is dead. On either side of the dirt road are trenches half filled with water and trash; the acrid stench of urine and rotting food swirls around toilet paper, discarded diapers, and single shoes floating sole-side up.

Inside the market, the labor of women is on full display: tall triangular mounds of potatoes, purple, red, and white; string beans, yellow beans, black beans, kidney beans, more varieties than I could ever imagine, which women dip from full burlap sacks with tin cups, selling them to other women. Carrots, cabbage, corn, cassava, spinach, sorghum, and all manner of grains from oats to barley to wheat create a color wheel of produce next to piles of polished avocados. The smell of coffee alone induces a euphoria in me, and I purchase a pound.

Deeper into the market, there are clothes of every kind: shirts, blouses, skirts and pants, new and used, and I duck to avoid brushing my head against all that is hanging above me. An acre of shoes stretches toward socks and bras and panties and briefs. Bolts of colored cloth, Indonesian batiks, some already cut to wrap around waists, are clothes-pinned on rope lines, flapping like sheets. Soccer balls; brushes and combs; creams and cosmetics; radios, records, and a tower of cassettes, from rap to jazz to African music; videos; magazines; dishes, pots, and pans; appliances. And then, at the far end of the market, I can first smell, then see, live chickens, eggs, baskets of fish, fresh and dried minnows from Lake Kivu. And then, hanging from hooks, is the red marbled meat of goats and cows. Anything you could want or need is here.

~

Jean Bosco explains the Rugerero Survivors Village to us. "After the war, the government thought about how they could help the survivors of the 1994 genocide to find security and shelter, so they set aside small tracts of land and built simple, adjoining brick structures covered in gray adobelike material for those who needed homes. One 'house' is built to accommodate two families."

The village in Rugerero is made up of genocide survivors from Gisenyi, Cyanzarwe, and Kibuye. The individuals and families are not related. And for the most part, they did not know each other before being placed together in this makeshift community. "The people in the Rugerero Survivors Village have nothing," says Jean Bosco. "Worse than nothing."

The memorial site is less than a mile from the village. It is a field of lava stones with the humblest of structures to protect the bones buried there, a corrugated-tin roof above a cement slab. Banana trees border the field. A primary school is adjacent to the memorial. Eldefons, one of the community leaders, says, "This is the place we buried our people with the little money we had to keep the bones safe. This is a matter of security to us, the safekeeping of our beloved. We will move the bodies while the new memorial is being built. There will also be new bones added as we uncover more loved ones' remains in the fields. And then we hope to make a big house where people can meet and talk about the genocide."

~

A small child stands against a brick wall, singing. I am sitting against a tree wishing I could disappear. The physical and psychic assault of Africa has deflated me. I close my eyes. Three girls suddenly grab my hands and pull me up, pushing me toward the school, where dozens and dozens of children follow, running, laughing, and tugging at my skirt. Meghan is behind me with her own group of children. Desperate to stem the chaos, I turn around and sit down on the ground, making a circle with my hands. Miraculously the children sit down with me. Louis gently asks the children to move back to enlarge the circle so more kids can join us.

"My name is Terry," I say, then clap, looking at the child sitting next to me. "My name is Olive," she says, and claps! "My name is Jean Claude." Clap! "My name is Vincent." Clap! The tempo picks up. "My name is

Yvonne." Clap! And so the children's names move energetically through the circle like an electrical current. And then, spontaneously, the children begin to sing. Olive sings with a deep, haunting voice. More songs emerge— many of them Christian songs the children learned in church.

Suddenly, the children start clapping their hands and calling my name. I don't know what they want. Louis turns to me and says, "They want you to sing them a song—teach them a song." My mind, in a panic, goes blank. A song? I can't remember any song. Finally (with Louis translating), I say, "Okay, this is a very silly song. It's about a food called Jell-O." I jiggle my body, they jiggle theirs, all of us laugh. I begin to sing:

> Oh, the big red letters stand for the Jell-O family.
> Oh, the big red letters stand for the Jell-O family.
> It's Jell-O—yum, yum, yum.
> Jell-O Pudding—yum, yum, yum.
> Jell-O Tapioca Pudding—try all three!

The children are laughing hysterically at me, at my singing, and I cannot believe that the only song that came to me was a Mormon camp ditty glorifying a food staple that I learned when I was eight years old.

Louis tries to explain to the children what Jell-O is. He looks at me completely puzzled. "What should I say?"

"Tell them it looks like a fat man's belly that jiggles when he's laughing. Tell them it's green and comes in cold square cubes." Louis raises his eyebrows. "Tell them it's like squishy candy that you can eat with a spoon." Whatever he tells them, the children burst out laughing.

At the genocide memorial site, there are more children still. Lily calls them together. All eyes are on her. She picks up two rocks and raises the lava stones high above her head. She then ritualistically places them down by her feet beneath the line of twine that Alan and Damas have used to stake out the boundaries of the site. Lily makes a rectangle in the air with her hands and then points to the children and claps. The children understand and begin gathering rocks and placing them below the twine. Within minutes, the children have enclosed the sacred space with lava stones. The boundaries of the memorial are set.

When I asked Lily how she had thought of this, she said smiling, "I'm Chinese, I know a workforce when I see one."

~

"Right now I think God is with us," Lily says to Alan, Meghan, and me, as we sit outside on the patio. "The Chinese contractor is here in Gisenyi once every two months. Mr. Yu works for a company based in Beijing with ties in Rwanda for the past eight years. I spoke with him on the telephone today. He will meet with me tomorrow. Cement is very expensive, eight times what it costs in China. I will show him the design. He said they will do whatever we need.

"The first stage will be to level the site. We will need surveyors. Mr. Yu promises to give me the best price because I speak Mandarin. But I have no idea how much it is going to cost . . . thousands, tens of thousands?

"Lava stones or bricks?" she asks Alan.

"We'll just have to price it out," says Alan, "and see what is available."

Lily tells Alan she will price out the room for bones with Mr. Yu as well. "There has to be an underground room for the bones with ventilation." Lily is thinking out loud. "Cement is too expensive. Lava with cement binder will be better. Mr. Yu will supervise."

Lily double-checks her drawing of the memorial. "Yes, the Bone Room is here. You will walk to the back of the pavilion and descend into this private space for families. Toward the front of the memorial will be steps ascending to the altar. The village will decide what words will appear here." She pauses. "The last stage will be to cover the memorial with mosaics. We can find broken pieces of tile that can be used to embellish the surface of the outside walls." She smiles. "I will teach the men and women in the village how to create beautiful mosaics with what has been thrown away." Lily turns to me. "We are all broken somewhere. Putting the pieces back together while using vibrant color creates joy in the bleakest of places."

She then looks at Jean Bosco. "So we start on Monday."

Damas stands up and begins chanting "Oh-oh-oh-oh" and clapping his hands. Jean Bosco lets out a deep belly laugh and raises his hands up to the sky. "God places his benediction on this," he says. It begins to rain.

～

A week later I meet Vincent Juarez, a U.S. Marine who arrived in Rwanda on September 1, 2005. He can't tell me why he is here. But he does say, "The government doesn't like the vibes in Kigali. We're here to protect the U.S. Embassy." He is the first Marine to be sent to Rwanda; five more troops are being sent in October. He is staying at the Kivu Sun Hotel with his new girlfriend, who works with USAID. He has been in the country all of five days. He is from New Mexico and recently served in Iraq but was sent home because of injuries. A long, jagged scar runs across his shoulder and down his right arm.

"I'm fine now," he says. "Listen, can you help me out with something?"

"Of course—if I can."

"There was a war here, right?" He looks directly in my eyes. He is serious. "I mean, could you sort of fill me in on what happened?"

~

Mr. Yu has delivered. The ground is being leveled. Hundreds of children stand on stone walls watching the rich black soil being moved. One Caterpillar with a central blade is clearing the lava field. There are twelve Rwandan men with shovels. Mr. Yu is helping. The Bone Room is being dug.

~

Sitting on the porch with a cup of ginger tea, my journal, and bird book, I am watching through my binoculars what I believe to be sunbirds in the garden—elegant, purple-iridescent birds with a decurved bill.

It is cloudy with intermittent rain. The roads are muddy, deep with puddles. Still, the sound of children playing creates joy, alongside the sound of chickens and roosters, birds, quiet conversations on the streets, and always the clicking of bicycle bells.

A wagtail, black and white, has just landed between the upright metal arrows that serve as a deterrent on the cinder-block wall. Its lyrical song softens the edges between this porch and the street.

I am touching only the surface of things.

~

At each memorial we visit, I read *Ntidigasubire*, which means "Never Again" in Kinyarwanda. But each time I see these coupled words and think about the ongoing genocides occurring in the Congo and Darfur, I want to add a comma between them: Never, Again.

And still, we look away.

~

The rivers are running red once again—not with the blood of the people, but the blood of the land. Steep quilted mountainsides are cultivated clear to the summits. The green and yellow squares look like a stretched quilt being pulled apart by rain and gravity. Every day, I watch women walking the winding roads of Rwanda carrying their burdens on their heads so they can continue to feed their children.

Erosion is the other genocide in Rwanda—the one no one mentions. Rwanda is a country that is literally slipping away. My hope is also eroding the longer I am here, even as my faith is deepening. I am too tired and overwhelmed to reflect on why. Who has time for reflection?

~

Our days here are taking their toll. I see it in our eyes. It is not the physical fatigue of working in the village, but the mental stress of moving in a world we don't understand. It's as if we are walking inside a hologram Rwandans can see but we cannot.

Echoes of war reverberate in each conversation. Every square inch of this country has been bled over. Nothing is neutral but perhaps the sky. Even the thought of God feels suspect. It is hard for me to reconcile myself to a god that allows this kind of suffering, and one that is indifferent to it. Both action and inaction cut into my conscience as a sharp-edged conundrum. Those who were perpetrators and those who were victims now all bleed together as one nation's casualty. We cannot tell who is Hutu and who is Tutsi. But the people we are working with know. There are tensions, I watch eyes. They see into one another's histories, but they remain silent.

How can I even begin to think about asking a woman about the war when it inevitably leads to memories of physical violence and revisiting the death of her children? And what are we doing disturbing the dirt where bones are buried?

Over and over again, I am reminded to live and work out of my strength, not my weakness, to stand in the center of my most generous self and trust what is good in humanity. But here in Rwanda, all these platitudes evaporate on the dusty red roads. Neighbors murdered neighbors. Priests called the machete bearers into their churches and allowed them to slaughter their congregations.

I think of the word *aftermath*—the aftermath of war. After the numbers, after the blood-drenched days of death, how does one reconstruct a life? "Alone, and now together, we are still displaced," one of the women in the Rugerero Survivors Village tells me.

So little makes sense. My heart trembles. I become my own darkness. At night in Gisenyi, the only buffer between me and the haunted streets of Rwanda is a torn mosquito net.

~

The sandy beach of Lake Kivu is utterly still. You would never know that less than a mile away is a prison packed with genocidaires dressed in pink, that the hospital has no more rooms left for the sick, and that the streets of Gisenyi are filled with orphans begging and wandering among the unemployed men who sit on the curbs of the dusty streets. Nor would you know that a stone's throw across the Congolese border another war is raging. The stillness and peace of this lake, barely a ripple, betrays its history. During the genocide, Lake Kivu's shoreline rose not by inches but by feet from the mass of bloated bodies floating like an enormous raft of death, a stinking sink of cholera and diseases.

Twelve white egrets skim the lake, their wings barely, just barely, gliding above the water. Beauty is not a luxury but a strategy for survival.

~

We have been invited to be guests at the local *gacaca* in Gisenyi, just down the road from where we are staying. "Gacaca," says Jean Bosco, "is pronounced *ga-cha-cha*. It refers to the traditional form of justice practiced in villages throughout Rwanda before colonial times. It was a way the community handled disputes over property rights, goats, cows, all manner of discord from marriage to theft. The community would sit on the lawn or hillside, listen to the quarrel at hand, and decide the outcome through consensus."

Jean Bosco tells us that throughout Rwanda, ten thousand gacaca courts are now trying genocide suspects in the communities where their crimes were committed. Perpetrators currently in prisons and jails are being tried by their friends and neighbors. If the suspected criminal shows proper remorse and tells who he killed, how he killed them, and where their bones are, the community will grant him forgiveness and fold him back into that community. But if the suspect lies or shows no remorse, or if the crimes he committed are particularly severe, the judges, empowered by the people, can exact a sentence, even execution, and send the perpetrator back to prison. Jean Bosco quotes statistics that are difficult to comprehend. There are 1.7 million displaced Hutus who are afraid to return to Rwanda for fear of reprisals. Many of them have taken up residency in the Congo. There are 400,000 widows and 500,000 orphans created from the 1994 war. And 130,000 individuals in prison upon suspicion of committing acts of genocide.

"Gacaca's goal is to bring restorative justice back into the country so we can live in harmony with one another," he says. "Gacaca is held once a week in every village, town, and city. Attendance is mandatory."

Louis whispers, "Gacaca is very difficult for me. All the terror returns to us." He pauses. "But I will come. You need to hear about the nature of these crimes and how we tell the truth from lies." I cannot help but look, once again, at the scar that traverses his left hand.

I look at my own two hands. On this hand, good. On this hand, evil. I am capable of both altruism and atrocities, blessings and brutalities. With both hands open, how can I judge another?

～

Genocide. The Holocaust. The displacement of First Nations in North America. Habitat destruction and climate change. It is not in our psychology as human beings to respond to the grand abstractions of catastrophe. Paul Slovic, a psychologist at the University of Oregon, calls it "psychic numbing." But we can respond to the suffering of another human being. To hear and share one another's stories becomes the open channel to compassion.

One man, Jean Bosco, inspired one woman, Lily Yeh, with his story of war and the need for healing. She responded to his call for help and came to Rwanda. She returned home with a vision and inspired three more colleagues to accompany her. There will be others who follow.

～

I take one last walk on the shores of Lake Kivu. Flecks of mica become tiny mirrors in the glistening sand. A pale chanting goshawk flies over me—the gift of a feather at my feet.

We are leaving tomorrow.

At night I dream that my husband, Brooke, and I are presented with bones—leg bones: femur, tibia, fibula—the bones by which we stand on the Earth, the bones that give us stature. We cannot see who is giving us these bones.

We hold them in hand as weapons. We rattle them. We play them like flutes. We bang them like drumsticks on hollow logs.

The bones of our ancestors are speaking. There will be nothing left if we do not listen. The scaffolding of our communities is collapsing.

In the continuing dream, we are presented with mounds of dirt in various colors—where life begins, where seeds are planted, where food is grown.

We place our hands in the soil. Our fingers wrap themselves around bones until they become trees, firmly rooted.

~

Eighteen months later, we return to Rwanda. The memorial rises from the volcanic rubble like a prayer. We walk down the center path of inlaid stones surrounded on either side by lawn. The white undulating wall defines the sacred space. Some of the tallest pinnacles, call them standing waves, are painted in Rwanda's national colors of turquoise, yellow, and green. A purple band is painted around the base of the white wall, the color of mourning.

We stop and look up from the base of the stairs that lead to the blue-roofed pavilion with turquoise pillars that houses the altar that will bear the word TWIBUKE in glass-jeweled mosaic: LET US REMEMBER.

Jean Bosco places his hands on his heart. Lily presses her palms together and bows. She walks up the steps first and greets Siboman Francois, the man she trained last year to oversee the mosaic work that is embellishing the altar. Dortea is completing a mosaic of a red flower with a green stem and leaves that will adorn the right side of the altar. Her eyes are focused on the work at hand.

Consulata is an elder dressed traditionally in a sarong and blouse with her head wrapped in a red scarf. She sits on an overturned bucket and breaks tile with a small hammer. She then takes the broken pieces of white, beige, and terra cotta tiles and tailors them to size with large clippers. I sit down beside her. She hands me another set of clippers and we cut and shape tiles together.

Francois points to the contour of one of the leaves and traces it with his index finger. "This," he says. "You must do." I nod.

For hours, we work on the mosaic. Cement on trowel, pick a piece of tile, set it, smooth the surface, and see that it is level.

A mosaic is like a puzzle. It engages the mind through a sequence of possibilities, trial and error. You look at the broken fragments of tile. Your eye assesses the space to be filled and searches for a corresponding shape. Piece by piece, you come closer to the desired form and effect. Mosaic is not simply an art form but a form of integration, a way of not only seeing the world but responding to it.

Consulata and I sit side by side creating a red flower together. She works on the petals.

Francois returns and points to the leaf I am working on. He runs his fingers across its uneven surface. "No good." I remove the green tesserae. He demonstrates quickly. His placement of new tiles chosen from the pile at my feet creates a much tighter and smoother construction.

"Murakoze," I say.

With his finger, he points to the line once again, the contour of the outer leaf, and walks away.

All of Consulata's children were killed in the genocide. She points to the brick house next door, now collapsed. "My home," she says. The work she is doing at the memorial is for her children. Every day, she mourns them. "Ten years, thirteen years—it was yesterday."

∽

A bank of clouds covers the green canopy of the Congo. The smell of rain is wafting on the wind. It is April, the Rwandan month of remembrance. What was hidden in our last visit is now exposed in a collective, public keening. Purple banners are everywhere and music, explicit and charged with lyrics of loss and lament, fills the streets.

Dortea takes my hand and leads me to the bone chamber. The last time I was here it was still a hole in the ground being dug by men with pick axes and shovels. She has just finished painting the cement floor green and the walls turquoise. The coffins will be brought in tomorrow, covered with purple and white cloth, and placed on the shelves. However, one coffin rests on a wooden platform that is displayed against the wall. It is made of glass with an intact skeleton inside.

"When I am here," she says, "I am not alone. I am here with my family."

∽

Dortea, Consulata, and I are now working on the flower on the opposite side of the altar. It measures close to five feet tall. As we finish, Francois' son surprises all of us with round jewel stones that Lily had given him. He places them like secrets in the white-tiled mosaic background. They take on the countenance of eyes.

Through the meditation of mosaic, both Hutu and Tutsi, perpetrators and victims, masons and mosaicists, are working toward a unity of expression by taking that which is broken and creating something whole. These tiles, now the structure of mosaic, are the fragments of war reimagined.

∽

April 5, 2007. The mosaic work is finished. The jeweled letters are complete:

TWIBUKE
ABACUBAZIZE GENOCIDE 1994
(LET US REMEMBER OUR BELOVED LOST TO THE GENOCIDE)

Young women are mopping the mosaic floor of the pavilion. Consulata continues to clean each tile, each letter. A few final paint touches are being made on the turquoise pillars. The dedication is set for four p.m.

Three mosaic sunflowers stand as guardians above the bone chamber, whose yellow doors, newly painted, are locked. Last night, the purple satin coffin covers edged with white lace had been washed and draped over the trees to dry.

Behind the memorial, dozens of men and women from the village are hoeing the ground, making it level for the thousands of people to come. A policeman is standing guard. His club is painted purple and yellow. Young women, bent over with straight legs, are sweeping the stone pathway to the pavilion with bundles of fine sticks.

Jean Bosco is slowly walking the grounds, his chin raised, smiling. I put my arm through his. "This is a great day in my life," he says.

Louis arrives in his best clothes. He will be translating the ceremony from Kinyarwanda to English and back to Kinyarwanda. Lily walks with her son, Daniel, to the altar. He leaves her at the steps. Dressed in purple, she walks forward alone, places her hands together and bows.

More policemen arrive with men in military uniforms carrying guns. "For security," Jean Bosco says to Lily. "Just a precaution."

A quarter mile away, on the side of the road, we can see a procession of children walking from the village, led by their teachers. As they approach, we can see they are dressed in gold and white costumes, prepared to dance, their faces sprinkled with glitter. The women dancers from the village are dressed in yellow chiffon caftans with gold headbands. They, too, have glitter sprinkled on their faces.

As we all stand outside the memorial entrance watching the dignitaries arrive, from the governor to the mayor to various local officials, extra security gathers anticipating the arrival of Joseph Habineza, the minister of culture, youth, and sports.

Habineza is well known for organizing a volleyball game between the Rwandan Patriot Front (Tutsi) and President Habyarimana's Rwandan

Army (Hutu), just months after the Arusha Peace Accords were signed in August 1993, establishing a truce on paper between Hutus and Tutsis, an attempt to stem the escalating violence of the previous three years. If the handshake meant something between the warring factions, then why not participate in good sportsmanship on the field? Thousands of people were packed into the stadium in Kigali to watch.

On January 29, 1994, the day after the volleyball match, Habineza drove home to find Hutu extremists waving machetes in front of his house. In a split second, he turned another direction, seeking refuge at his neighbor's, where he found his family in hiding. A moderate Hutu who suddenly found himself at risk with many others during the buildup to the genocide, Habineza joined the Rwandan Patriotic Front and fought alongside Tutsi leader Paul Kagame in the bush. As he tells the story, the two men were actually talking about the volleyball game when they received the news on April 6, 1994, that Rwandan President Habyarimana's plane had been shot down, the event that triggered the war.

Paul Kagame never forgot Joseph Habineza and his daring volleyball match. In 2000, when Kagame became president of Rwanda, he appointed Habineza as part of his cabinet.

Over an hour passes in the hot Rwandan sun as we wait, listening to the music played only during the month of April. Genocide music. Music of remembrance.

The minister's entourage of black SUVs arrives. The crowd backs up. Joseph Habineza steps out of the black shiny vehicle, dressed in a black, well-fitted suit and black patent-leather shoes, an impressive man in his early forties. He adjusts his aviator sunglasses and is greeted by the governor of Gisenyi. He is then introduced to Jean Bosco and Lily.

Dortea, now dressed like a Greek goddess in a sleeveless white chiffon gown with a purple sash over one shoulder, holds a silver tray with scissors at the entrance of the Rugerero Genocide Memorial. She stands stoic and regal, her eyes focused down. The minister of culture, youth, and sports steps aside as Lily is invited to cut the purple ribbon. The ribbon flies open and the crowd claps.

There are many speeches, many songs, and many tributes to the genocide survivors and those who died and are buried here.

Joseph Habineza delivers his speech in both Kinyarwanda and English. "May we never forget that the genocide was a result of bad governance. May we never forget the consequences of prejudice. May we never forget our loved ones who are buried here and all over the countryside of Rwanda. May we never forget the power of forgiveness and reconstruction. We are no longer Hutu or Tutsi, we are Rwandans."

Lily rises and walks to the podium to deliver her speech. It begins to rain. A woman appears behind Lily with an open umbrella. Jean Bosco whispers to me, "In Rwanda, when it rains it is a sign of blessings."

The dedication ends. Music resumes. Many people walk up the steps of the pavilion to lay bouquets of flowers at the base of the altar. "More of our dead are at peace," Consulata says, wiping her eyes. "But we will never be."

∼

At a dinner following the dedication, Habimana Martin, director of good governance in Gisenyi Province, said to me in an unguarded moment, "It would be a beautiful place if the dark things in your heart hadn't happened. But things change. What I would want you to know is this: Please do not close your eyes or ears when you know people are being killed. Because if you close your eyes, I will go out and act on it. While you are sleeping, people are dying. The world was told, 'People are dying.' They closed their eyes. Right now, people aren't sleeping. They regret what they did and did not do."

∼

They walk. They walk with the memory of the genocide. They walk in remembrance of those who died, their loved ones among them. We walk with them. It is a river of solemnity winding through the roads of Rwanda.

It is April 7, 2007, the thirteenth anniversary of the day when Hutu extremists turned simple machetes into sabers of war and filled stadiums with young men whipped into a frenzy, waving their farm tools, crying "cockroaches" and "snakes." Machete season. April. May. June. The people walk with their memories. Eyes straight ahead, covering familiar ground.

We stop. A particular family is remembered. Here. This house. See the burnt foundation. Still. The names are read. A silence is held. We walk. We remember.

The procession gathers in size as men, women, and children, the young and the old, enter into the respectful flow of feet walking together to mark the National Day of Mourning. We walk. We stop. We remember. The names are read. The soil is red. A silence is held. We walk. We walk together. This is storied ground.

The governor of Gisenyi walks wearing a black pinstripe suit; his hands are clasped behind his back. The mayor walks next to him. The colonel walks to his right in full uniform with a purple scarf tied around his wrist.

Purple scarves are being worn by most around their necks or arms or wrists.

We cross the river on a wooden bridge. We stop. Stories are recounted. Jean Bosco whispers in my ear that this river ran red, choked with bodies. The bodies created a dam and the bloody river flooded people's homes.

The procession turns. We pass a graveyard. We walk past a Catholic church. We stop. The story is told that only two people survived the mass killings here. Those two survivors step forward and speak. We listen.

We hold the silence between the names that are read. We walk through the religious grounds that are now graves. Buzzards and kites follow the procession.

"These are the same birds that followed the Interahamwe," Jean Bosco says to me as he looks straight ahead. We walk and we walk. The width of the road is the measure of feet, walking, in front of us, behind us, on either side, all sizes of feet, some in leather shoes, some in sandals, some bare, worn, walking, slowly walking, belonging to the memory of genocide.

"No one asks God who is a Tutsi or a Hutu," the voice from the loud-speaker utters. "We are all God's children. We only ask God to stop the genocide."

The procession is a spectrum of colors. The woman in front of me is draped in orange cloth with designs of gold dolphins. Her shoes are black patent leather. Next to me is Aimee, a young woman in her twenties. She lost all her family in the war and is dressed in a black suit with a long narrow skirt, a purple scarf tied around her neck. She carries a handbag with a photograph inside: a picture of herself kneeling in front of a line of skeletons, identifying her family.

We pass another church, this one made of lava stones. We stop. Another story is told. The priest and sisters were murdered. They tried to hide Tutsis. Grenades were thrown. Houses were burned. All were killed.

Names are read. Prayers are given. We proceed. We walk. Bits and pieces of broken tiles are everywhere.

Another turn. We walk on a dirt path through green fields, feet traversing over red and black lava stones, uneven ground, the glint of mica. Banana palms are waving in afternoon breezes. Blue sky. Cumulus clouds. The cry of kites. Always, the circling of kites and buzzards.

Jean Bosco wipes his forehead and then takes my hand as we enter the grounds of another genocide memorial. We follow the procession inside. Public officials take their seats. Some people stand, others sit on the lawn. Jean Bosco follows the governor of Gisenyi who leads us down to the bone chamber. We hesitate. His eyes say, *come.* We follow.

Inside there are fifteen coffins, each draped in white cloth with a purple cross appliqué. On top of each lies a wooden cross. Each person is invited to sign the guest book, which we do. The room is small and crowded.

We walk around to the other side of the memorial to find a place to sit. There is another bone chamber. Aimee takes my hand and pulls me inside. It is damp. We are the only ones here. Suddenly, as if in a gesture of defiance, Aimee walks up to a coffin, pulls the cloth away, and opens it, then, just as quickly, lets the lid slam shut. Exposed were small cloth bundles of bones, bones wrapped in the brightly colored, now faded fabric of women's sarongs, holding the remains of their loved ones together in motifs of flowers and birds.

We leave quickly. Aimee says nothing, just walks outside where people are singing and sits down. I sit beside her on the cement steps against a chainlink fence. Jean Bosco joins us. Lily is sitting with her back against a white cement wall. Her eyes are closed. Meghan and Alan are sitting on the other side of the memorial. The midday sun is bearing down on the speakers, on everyone. All of us are dripping wet with sweat. Thousands of people are gathered on these grounds.

A woman stands in the center and speaks. The crowd is rapt. Many women are wailing uncontrollably. Jean Bosco shakes his head. "I am sorry, I cannot translate." He wipes his eyes and pauses. "This woman's name is Ubuhamya. She is very strong," he says. "She calls for unity. Unity. This is what she wants."

At noon, everyone stands in silence. All over Rwanda, silence. There is no one working in the vertical fields, no cars, no motorbikes, no ringing bells of bicycles, even the birds are quiet.

Silence.

On our way back, graffiti appears on a collapsed building: STRIP US OF OUR SKIN AND WE ARE ALL THE SAME WITHIN. At night, bonfires burn across the land.

∾

"I want to tell you a story," Louis says as we sit on the porch where we first met almost two years ago.

"There is a woman who was married to a pastor. It was a happy family. Some people say they were a family of six, others say they were eleven. The woman was away and when she returned she saw how the Interahamwe were butchering her children on the ground along with her husband.

"After the war, the man who murdered her family came back from the Congo, and when gacaca called him to explain what he had been accused of, he said, 'I accept everything I have been charged with and from the depth of my heart, I apologize.'

"The woman said, 'I saw everything happen. I know you killed my family. I loved my children and my husband. I am alone, I have nothing, but I now choose to forgive you and take you into my home. You will live with me, and I will do whatever it takes to make you feel like my own son.'

"Can you be in the same shoes with this woman?" Louis asks.

Louis then says, "Rwanda is struggling with peace one person at a time. This is as hard as growing wheat on rock. We are finding our way toward unity and reconciliation on a walkway full of thorns and we are walking barefoot."

He stands up and walks over to the balcony that overlooks Gisenyi into the Congo where he was born. "We are trying to forgive, but to forgive is to forget, and we cannot forget. Perhaps there is another word. I am searching for that word."

CHAPTER 11

When Words Fail

Climate Change Activists Have Chosen a Magic Number

BILL MCKIBBEN

I ALMOST NEVER WRITE ABOUT WRITING—in my aesthetic, the writing should disappear, the thought linger. But the longer I've spent working on global warming—the greatest challenge humans have ever faced—the more I've come to see it as essentially a literary problem. A technological and scientific challenge, yes; an economic quandary, yes; a political dilemma, surely. But centrally? A crisis in metaphor, in analogy, in understanding. We haven't come up with words big enough to communicate the magnitude of what we're doing. How do you say: the world you know today, the world you were born into, the world that has remained essentially the same for all of human civilization, that has birthed every play and poem and novel and essay, every painting and photograph, every invention and economy, every spiritual system (and every turn of phrase) is about to be . . . something so different? Somehow "global warming" barely hints at it. The same goes for any of the other locutions, including "climate chaos." And if we do come up with adequate words in one culture, they won't necessarily translate into all the other languages whose speakers must collaborate to somehow solve this problem.

I've done my best, and probably better than some. My first book, *The End of Nature*, has been published in twenty-four languages, and the essential idea embodied in the title probably came through in most of them. It wasn't enough, though, nor were any of the other such phrases (like "boiling point" or "climate chaos") that more skillful authors have used since. So in recent years I've found myself grasping, trying to strip the language down further, make it communicate more. This year I find myself playing with numbers.

When the Northwest Passage opened amid the great Arctic melt last summer, many scientists were stunned. James Hansen, our greatest climatologist, was already at work on a paper that would try, for the first time, to assign a real number to global warming, a target that the world could aim at. No more vague plans to reduce carbon dioxide in the atmosphere, or keep it from doubling, or slow the rate of growth—he understood that there was already enough evidence from the planet's feedback systems, and from the quickly accumulating data about the paleoclimate, to draw a bright line.

In a PowerPoint presentation he gave at the American Geophysical Union meeting in San Francisco last December, he named a number: 350 parts per million carbon dioxide. That, he said, was the absolute upper bound of anything like safety—above it and the planet would be unraveling. Is unraveling, because we're already at 385 parts per million. And so it's a daring number, a politically unwelcome one. It means, in shorthand, that this generation of people—politicians especially—can't pass the problem down to their successors. We're like patients who've been to the doctor and found out that our cholesterol is too high. We're in the danger zone. Time to cut back now, and hope that we do it fast enough so we don't have a stroke in the meantime. So that Greenland doesn't melt in the meantime and raise the ocean twenty-five feet.

For me, the number was a revelation. With a few friends I'd been trying to figure out how to launch a global grassroots climate campaign—a follow-up to the successful Step It Up effort that organized fourteen hundred demonstrations across the U.S. one day last spring and put the demand for an 80 percent cut in America's carbon emissions at the center of the political debate. We need to apply even more pressure, and to do it on a global scale—it is, after all, global warming. But my friends and I were having a terrible time seeing how to frame this next effort. For one thing, the 180 or so countries that will negotiate a new international treaty over the next eighteen months are pretty much beyond the reach of effective lobbying— we can maybe influence the upcoming American election, but the one in Kenya? In Guatemala? In China? And for another, everyone insists on speaking those different languages. A Babel, this world.

But a number works. And this is a good one. Arcane, yes—parts per million CO_2 in the atmosphere. But at least it means the same thing in every tongue, and it even bridges the gap between English and metric. And so we secured the all-important URL: 350.org. (Easier said than done.) And we settled on our mission: To tattoo that number into every human brain. To make every person on Planet Earth aware of it, in the same way that most of them know the length of a soccer field (even though they call it a football pitch or a *voetbal gebied*). If we are able to make that happen, then the negotiations now under way, and due to conclude in Copenhagen in December of 2009, will be pulled as if by a kind of rough and opaque magic toward that goal. It will become the definition of success or of failure. It will set the climate for talking about climate.

So the literary challenge—and the challenge for artists and musicians and everyone else—is how to take a mere number and invest it with meaning. How to make people understand that it means some kind of stability. Not immunity—we're well past that juncture, and even Hansen says the number is at best the upper bound of safety, but still. Some kind of future. Some kind of hope. That it means kids able to eat enough food, that it means snowcaps on mountains, that it means coral reefs, that it means, you know, penguins. For now 350 is absolutely inert. It means nothing, comes with no associations. But our goal is to fill it up with overtones and shades and flavors. The weekend before we officially launched the campaign, for instance, 350 people on bicycles rode around the center of Salt Lake City. That earned a story in the paper and educated some people about carbon dioxide—but it also started to tint 350 with images of bicycles and the outdoors and good health and pleasure. We need 350 churches ringing their bells 350 times; we need 350 spray-painted across the face of shrinking glaciers (in organic paint!); we need a stack of 350 watermelons on opening day at your farmers' market; we need songs and videos; we need temporary tattoos for foreheads. We may need 350 people lining up to get arrested in front of a coal train.

It makes sense that we need a number, not a word. All our words come from the old world. They descend from the time before. Their associations have congealed. But the need to communicate has never been greater. We need to draw a line in the sand. Say it out loud: 350. Do everything you can.

CHAPTER 12

The Blood Root of Art

RICK BASS

L ET'S DO THE NUMBERS.

In trying to sing the praises of a place, in fighting to earn or draw respect to an endangered place, you can only say pretty things about that place and think pretty thoughts for so long. At some point, you can no longer ignore the sheer brutalities of math, nor the necessity of activism. It's always a tough choice. You have to decide whether to use numbers or images: you have to decide whether the fight requires art or advocacy—and to try to have an awareness of where the one crosses over into the other.

I think it is like a rhythm—deciding when to choose the "soft" or supple approach of writing pretty about a place—writing out of celebration—versus writing about the despair of reality, the enumeration of loss.

The numbers are important, and yet they are not everything. For whatever reasons, images often strike us more powerfully, more deeply than numbers. We seem unable to hold the emotions aroused by numbers for nearly as long as those of images. We grow quickly numb to the facts and the math. Still, the numbers are always out there:

- Logging on the public lands in the Forest Service's Region One (the northern Rockies) cost the government between $100 million and $200 million more than they received for those sales in 1993; and,
- Siltation levels in streams are 750 times higher near logging roads than in undisturbed sites, often contributing to excessive erosion, flooding, scouring, road-slumping, and destroying water quality for sturgeon, trout and salmon, which—tough break!—have evolved to require clear, cool water. . . .

- *Forbes* notes that in the Gallatin National Forest—where recreation provides sixteen jobs for every one logging job—the unemployment rate is 1.8 percent. Dr. Michael McGarrity writes, "The pristine environment, not logging, is the driving force in the current economic boom"; and,
- The Forest Service ranks as the world's largest road-building company in the world. Almost half a million miles of logging roads exist in this country—more miles than the federal interstate system—and another quarter million miles of logging roads are planned, paid for by taxpayers, for use by international timber companies; and,
- The Forest Service survey of 1993 showing 70 percent of Montana and Idaho residents oppose any further entrance to the last roadless areas in their states; and,
- Despite the influx of cheap Canadian timber—the results of the obscene forest liquidation going on up there, which rivals Brazil's deforestation rates—the timber companies working on public lands in the West continue to post record quarterly profits for their stockholders. By the end of 1994, despite a drop in timber prices, Plum Creek posted a record profit of $112 million; Georgia Pacific, based in Newt Gingrich's home state, had a 1,000 percent increase in profit. . . .

This nonsense about the last wilderness areas putting timber workers out of work, this big fat greed-suck lie about the last tiny wedge of remaining unroaded public lands being all that keeps sawyers and millworkers from reaching the eternal Big Rock Candy Mountain of secure futures and high finance—that myth (sold and packaged to workers by the timber products industry) runs counter to the *Washington Post*–compiled data that found that 80 percent of downsizing corporations neglect to pass on the savings to their workers in the forms of higher wages or more jobs. Instead, it all goes to the stockholders—and 45 percent of those companies use the savings from downsizing to buy more labor-saving machinery, which then triggers a second round of layoffs within twelve months.

More numbers.

Not a single acre of the valley where I live—the Yaak Valley of northwestern Montana—is protected by our government as wilderness for our future. It's the wildest place I've ever seen in the Lower Forty-eight. We all have special places that nourish our spirits, that ignite the sparks of our imaginations, that help make life more tolerable by sharpening the sacred edge that human lives can still hold. We all wonder daily how we should go about saving these places.

I'll go for long stretches at a time asking men and women and children to write letters to Congress and to the Clinton administration, as well as to the Forest Service, pleading the case of the unprotected Yaak, believing that if enough people write letters, the roadless areas that remain there—the wilderness—can be saved; that an invisible thing like passion can hold a physical thing that is fragmenting.

But then, almost as if in response to some seasonal change, I'll succumb to the weariness of the activist—the brittleness, the humorlessness of the activist, the wearing down of one's passion and effectiveness—and I'll go for a long period (two or three months, sometimes) during which I believe that art helps achieve cultural change more effectively than does activism and the statistical rantings of fact. I'll believe that the bright primary colors as well as the pastel tones of art can carry more power than the black-and-white polarizations of activism. For a while, I'll think that *that's* the way to save a place—to write a pretty story about it, a pretty book—and so I'll change to fit that rhythm and belief, as if I'm in some cycle I do not understand but am nonetheless attentive to.

Later on in the year—for three or four months—I will then find myself trying to do both: art in the morning, and hard-core activism in the afternoons and evenings.

And then I'll wonder why my eyes drift crookedly; why I sometimes find myself staring at the sun, or why I feel off-balance.

Beginning in September, I disappear into the grace of hunting season for three months with my bird dogs. We chase grouse and pheasant; I hunt deer and elk, too, by myself, while the dogs stay home. It is like a submergence—like being in a cocoon or hibernation. I take from the land, in both meat and spirit—in what I believe is a sustainable manner—and I rest myself during that time for another year, another round in this fight to try and save the last parts of a place that has not yet been saved, in which and for which I am asking your help.

I don't mean to be insulting—traveling beyond my valley to ask your help. I know you have similar stories—identical stories—about places there: about every place that's loved.

What would you do?

How can the Yaak be saved—the last unprotected roadless areas in it?

I meant to use numbers throughout this essay—I had a bunch of them lined up, all of them perverse and horrible—but I got tired of them right away.

Writing—like the other arts—is not a hobby, but a way of living—a way, in the words of nature writing scholar Scott Slovic, of "being in the world." There is a rhythm that we must all find, in loving and fighting for a place— the integration of advocacy into your "other," peaceful life. I do not think it will always seem like a balanced or even pleasant rhythm. There will probably be long summer days of peace with only short stretches of darkness, in which you might be able to go a couple of weeks without panic and despair at the impending loss of the loved place—but there will also be long winters where advocacy and its inherent brittleness lasts for months at a time— times when the sun barely, if ever, gets above the horizon.

Even if you're not doing your art (or living your "other," peaceful life during this period), reading a great novel or viewing a great painting can be necessary solace during this dark time: and you continue your advocacy as intensely and passionately as you can, daring to take it all the way to the edge of brittleness—like a starving deer in winter. In the cycle, you begin, or your body begins, to create space within you for the return of art, or peace—order constructed out of disorder; a return to suppleness; sometimes you even warn, or mention to your fellow advocates, that you feel this internal space growing within you, and that because of it you may be stepping aside for a brief time; so that in this manner those just entering the crest of their advocacy cycle can help pick up the slack and continue forward as you rest (hopefully in peace) before you return to the advocacy at a later point, strengthened and invigorated. . . .

The writer, naturalist and activist Terry Tempest Williams is fond of the D. H. Lawrence quote "Blood knowledge. . . . Oh, what a catastrophe for man when he cut himself off from the rhythm of the year, from his unison with the sun and the earth. Oh, what a catastrophe, what a maiming of love when it was made a personal, merely personal feeling, taken away from the rising and setting of the sun, and cut off from the magical connection of the solstice and equinox. This is what is wrong with us. We are bleeding at the roots."

～

This is how I try to help protect the last roadless areas in the Yaak: with both brittleness and suppleness. It's been said that 10 percent of the world wants the world dammed, 10 percent wants it healthy, and the other 80 percent just doesn't care. I can rarely decide upon a fixed strategy—do I try and motivate further the 10 percent already committed to a healthy world, with brittle, angry urgings? Or do I try and coax the other 80 percent into the camp of the wild by writing as hard and as well—as pretty, as peacefully—as I can?

Again, it blurs. It becomes a weave, a braid, of rhythms; I do both, and I try and stay in touch with what Lawrence called "the blood root of things"; I try to make the right choices based on invisible feelings and rhythms, which are anchored in the realities of rock, trees, ice.

I think in large part the brittleness we feel when fighting—when advocating—for a place (versus the suppleness one feels when deep in art) comes from the almost totally dependent nature of the relationship: the relative lack of reciprocity. We receive far more nourishment from the grace of the woods, or the spirit of a place, than we are ever able to return. We can only learn to mimic the rhythms of the place we love—joining more tightly, in some small manner, in that larger weave before we extinguish ourselves: before brittleness wins out over suppleness.

Thomas Merton wrote of this fragmentation, this too much brittleness, in one's passions for justice:

There is a pervasive form of contemporary violence to which the idealist fighting for peace by nonviolent methods most easily succumbs: activism and overwork. The rush and pressure of modern life are a form, perhaps the most common form, of its innate violence.

To allow one's self to be carried away by a multitude of conflicting concerns, to surrender to too many demands, to commit one's self to too many projects, to want to help everyone in everything is to succumb to violence. More than that, it is cooperation in violence. The frenzy of the activist neutralizes his work for peace. It destroys his own inner capacity for peace. It destroys the fruitfulness of his own work, because it kills the root of inner wisdom which makes work fruitful.

A little art can go a long way. This phenomenon is again a measure of the unevenness of the relationship between man's love-of-place and a place itself—the differential in that equation equaling, perhaps, the definition of grace. A love of place can fuel art, can fuel the imagination—can give nourishment to the supple, questioning, creative spirit in excess of whatever that place might receive back from the taker.

Art can be its own sort of advocacy for place; can advocacy—on the other hand—be art? Some say yes. I don't know. I'm not sure.

~

I had, once again, meant for this whole essay to be numbers: a landslide of numbers, like brittle talus. But I cannot tolerate them, at present. There is a space in me, this short winter day, that cries out for words.

I just read that when the freshman United States Representative from Idaho, Helen Chenoweth, addressed a Wise Use–Endangered Species Conference, she told the audience that the Yaak Valley was in northern Idaho, not northern Montana, and that it was so dead and sterile that there weren't even any bugs there.

I wish to differ with the representative. I live in this vanishing valley and it is still in Montana. Many of the logs from this valley, it is true, are trucked over to mills in Idaho (did you know that the recently developed single-grip tree fellers now require only two men to run them, whereas it used to take sixteen sawyers to fell a comparable number of trees?), but the Yaak is still in Montana.

Words.

Here is a list of some of the species still found in this place: Bull trout, gray wolf, woodland caribou, grizzly bear, wolverine, lynx, fisher, harlequin duck, golden eagle, bald eagle, torrent sculpin, sturgeon, Coeur d'Alene salamander, great gray owl, Westslope cutthroat trout, flammulated owl, shorthead sculpin, northern goshawk, boreal owl, peregrine falcon, wavy moonwort, Mingan Island moonwort, Townsend's big-eared bat, small lady's slipper, common loon, sparrow's egg lady's slipper, kidney-leaved violet, maidenhair spleenwort, black-backed woodpecker, round-leaved orchid, green-keeled cottongrass, bog birch, crested shield-fern, Spalding's catchfly, linear-leaved sundew, northern golden-carpet, northern bog lemming, water howellia. . . .

There are more, of course—a Noah's ark of diversity in this magical, totally unprotected wilderness—lions, moose, elk, bobcats, black bears, geese, grouse. The thing the earlier names all have in common is that they are on the threatened, endangered or sensitive species watch list: all imperiled, but still here, still hanging on—numbers be damned—as is my love for this place, and my hopes, in all seasons.

PART III

Interviews on the Communication of Numerical Information to the General Public

Introduction

SCOTT SLOVIC AND PAUL SLOVIC

L ITERARY ARTISTS, JOURNALISTS, VISUAL ARTISTS, AND ACTIVISTS tend
to have an intuitive sense of why they're using particular communication strategies, even if they do not explicitly comment on how they are
using language. Several of the essays in the previous section not only experiment with both quantitative information and emotionally provocative
stories and images, but also comment on the issue of desensitizing information and modes of discourse. In order to produce a more direct and
explicit response to the question of how quantitative information might take
on emotive meaning, we decided to conduct detailed interviews with several leading writers and artists from various countries, people whose work
powerfully confronts important social and environmental issues.

Husband and wife Homero and Betty Aridjis became prominent leaders
in the Mexican environmental movement in the 1980s when they launched
El Grupo de los Cien (the Group of 100), an organization of artists and scientists concerned with various environmental programs ranging from air pollution to habitat degradation. Scott Slovic traveled to their home in Mexico
City in January 2007 to talk with them about the history of their work with
the Group of 100 and about how to communicate effectively in politically
charged and sometimes scientifically murky territory, such as climate change
and species preservation. In their interview statements, they emphasized

the initial importance of maintaining credibility with the general public by gathering and publicizing data about air pollution in Mexico City at a time when such information was difficult to obtain. They do not downplay the importance of presenting quantitative data. However, they hasten to explain that technical information is not enough to make people care about the subjects under investigation. Betty Aridjis explains that one of the key elements of their publicity style is "to particularize without trivializing." This entails using specific examples that resonate with readers or listeners so that they can see the relevance of a large, abstract topic—such as the presence of harmful chemicals in gasoline, paint, or children's toys—to their own lives. Homero, on the other hand, considers the challenge of spurring the public to think in the opposite direction—to "personalize the volume," as he puts it. This means that although each of us may well be complicit in causing the air pollution, deforestation, and decline of water quality that we find unacceptable, we tend not to multiply our personal behaviors to a societal level, a thought process necessary for the alleviation of these problems.

While Homero and Betty Aridjis approach their concerns for public health and environmental protection as literary artists who venture regularly into the realms of science and public policy, Vandana Shiva was trained as a physicist in Canada before developing her focus on environmental protection and social justice as head of the nonprofit organization called Navdanya, based in New Delhi, India. Scott Slovic visited with Shiva in September 2006 at the small café operated by her organization and talked with her about language, numbers, and how to "communicate in ways that touch people's hearts," as the Indian author put it. Although Shiva makes it clear that she is at home with numbers and works comfortably with such information, she also explicitly condemns the complete reliance on numerical communication and suggests that experts and people with political power use such discourse as "the anesthesia of destruction," numbing the public into complacency by relying on inaccessible, unassailable forms of data. As she puts it, "around a number you create a wall. Because ordinary people can't reach it." So, for a numerate activist and writer like Shiva, it is necessary, first, to use what she calls "counter-expertise"—that is, to take the experts' numbers and deconstruct and contextualize them. Next, she uses these numbers to construct a story, a "lived reality." She argues for a flexible, varied toolbox of communication strategies, depending on the situation, with one mode likely to be effective when meeting with the Indian Supreme

Court (she had just come from the court when we had our conversation in Delhi) and another likely to strike a chord with general readers making their way through her books. This situational calibration of her communication style is central to Shiva's work as an expert witness, an academic lecturer, and a writer of books on social and environmental justice for specialists and lay readers.

We find a similar balance of technical expertise and personal conviction in the work of American author Sandra Steingraber, whose background includes a master's degree in poetry and a Ph.D. in biology. Scott Slovic interviewed Steingraber when she was visiting Reno, Nevada, in March 2007 to give several readings and join public discussions on science writing and the human health effects of environmental contamination. Much of this interview focuses on her 1997 publication *Living Downstream*, which directed public attention to the presence of carcinogens in the environment and particularly to the question, "What is the evidence for a link between environmental exposure and rising rates of cancer?" Steingraber addresses many of her comments to the issue of how one goes about ascertaining the link between environmental causes and human health effects and explains that she herself is rather cautious and conservative in making such claims, requiring a lot of "data under [her] feet." In the 1997 book, she packed her discussion with data from numerous scientific studies, inserting only brief (but vivid) narrative passages to bring the discussion to life by sharing her own story as a cancer-cluster survivor. Several years later, when she published her 2001 book *Having Faith: An Ecologist's Journey to Motherhood*, she was more confident in her ability to keep the technical information "behind the scenes," as she states in the interview, relegating evidence of the research supporting her claims to footnotes rather than giving it center stage. Her comments in the interview focus on her intuitive efforts to find effective ways of juxtaposing "the big picture" to personal stories, of making topics interesting enough so that readers will "open up" and absorb more of the technical data, and of holding back on explicitly advocating how readers or listeners should act in response to particular information. Her strategy of addressing broad public health issues by way of individual stories is an example of what psychologists call "scaling up." When she refers to herself in the interview as being "one data point," this is what psychologists would refer to as "singularity" and "identifiability." This kind of individualized narrative meaning does not nullify the importance of the broader statistical information about public health issues or other large-scale phenomena—both matter. As Steingraber puts it, the "human stories and math can . . . work together."

Scott Slovic traveled to Seattle, Washington, in June 2011 to interview visual artist Chris Jordan, who has been attracting considerable attention throughout the United States in recent years for his beautiful and provocative photographs and digital compositions. After practicing law for ten years, Jordan became a full-time photographer with a particular focus on the wastefulness of American consumer habits. He produced an initial collection of large-format photographs on consumption titled *Intolerable Beauty: Portraits of American Mass Consumption (2003–2006)*. These images are, in a sense, "landscapes of consumption," showing enormous stacks of tires and shipping containers and sawdust. The 2005 book *In Katrina's Wake: Portraits of Loss from an Unnatural Disaster*, which includes essays by the prominent environmental writers Bill McKibben and Susan Zakin alongside Jordan's photographs, tells the story of the human cost of Hurricane Katrina, depicting post-storm images of dilapidated homes and natural debris with an eerie beauty that provides access to the intrinsic aesthetic dimension that Jordan finds in all aspects of experience, even (frequently) in "terrible" or disturbing circumstances. Media scholar Sean Cubitt wrote in 2013 that "appearances can deceive, as everyone knows, but the industrialized and informatic cultures of the developed, and increasingly the developing, world place a great deal of faith in numbers" (p. 280). Although numbers may have inherent credibility, there is an essential popularism, a broad accessibility, associated with visual imagery, whether moving or still. This urge to reach the public, not only small technocratic audiences, has increasingly inspired filmmakers, visual artists, and communicators working in other media (such as literature and journalism, and even music) to seek techniques for "visualizing" (making palpable and emotionally resonant) the abstract numerical data associated with various issues, from climate change to poverty. Jordan's photography contributes precisely to this effort.

More recently, Jordan has exhibited large-format digital compositions from the *Running the Numbers* series at galleries throughout North America and as far away as Australia. A 2009 exhibition at the Washington State University Museum of Art resulted in the book *Running the Numbers: An American Self-Portrait*. A typical image from this series is the one titled "Plastic Bottles, 2007" (Figure 16.3), which, from a distance, depicts an abstract and appealing field of multicolored dots, akin to the appearance of a pebbly ocean beach. The caption to the image, however, reads, "Depicts two million plastic beverage bottles, the number used in the US every five minutes." As the gallery viewer steps toward the composition, the individual bottles become increasingly visible, offering a powerful perceptual experience of American consumption (Figure 16.2). The experience of moving from the faraway view to the close-up view, from the many to the more individualized objects of consumption, is what Jordan refers to as the "trans-scalar imaginary." At present, Jordan continues to produce new compositions for a second *Running the Numbers* series. He has also been working on a film and still photography project in the central Pacific Ocean concerning the endangerment of seafaring albatrosses, a unique aquatic bird whose existence on Midway Atoll (the only place in the world where the species nests and raises young) is imperiled due to the ingestion of plastic garbage: all the oceans of the world have become a plastic soup, deadly to many animal species that depend on the sea for survival. Jordan's work is also available at his website (www.chrisjordan.com), and by clicking on the large-scale images, viewers can activate unique software that creates the trans-scalar impression of "zooming in" to perceive the specific items of consumption represented in the images. The meaning of Jordan's work is the result of a sort of mosaic technique, calling the attention back and forth between the specific elements or pieces used in making the images and the "big picture" available when the compositions are viewed from afar. The social critique that emerges in his work is powerful but usually inexplicit. The fact that he tends to avoid entirely obvious criticism of his viewers' lifestyles, requiring viewers to inspect his work closely and *derive* the meaning with their own imaginative interpretations, reinforces the impact of this work.

One of the major facets of Jordan's digital compositions is how they raise the issue of how the individual human observer is a member of "the collective," the broader society whose actions have a deep impact on the planet. The interview explores the artist's thinking about how his audiences respond to his work and are challenged when they deflect or deny responsibility for their own participation in the consumerist phenomena depicted in Jordan's art. Jordan also comments insightfully on the individual observer's feelings of empowerment and disempowerment when contemplating the possibility of responding effectively to the destructive impacts of modern society. Although he resists attributing a moral or didactic effect to his visual work, he vividly describes the psychological processes he hopes to spark in his viewers, including his belief that anxiety, anger, fear, and grief will eventually motivate collective action.

It is clear from the four interviews that all of these writers and artists think carefully about the need to balance raw information with evocative, humanizing modes of expression. While none of these writers explicitly invoke terms such as "psychic numbing," "pseudoinefficacy," and "the prominence effect," used by social scientists to describe intuitive and emotive processes, the writers are working with their own equivalents of these and other psychological concepts. What emerge most poignantly from these conversations, perhaps, are the interviewees' individual quests, contingent upon educational background and cultural context and other personal factors, to tease out and communicate the ideas needed for themselves and their audiences to live meaningful and responsible lives in the world today. "Information" is not the same as "meaningful information." In this age of "data smog," as author David Shenk put it in the title of his 1997 book, we sometimes struggle to discern the most essential facets of the information available to us. It is easy to drown in information. The many contributors to this entire book suggest that we must each find our own ways, as producers of language and also as recipients of language, to appreciate the balance of big pictures and specific cases, technical vocabulary and poetic descriptions, numbers and nerves.

REFERENCES

Cubitt, S. (2013). Everybody knows this is nowhere: Data visualization and eco-criticism. In S. Rust, S. Monani, & S. Cubitt (Eds.), *Ecocinema theory and practice* (pp. 279–296). New York, NY, and London, UK: Routledge.

Shenk, D. (1997). *Data smog: Surviving the information glut*. New York, NY: Harper-Collins.

CHAPTER 13

Reacting to Information in a "Personal, Moral Way"

An Interview with Homero and Betty Aridjis

MEXICO CITY, MEXICO, JANUARY 12, 2007

SCOTT SLOVIC: How does your work as writers, translators, and activists try to bring together information and emotion in particular ways?

HOMERO ARIDJIS: Well, for me the connection between information and emotion has happened since the foundation of the Group of 100. Because what makes the Group of 100 so special—I'm referring to our press releases, articles, position papers, etc., concerned with the environment— is the mix of information and emotion. What makes our work special is the way we give a personal interpretation to this information and a moral dimension because sometimes that is the difference between merely presenting scientific or technical information and giving the same information a cultural, spiritual, or moral position we have. Without the emotional connection, we wouldn't be called to this information. In our work as activists and writers, we try to react to information in a personal, moral way, as human beings.

SCOTT: So, in a sense, that is the goal of El Grupo de los Cien—to help Mexican society respond to environmental issues in a deeper, more emotionally powerful way. When exactly was the group started?

BETTY ARIDJIS: On March 1, 1985, our initial statement was made public, was released to the press, and then it kind of mushroomed.

SCOTT: At that time were you primarily focused on air quality issues here in Mexico City?

BETTY: Yes, the initial statement of the Group of 100 was concerned with air quality in the Valley of Mexico, with the fact that no one was doing anything about it, nobody was paying any attention to it, nobody knew anything about it. It was our main focus initially. And we had to use figures—numbers—because at the time when we started the Group of 100 the government had a monitoring system in place and they translated all of the data into a sort of homegrown measuring device called "EMECAS"—the Mexican pollution index—so that people could not readily compare the data with the international or American standards. Although we soon found out exactly what it corresponded to.

SCOTT: Therefore part of your project was simply to get information—even quantitative figures—out to the public.

HOMERO: When we began our work, there was almost no information reaching the public at all. There was really fragmentary information about the effects of pollution on human health in Mexico City. We tried to find information in newspapers—it was really dispersed, incidental information, not complete. Most people in Mexico City—or in the country as a whole—didn't know the effects of pollution on human health. They didn't react—sometimes they thought that a terribly polluted day was simply a cloudy day! They didn't understand.

But since the beginning of the Group of 100, our idea was that there is a relation between politics and the environment—this is true in Mexico, just as it's true in other countries. I find it necessary to say that in order to decontaminate Mexico City, first you have to decontaminate the politicians and the people in the government because they are the principal polluters, not only materially but also morally. And in Mexico this was the condition until now—that behind almost every environmental problem there is a politician or a businessman.

SCOTT: For this book, we're especially interested in questions of numbers—in this idea of "data." We're asking, what are the limits of data, and what can we do to move beyond data, what are the alternatives to abstract data?

BETTY: If I could just say something with that in mind about the specific air pollution battle we've just been describing. As far as the data was concerned, the main thing this was anchored in were the readouts, which is why we had to go to so much trouble to get the information, to analyze it, and to present it to the public in a digestible form. We'd say, "Okay, the readouts indicate that these were the pollution levels, and this is three times the levels allowed in Europe and the United States." We wanted it to be comparative because otherwise it was all abstract to the public. More or less 100 units was the permissible level. This battle went on for years, until 1991, I think, when in March there were some really critical days and the readings went over 400. We happened to be in New York then for some meetings leading up to the Earth Summit. We got a call from Mexico City because Homero had published some articles and the group had done some press releases—this was a crucial moment when they finally decided to put in a contingency plan that said when the readings went over 350 they would begin shutting down some industries. By then we already had the one-day-without-a-car program, which was our idea originally. This was very closely tied to numbers, and any actions that were taken occurred because the numbers went above a certain level. Recently they lowered the contingency level.

SCOTT: In a way, Betty, you're pointing out that some issues or contexts seem to require using numerical information.

HOMERO: Well, to finish what Betty's talking about, it was very important for me to collect information from many monitoring stations throughout Mexico City, eleven stations, perhaps thirteen. This is because the government officials were averaging the data from various stations. In some areas of the city the pollution levels were low, and in other areas the levels were very high. I read these readouts very carefully, checking hourly how much of each pollutant was in the air. One of the things the newspapers liked was the fact that we were the only ones providing this kind of detailed information—in this place at this hour this particular pollutant is at such and such a level. For us this credibility was very important.

BETTY: That's exactly the word I wrote down. In all of our campaigns, it's been very important for us to have credibility based on scientific—or "real"—information about everything we're talking about. From the very beginning, there were always people, especially in the government, who would say, "What do they know about anything? They're writers and artists—"

HOMERO: "—He's a poet—what does he know about pollution?" And another thing they did to discredit us was to ask if we were working for a foreign government.

BETTY: Oh, yeah. That's always the typical smear in Mexico: "He's representing dark or murky interests." Or, when we were defending the dolphins: "He's being paid off by the American tuna industry." But the whole point, after gathering data on whatever issue we were talking about, to back everything up, was to translate it into terms that would have an impact on the public, on the government, on whoever—and that is where the particular talent of being a writer came into play. As opposed to having some dry presentation of numbers that would produce a glazed-eye reaction—something people couldn't really react to—in the case of pollution, this data about the excessive levels was always accompanied by what are the effects on *you* of carbon dioxide, of ozone—what are the health effects.

SCOTT: Perhaps we could turn to some of the more general questions I have about numbers. Maybe you recall the passage by Annie Dillard that I sent to you before coming here, the passage in which she both playfully and profoundly suggests that in order to understand a vast phenomenon, such as the population of China (or, for that matter, of Mexico City), we need only multiply ourselves, with all of our unique qualities, by this number. Do you have any response to this idea?

BETTY: I think it's absurd because nobody could actually internalize that and say, "Yes, I understand what that means."

HOMERO: The only thing is that sometimes when you describe particular issues is that people can personalize the volume. For example, the Mexico City traffic or in California or anything. When we discuss the traffic in Mexico City and the pollution, they will say, "I have a right to drive my car, but why are all these other people driving their cars and making traffic?" Personal, individual actions affect global issues. Think about the Brazilians and their logging of the Amazon jungle. They say, "Why, if the Europeans and the Americans can cut their forests, should we not be able to do the same to our own forests? They have the right to do it, but not us?" It's a matter of seeing the *volume*. If you multiply this *ego*—this *myself*—by millions or billions, then the planet is finished. It's what they say about India and China—if every American has a refrigerator or a car, why doesn't everyone in India or China have such a right? But, you see, this would be a catastrophe!

BETTY: Yes, but people can't understand that! This message doesn't get across.

HOMERO: The big problem is how you can understand your own actions— your *ego*—in this large volume. Millions or billions of people can affect the environment. Because you have certain rights, but others don't. If everybody has the same rights, you have millions of cars, millions of refrigerators, millions of planes, etc.

When we were defending the Lacondan Jungle, these Lacondan Indians came to Seattle to talk about the destruction of the Lacondan Jungle in Mexico. And when we said to them, "What do you want? What do you need?" the first thing they said is, "A truck."

BETTY: And so a truck—that means a road, right? It means cutting down trees.

HOMERO: Exactly. Then we said, "No—you have to live in your natural environment." But they said, "No—it's really useful because if my wife or child is sick, I have to take them to a hospital or another village. I can go really fast, much faster than by horse. Or if I need to buy supplies." But that is the big problem. If someone in California, or Nevada, can have the right to own a car, why is this not a right for someone living in the Lacondan Jungle? This is the big problem.

BETTY: Who is to determine what is enough and what is enough for whom? Enough for everybody? Who is to determine that everything is distributed equitably on a global scale? Obviously this is not going to happen.

HOMERO: This concerns the limits of the individual. This is the big thing—what kind of individual and where. Because Europeans and Americans feel they have the right to have everything—civilization, material comfort, appliances, everything—but when everybody in other countries wants to have the same thing, it becomes a disaster, a disaster.

SCOTT: Well, why should Lacondan Indians or people in China or India be forced to think in this manner, to extrapolate from their individual needs or desires to a vast level, when people in Europe or North America aren't doing the same calculation? You could just as easily say that people everywhere should be asking, "If everyone lived as I wish to live, what would the implications be?" But because human beings cannot think in this way, are we doomed?

HOMERO: Yes, exactly. This is the big problem.

SCOTT: I wonder if we could talk about this issue specifically in relation to language, in relation to various strategies that might be used to convey the connection between the vivid, individual example and the large-scale phenomenon.

BETTY: I just wanted to talk about using numbers to get an issue across in the specific case of the monarch butterflies. Every year when you talk about the number of monarch butterflies that have come to winter in Mexico and the number of hectares that have been logged, the number of butterflies per hectare, the effect of winter storms, the government comes right back and announces, "Last year there were 250 million butterflies." Then people say, "Well, what are they worried about?" The numbers are very important in terms of credibility, but the numbers can also be countered and contradicted.

SCOTT: Important in terms of credibility, but perhaps not in terms of emotional impact on audiences. I have an article here from the *New York Times*, dated March 2005.

BETTY: Is that Jim McKinley's article?

SCOTT: Yes, and it leads with a quotation from Homero, where he offers an image: "There used to be rivers of butterflies but now there are years when there are no butterflies at all." Obviously, this writer—the journalist—understands that the image of a river of butterflies is very vivid and powerful, and the idea of a huge, flowing river of this organism suddenly stopping is interesting in contrast to the end of the article, which goes back to the numbers—the populations, the winter storms, and the radical decline in butterfly population. So the article tries to use both the numbers and images, and I wonder if you have any thoughts about how these different forms of communication—numbers and images, or science and poetry—fit together and support each other.

BETTY: That's Homero's power as a writer! He's able to convey these things in terms of images which do impact people, but always backed up by science and the numbers, which give credibility to what he says.

SCOTT: In the context of journalism you can use them both together, but in a poem you often don't want the numbers—just the images or just the story. So my question is whether there's something missing when you don't have the scientific information, the data, or does the poem have another sort of power that's completely different than what might come through a journalistic article?

HOMERO: This reminds me of the efforts of socialist poets to comment on real issues, like hunger, in their work, but the results were ridiculous. It didn't work well. I learned from this that it's always important for a poem to be a good poem or a story to be a good story. This must be your first goal.

SCOTT: What do you mean by "a good story"?

HOMERO: It has to be more than information. When you write about concrete issues, you can use data. When you write a literary piece, you can use metaphors, images, remembrances, etc. Because your language is different. But when you're writing about the monarch butterflies, sea turtles, gray whales, forest or trees, sometimes you have to use an image so that people can understand. When you want people to understand the disappearance of butterflies in your village, you have to use an image. When I was ten years old, I couldn't even begin to count the ten million butterflies in my village. I couldn't use an exact number or even a very approximate number, but I could use the image of rivers of butterflies crossing the streets because that's what I saw—I saw the *presence* of butterflies.

This is very special. For me, there are two realities: the informative reality and the poetic reality.

SCOTT: But I think when you say "the poetic reality," you're also talking about an emotional reality, an experiential reality—

HOMERO: —yes. For example, you can say you saw millions of butterflies flying together in the air. There is no scientific language that can capture that situation in the moment, but for me watching the butterflies is like listening to the musical patterns in the *Goldberg Variations*.

SCOTT: The experience has an aesthetic dimension—

HOMERO: Exactly.

SCOTT: It's interesting. You talk about a ten-year-old child being unable to count so many butterflies, to fathom the meaning of such a large number of butterflies, but when I gave the Annie Dillard calculation earlier, you said very few people could do that sort of calculation, not even scientists, who might use numbers all the time in their work.

BETTY: When you think about it, eight hundred thousand people were killed in Rwanda, but what does that number mean? Whereas if you said the city of Albany disappeared, that is something people can understand. That's why when people talk about the size of something they say, "Oh, it's the size of six football fields," or they say, "An area the size of Italy disappears in the Amazon every year"—perhaps that's a bit exaggerated. If it's comparative, people can understand. And I think people can understand the difference between *some* (no matter how many that is) and *none*. That's why the idea of extinction is so important to insist on, even though people don't want to believe it.

SCOTT: Homero, in the McKinley article on the monarchs, I was interested in the discussion at the end about the local people in the mountains of

Mexico. They seem to be interested in the monarchs. They care about them and they want them to keep coming back to the mountains in the winter. But often simple issues of survival complicate things. Either they go into the forests and cut trees in order to take care of their families or leave the trees alone. How do we ever overcome this dilemma?

HOMERO: Well, that is the big problem. It's related to larger economic issues in countries like Mexico. You have to make jobs available in these countries so that people can survive without destroying the natural resources of their homes. This big logger once said to me that either the butterflies must die or his children must die. I said to him, "Sorry, but the butterflies are not responsible for your human problem." It's like me saying a cloud floating in the sky is responsible for my personal problems. It's not responsible. The butterflies, a cloud, a tree—these things operate on a different level of experience. They have a right to exist, and they are not responsible for our problems. We need to find human solutions to our problems, because killing a butterfly or knocking down a tree will not solve our human problems. I see a tendency among people to blame nature for their own problems, but nature has no relation to the problems. It's just an excuse.

SCOTT: You seem to be talking about the question of people taking proper responsibility for their own lives, and this is also related to the issue of power—

HOMERO: That's right. This brings to mind the issue of poverty. If you wait until poverty is solved before you try to solve the problems of the environment, it never is going to happen. It's tied together with governments and industries, with location, with corruption, with lack of equal opportunities—there are so many issues.

I grew up in the mountains where the monarch butterflies come in the winter. When I lived there we had about five thousand people in the village. There are now about half a million people in the area. It has become a demographic problem. You have to work with the local people on the issue of family planning, birth control, because unlimited population growth is not possible with limited resources. The solution is not to go on cutting trees. The solution is to limit the size of families.

SCOTT: You might be able to limit the size of families that are not yet too large, but now that we have so many people living in these sensitive areas, what is the solution?

HOMERO: This is the problem. Let's talk about the butterfly sanctuary. In this country we have freedom of movement, so if you send money to a place, suddenly you have millions of people moving to that place. People come for the opportunities. They say, "Oh, there is money here," and they come. This is my big frustration in Mexico. You see governments come and governments go, but you see the same corruption. In this country you see extreme poverty and you see people who are worth billions. The economic injustice is extreme. Some of the richest people here don't give a penny to social or environmental causes. They want to be richer and richer and richer. And then you have ten million poor people in this country, people whose poverty is partly the result of a corrupt government that is not really dedicated to helping them out of this poverty. If you think you can simply wait to help the butterflies until the problem of poverty is solved, it's impossible.

SCOTT: My question, though, is what would happen if we could suddenly create an ideal society—with no corruption, with justice and the equal distribution of wealth. If you could make the obscenely rich people less rich and the obscenely poor people less poor, would society behave differently or would people simply consume as much as they are able to consume? Would the poor people consume more if they had more money? Maybe we're talking about human nature—

HOMERO: This is a big problem. In the case of the monarch butterflies, you have thousands of people conducting business in three countries—Canada, the United States, and Mexico—full of technical and economic resources, and if they had the political will, these governments could protect the areas vital to the butterflies by declaring a moratorium on the logging of the forests needed by the butterflies—the *oyamel* trees in Mexico. They could try to establish new models of living for the local people, saying that they shouldn't cut any trees, telling people they will be punished as criminals for cutting trees, but offering economic alternatives. You see problems also with local people killing sea turtles in the Pacific in order to sell eggs for a peso—for ten U.S. cents—it's just terrible. When you're looking for the origins of life on the planet and people are killing these ancient animals to sell their eggs for a peso, our big companies and environmental groups could dedicate millions of dollars to stop this killing. But you never see these people providing a penny, and that's why you see the desperation of the local people. The locals say,

"Oh, here the environmentalists come to preach, to say 'Don't do it.'" But when the people need help, the corporations and big environmental organizations don't give a penny. But the problems of the local people are also the problems of the companies and organizations.

SCOTT: So, Homero, in a way it sounds like what you'd really like to do is not only communicate to the average reader but I sense from your comments that you'd also like to communicate to the leaders of big corporations and governments, to make them care more about these issues and become more generous and more—

HOMERO: —committed.

SCOTT: So how do you write for an audience of self-interested people with a very short sense of time? They're not thinking of the long-term, but of keeping their power for a few years. What way do we have to get through to our leaders and inspire them to be committed to something other than their own power?

HOMERO: You appeal to their sense of individual responsibility. But because I am a pessimist to start, I am very skeptical of human actions; but as a poet I have to do anything in my power to help, even small things.

SCOTT: It's interesting to hear you say you're skeptical because when I read your work, it doesn't feel as if it's skeptical. Your voice is idealistic and pained, but it's not a voice of skepticism and irony and anger. In a way, it's as if you're trying to reach toward a more innocent part of your readers—

HOMERO: Well, as an environmentalist, I am very pessimistic. But as a poet, I celebrate life. I love nature. I love trees, animals, birds, light—I celebrate life, and I feel we are living in a terrestrial paradise. For me, it's a fantastic planet. I am never tired of enjoying the beauty here.

SCOTT: We've been talking for quite some time now, but I wonder if I could try to return to the central focus of this interview. What you've just been saying is related to the sense of a personal, ethical commitment to the world, even to other species. What I hear you saying is that many people are more concerned with their personal comfort—their power, their economic status—and they feel a kind of numbness, a lack of sensitivity toward other things happening out in the world, particularly when these phenomena seem so monumental, impossible to approach. Psychologists refer to this as "psychic numbing"—the insensitivity to street crime, to genocide, to species depletion, to lost habitat. How do you overcome psychic numbing—how do you begin to chip away at this numbness, this lack of sensitivity? How might art, literature, public speaking—various strategies—help with this?

BETTY: This goes right to the heart of the issue. How can you change people?

HOMERO: For me, what's required is an active conscience. The conscience has to be active—moving, spreading. For me, the only way to change things is through a movement of conscience, and this will take years. It has to be spread through individuals, in waves of conscience. One of my frustrations with writers is that most of them in the United States, France, Spain, throughout Europe—except for a few exceptions—is that they are closed to what's happening, they don't understand. They are busy with their own literary careers, their literary business, not so different from the man selling cars. I feel it's a lost opportunity when writers have access to information and could help to propagate this information, not as preaching but as a way of providing information. But they don't care, they don't help.

SCOTT: So, earlier I said maybe your ideal audience would consist of government and corporate officials, but what I'm hearing now is that even artists, imaginative people, are not open, are not aware of what's going on in the world or don't care.

HOMERO: They don't care. Sometimes they have enough information because they read newspapers, and they're not stupid people, but they don't care. And that is the big frustration. You see what's happening, you see species disappearing, you see that the climate is changing, disasters are coming—and people don't care.

BETTY: And back to the idea of psychic numbing, there's simply the overload of information and the feeling of individual impotence. Or fatalism. Or just lack of interest—people are involved with other issues or they're not involved with any issues.

SCOTT: All of these are underlying psychological phenomena, and all of us are susceptible to them, even those of us who may have these kinds of concerns. We all have daily distractions and needs.

HOMERO: Yes, and that is the reason I consider that besides your own professional activities, there is nothing more important for a human being than to defend life. There is nothing more important. I am a poet, a professional writer, but besides that, for me, there is nothing more important than the defense of nature, the defense of life.

CHAPTER 14

Countering the "Anesthesia of Destruction"

An Interview with Vandana Shiva

NAVDANYA CAFÉ, NEW DELHI, INDIA,

SEPTEMBER 18, 2006

SCOTT SLOVIC: First of all, I'm interested to know what you think about the assertion that for information to have meaning it has to be infused with emotion, with feeling. Information—does it need an emotional dimension in order to have some kind of meaning? And would you say that your own work seeks to bring together information and emotion in particular ways?

VANDANA SHIVA: I definitely think that if you're not just writing for yourself or for three friends who understand your particular vocabulary, then you need to communicate in ways that touch people's hearts. And obviously that is the word—we use the word "emotion" for something that touches people's hearts. I am trained as a physicist, and my whole grooming is dealing in numbers. For me, it's still the easiest mental framework. But I'm also fully aware of the fact that communication through the head alone requires specialized training. So if you have to create a public discourse and a public concern and give meaning to phenomena that are going unnoticed because those who talk about them talk in mystified language, then, in the case of ecological destruction, bringing the feeling for that is part of the responsibility of communication and transmitting information.

SCOTT: So in a way, you have to move beyond your specific background as a physicist and reach out toward a public you understand not to be trained in the same way.

VANDANA: Absolutely, absolutely.

SCOTT: When we began doing this work, we found ourselves using a particular quotation whenever we tried to get the message across to our own
audiences about the difficulty of thinking about numerical information.
I don't know if you're familiar with the American author Annie Dillard,
but she writes in her book *For the Time Being*, without any detailed explanation, that all you need to do in order to understand a huge number,
such as the number of people living in China today, is to multiply yourself by that number. Do you have any response to the idea that we might
simply imagine a billion-plus carbon copies of ourselves?

VANDANA: My response is that the Chinese represented by that number are
anonymous, inconsequential, etc., but by making the connection through
you, your feelings, what you are, and then multiplying it, it has personalized the connection. So you have made it your own.

SCOTT: That's the goal—the goal is to make personal and meaningful each
member of that large society. But in the original passage, the author
calls for this act of multiplication and then says, "See? Nothing to it,"
implying that it's really very difficult. That we wish we could do that—
we understand that each person in China or in India is an individual
person with feelings, with singularity, with complexity. But maybe such
a computation is more easily said than done as we try to work with vast
numbers of this kind. So I'm wondering which aspects of your own
work—what you're working on now or what you've done over the years—
seems to require using numerical information. What can't you get away
from?

VANDANA: All aspects of my work—because all environmental assault is
through numbers. And in fact quantification is the anesthesia of destruction, so the point is society is anesthetized to destruction, whether it be
social destruction or the pain being caused through globalization or the
ecological destruction of how our rivers are dying. The way immunity is
created is to communicate that in the numbers of economic growth—
the 8.5 percent figures of India's recent growth. That basically takes the
subject matter beyond the reach of people—that is what it is intended to
do. It's supposed to create social immunity, ethical immunity.

SCOTT: Immunity?

VANDANA: Immunity—that, in a way, around a number you create a wall.
Because ordinary people can't reach it.

SCOTT: It's unassailable. You can't criticize it.

VANDANA: Exactly. That's the beginning of a lot of destruction. When rivers are dammed, all you find out is a figure of the amount of water impounded, the acreage of irrigation, and the megawatts of power. Those are the three magic figures that will justify the submergence of millions of acres, of hundreds of thousands of people being uprooted from their homes, etc. Since the destruction comes through numbers. When I left the university, when I created the Research Foundation for Science, Technology and Ecology, people said, "Oh, you're giving up research." I said, "No, I will still do research—I'll do it with a different purpose, and my purpose will be to connect it to people's lives, to the planet. And I will do counter-expertise, and counter-expertise means—"

SCOTT: Counter-expertise?

VANDANA: Yeah, for me, counter-expertise is the ability to do three things simultaneously: take the numbers of destruction and domination and deconstruct them, embed them in society, and determine what are the consequences. So many car sales in Delhi, and then they build roads. Connect—connect those anonymous numbers.

SCOTT: Context.

VANDANA: Connect—embed them, contextualize them. The second is, in the contextualizing, generate a different set of numbers that had never been generated before. So I'll give you a simple example—one of the very first studies I did when I formed this independent institution was on mining in Dehra Dun. The Ministry of Environment had commissioned this. We had figures of how much revenue was collected, royalty payments come, how many million tons of mining had been done of the purest limestone. We did that, of course, but I also went and said, "Okay, what does the limestone really do—it conserves the water. Therefore, when this mining happens how much water conservation are you destroying and what will it take to supply that much water that nature is supplying to you for free if it had to be supplied from man-made structures?" We generated a figure of two hundred billion rupees that would be needed to reproduce that capacity of water generation. That's the second job, you know—to quantify the destruction. But the third and most important job is to bring life to it all, and that means the lives of people who are impacted and the life of the ecosystem, and to make that come alive beyond numbers.

SCOTT: But how do you move beyond numbers? How do you take numbers and bring them to life?

VANDANA: Largely, as far as the methodology is concerned, it's by doing participatory research. It's not just going into a place and treating that place as an object of study and generating the numbers, but treating every person as a subject. And as a subject who's a knowing subject, and that knowing subject is transmitting to *you* the information that is then helping generate the *numbers* but in addition to that generating a *story*, a lived reality.

SCOTT: So when you present the findings of this participatory research, what type of voice do you use in order to provide the new kind of numbers but also to embed them in a story—how do you fit numbers and story together?

VANDANA: Yeah. Well, one has to use different voices for different platforms. If I'm filing a case in the Supreme Court against the numbers of Monsanto, then I'll just cite numbers because stories don't count in legal matters. If I'm writing a scientific report for the Ministry of Agriculture or the Ministry of Environment, again it's numbers. But when I'm writing my books, where there is no precondition of what should be an expert's voice—you know, there isn't a shutting out of voices—then I'll use the full experience that I have had of working on an issue with a particular community. So you will see my book *Staying Alive* is really spoken in my voice as a human being called "Vandana Shiva," a woman, a feminist, a physicist. And there are other reports that get submitted that are about the same issue, but all they will have is tables and all they'll have is graphs.

SCOTT: So you have a very acute sense of audience.

VANDANA: Oh, I have a very acute sense of audience—very, very deep. So deep that when I'm speaking—and I do a lot of public speaking—I literally am watching people's eyes to see when something is going above their heads, and I totally change metaphor, change track—

SCOTT: —in the middle of a speech, when you know what's connecting and what isn't.

VANDANA: Yes. Absolutely, absolutely.

SCOTT: I spend much of my time teaching writing, and the hardest thing with young writers is to get them to care about audience. They often think it's only the teacher who is the audience, but what you're saying is a good lesson that the more opportunities you have to reach audiences, the more precisely aware you become of what your audience needs. I'd be interested to hear whether there are some audiences that you would very much like to communicate to but you're not sure that your work is yet reaching these audiences. If you could really communicate with any group of people that you don't feel you have contact with—

VANDANA: Yeah. I think the problem is not about not having the communication *means*—it's really about not having the time to have multiple communications because I don't trivialize communication. For me, communication is part of a long-term commitment, so we have, for example, commitments to schools in the city. I don't find the time to go to the schools, but my colleagues do. Yeah? Now if I was there, I think I'd have to develop a completely different style of communication to reach six-year-old kids, you know. It's something I haven't had to do so far. I've done it—I've done it probably once in five years. So it is with farmers— every week I'm with a big farm group, one day in Punjab, one day in Tamil Nadu. You communicate taking their context as the beginning. You begin from there—not from where you've been, not from where your research is, not from where your latest analysis is, but you begin from where they are. And so you build up a connection. So I would say children, young people, is one group I haven't had the time to dedicate myself to. It is something I've started to realize I have to make the time for somehow.

SCOTT: And with the children, even if you had to change your voice, you might find a rather willing, enthusiastic audience. There might be others who would be a more resistant audience—like corporate officials. I wonder if you've had many occasions to communicate your ideas to corporate officials.

VANDANA: Oh yes. It's probably because I've had to be involved in huge debates, whether it's with Coca-Cola or with Monsanto. And it's frustrating. The reason it's frustrating is because it's very difficult in human communication to bridge deliberate falsehood, you know. And for me it's often happened that I've talked in the room where it's a formal debate, and the person from the corporate side is saying a certain thing— this has happened on every issue, whether it's McDonald's or Coca- Cola—and you step out in the corridor with the person who's now their own person, and they'll always turn round and say, "I totally agree with you." And I'll say, "Isn't it frustrating to have to live two minds? Speak two voices all your life?" So that's frustrating—it's a noncommunication—and now I've done this for twenty years, for twenty years as the global corporations became bigger in our lives. They weren't here when I first began my work. They only really entered in the late 'eighties, early 'nineties. Over time I've realized that ultimately the best communication even with them is through society.

SCOTT: So you reach out to society and then you let society communicate to them.

VANDANA: Yes, exactly.

SCOTT: Through what means?

VANDANA: So, for example, if you see that [points to poster on the wall of the café that reads, "THIS IS COKE PEPSI FREE ZONE"]. Well, that's one of our methods of communication. Five thousand institutions—five thousand have gone that way. Five thousand more by November, in India alone. Coke and Pepsi don't get sold or consumed in those places. That especially excludes schools and colleges, which are the big targets. Thirty percent decline in sales of Coca-Cola and Pepsi in the last few months in this country—seven states have banned those products.

SCOTT: So abstinence, a kind of divestment.

VANDANA: A boycott—basically a boycott, a very Gandhian method of exercising democratic rights. That's the message they do hear.

SCOTT: But the way corporations work is they'll now sell other products.

VANDANA: Yes, well, they already went into water. Now they get into healthy water. Again, that's another level of communication where you have to educate people on the issue of water as a commons—they have to conserve, and they have to have access. I think for me this is important because the problem with the rule of experts, which is also the rule of numbers, is that some people speak on behalf of society all the time. And I think *these* modes of communication allow society to speak for itself.

SCOTT: Society speaks in a very material and concrete way. I'm wondering if you can speak specifically about language, about whether there are any specific strategies or techniques that you use in your writing that might be especially potent or powerful. And have you learned anything in particular over the years, through your public speaking or through the ways people respond to your writing, that convinces you that particular styles of expression have special power?

VANDANA: Well, you know, I'm very careful about the facts on which I write. Because I have very strong adversaries, and I don't want them to be able to trivialize a piece of work because of a fact I got wrong. But the place where I use huge creativity is allowing my writing or my speaking to express things exactly as I feel them. Obviously the way I feel them is already a result of communication. So if I am down in Kerala supporting the women who are fighting Coca-Cola, and my colleague was telling me, "Tell the people when they drink Coca-Cola they are drinking the blood of my people." You know, there's already that communication. That's telling me how she's feeling, and that's telling me how I need to communicate her story.

SCOTT: By taking your cue from the kind of voice she's using.

VANDANA: Exactly. Obviously that also means I've had to shed the physicist's training of antiseptic communication in this process. And of course in the process people get very nervous and say, "Oh, she uses very strong language." I always say, "You know, the language I use is the language people are using about what they are having to live through. So listen, don't ignore it because you're not used to a spade being called a spade, since you juggle figures of one dollar a day, 8 percent growth, half of India under the poverty line, without ever seeing what really is happening to India." Unlike you I'm not a literary person—I write a lot, but my upbringing is not literary, and if there is a component of literariness in my communication today, I am communicating what I hear.

SCOTT: So in a way you echo the environment that you find yourself in, and you have a strong sense of ethical necessity, a sense of purpose, that compels you to speak emotionally.

VANDANA: Yes, yes.

SCOTT: You mentioned earlier the idea of anesthesia. The term we tend to use to describe this phenomenon is "psychic numbing."

VANDANA: Yeah, same thing.

SCOTT: It's a psychological concept. "Psychic numbing" indicates that feeling and meaning tend to decline when the numerical magnitude of a phenomenon increases. You've already talked about this a bit, but I wonder, with this phrase in mind, if you've encountered this when you've tried to present information to the public or to farmers.

VANDANA: I've been able to avoid this because I communicate at the level where there's a certain facility in the particular communication, and because I'm so fully aware that numbers are used for psychic numbing, I do not burden people. If it's necessary, I will use a number to counter another number, but that is in fact to undo the psychic numbing and to in a way allow the intelligence of every person to come into play on their own terms to make decisions, judgments, assessments. You know, this phenomenon of farmer suicides I've been working on for ten years. To me, it is a result, a direct result, of psychic numbing. If the package of farming practices and that model had not been brought through numbers, those farmers would have been making sane decisions that would not have driven them down the debt and suicide path. The fact that they are getting so desperate is because they've been numbed, and they don't know why they're in a mess. They worked hard—in the past when they worked hard there was no problem. To me, the suicides are a result of psychic numbing—they are a symptom of helplessness that comes out of psychic numbing.

SCOTT: So what is the antidote to that numbing?

VANDANA: The antidote to that numbing is to make the life of each of those farmers count, which is why we do the reports like this. We were the first in this country, starting in '97, to start bringing out lists of farmers and their stories. We started doing public hearings, and the public hearing concept made people real—that this was not just a number, not just one of the ten thousand, one of the fifty thousand, one of now the hundred and forty thousand in India—that's the number that it has reached.

SCOTT: During what time period?

VANDANA: Ten years. But this is a person whose wife today is struggling without land, who's got a baby of eight months and another child of five years. So that is one antidote. And the second is to go behind those numbers of psychic numbing and give meaning to those numbers in terms of power. That's why I am naming Monsanto all the time—to say, "You know, these seeds, you're not just getting them to improve your agriculture. You're getting them because it works for Monsanto to have genetically engineered seeds."

SCOTT: This is what you say to the farmers.

VANDANA: Yes. So there are two antidotes: make their lives real in the larger public, and the second is, make the anonymity of numbers that is causing the psychic numbing, make that real by saying this is not just a number. There's this million-dollar market or that million-dollar market for this particular company. I'll give you an example. We're having a huge wheat crisis now. The U.S. government has created it so that Cargill can sell more wheat. Cargill is the biggest grain trader of the world—biggest private company of America, from Minnesota. They control 70 percent of the grain trade the world. They're the ones who wrote the agreement on agriculture in WTO. They're big—and they bought up the second biggest, Continental. So they're super, super, super big. There was suddenly a little package from the government about how they're going to increase productivity of wheat because first they import it and now the prices are going up, so they say we'll increase productivity. You read through the lines, and there are figures against it. Now people who just see the figures and technical language—reseed replacement 160 krores, no-till farming this much krores (ten to the power of seven, ten million—that's an Indian figure, we count in lakhs and krores). That's a psychic numbing—that package means the government will go to farmers and give this packet, and the farmer won't know why he's doing what he's doing. The way I deal with this psychic numbing is to say, "You know, when you see 'seed replacement for 160 krores,' basically it means the seeds you grow will be replaced by seeds Monsanto can sell, and this 160 krores will be a government subsidy to Monsanto to help distribute their seeds." That's how I deconstruct it. Or the "no tills"—the word "no till" usually goes hand in hand with when Monsanto wants to sell Roundup, this broad spectrum herbicide, so when there is 180 krores for that, that is basically another 180 krores of Roundup sales. With the subsidy from government—public money is being spent. That's how I take it to the public, which is why we do have a broad base of concern. And I think we now have a consensus on the causes of this tragedy.

SCOTT: So when you raise the public's awareness and you stoke their emotional outrage, does it work simply to do that or do you have to have an outlet for those feelings—do you have to tell them that the appropriate response is not simply to feel frustration and despair but to take action in appropriate ways?

VANDANA: No, that's another element. When you take on this kind of work, you have to take responsibility for creative change all the way down. You just don't bombard with another piece of information—

SCOTT: That results in another kind of numbness.

VANDANA: Yeah, it does. So you work on a very long-term basis and keep coming back to the communities, and I guess my style of organizing is very feminist in that way. It is based on self-organizing. It is based on constant communication for self-organizing. So I go with a lot of ideas. What a Punjab farmer union will pick up will depend on them, but you go with ideas. Say, "You could do this and you could do this, you could do this." It means their frustration doesn't numb them, it energizes. The communication-knowledge energizes them.

SCOTT: There are so many ways to make people passive.

VANDANA: Yeah.

SCOTT: The trick is to make them excited and concerned and give them a constructive outlet.

VANDANA: Yeah, right.

SCOTT: So when I was reading this book—the 2006 edition of *Seeds of Suicide: The Ecological and Human Costs of Seed Monopolies & Globalization of Agriculture*—earlier today, I noticed that you have stories of individual farmers. What is the effect when other farmers read these stories?

VANDANA: I think, because we do it in a long-term context of denumbing, the effect has been farmers organizing. So that instead of hearing anonymous stories from newspapers, when this kind of material is from the farmer's communities, they start to organize and say, "This is the cause of the suicides, and this is the solution." They are able to organize and start making demands on the system for a policy shift.

CHAPTER 15

The Meaning of "One Data Point"

An Interview with Sandra Steingraber

RENO, NEVADA, MARCH 6, 2007

SCOTT SLOVIC: Much of what you discuss in your books and lectures and magazine articles is actually rather technical biology, and much of it is based on numerical data. You don't simply tell autobiographical stories in your work. For instance, in talking about the environmental causes of cancer in *Living Downstream,* you have a whole section where you explain how these diagnoses form a collective statistical story, and you proceed to offer some of the general statistics, but you don't let the explanation remain in the form of raw statistics, simply presenting the cancer-registry data. Instead you return to the specific story of your friend, Jeannie Marshall, who is suffering from cancer of the spinal cord. Could you talk a bit about the importance of using statistics, numerical data, in your work, and the limitations of this kind of information?

SANDRA STEINGRABER: Sure. I think statistics are really important. There are real limits to an autobiographical approach to things. One doesn't know simply by an individual story whether this story has anything in common with the rest of humanity, whereas if you look at statistical trends, another kind of truth emerges from the numbers. So I like to tell that story, too. For me, as a writer, all the stars kind of have to align themselves. There has to be a really good human story to help my readers through this kind of narrative arc, and in *Living Downstream* the story of the life of Jeannie Marshall, who is one data point among the cancer non-survivors, helped me talk about bigger issues, which require lots of statistical information. The narrative arc carries the water for the statistical scientific stories. But readers have a limit on how much quantitative information they can hear before their eyes glaze over.

SCOTT: What is that limit?

SANDRA: I don't exactly know. I mean, I have a limit too, right? My limit is probably different than other people's. That's why I've kind of created this kind of juxtaposing approach to my writing. Let's talk about the whole big picture here: How many people really are suffering from Parkinson's disease? Is it going up? What do we know about paraquat exposure in relation to Parkinson's disease (paraquat being an agricultural chemical)? It turns out we know quite a lot, and there is a lot of interesting statistical correlation. Just as when the surgeon general in 1964 declared that smoking caused lung cancer, you base such assertions on a massive amount of statistical correlation, on correlative evidence. That's important because social change like anti-smoking laws in the workplace came about because of statistical information. That's a story that people now know and understand: smoking causes lung cancer. There are other stories, like paraquat's relationship to Parkinson's disease, that people don't quite know yet. That's not a common story, so the statistical data are really important, but I wouldn't tell that story unless I had a person with Parkinson's to be the water bearer for the story. I need that person, too. That helps my readers.

I don't think our ability to absorb statistics is a fixed quality. I think we'll open up and absorb more if we're curious. I was really pleased that your student found my basic description of embryology thrilling because that is actually another big goal of mine as a science writer: to describe the biology in such lovely language that people are intrigued to know more. Then they'll accept a lot more numbers. I can open up their capacity— increase their capacity to be curious about the numbers.

I'm trying to do that with a project I'm doing on puberty now [published in 2011 as *Raising Elijah: Protecting Our Children in an Age of Environmental Crisis*]. "Puberty"—it's an ugly sounding word, so I don't even like it as a poet. Puberty—it's icky. You know, pubic hair. It's just an icky word. It's not a good word, and there are really no other good substitutes. "Sexual maturation," that's not so great either. People think of it as adolescence, but they're not actually even synonyms of each other. But if I can get you to see that puberty is not just an event—it's an actual parade of events and involves sculptural remodeling of the brain under the direction of sex hormones so that when you enter puberty you can no longer learn to speak a language without a foreign accent because you've lost brain plasticity even as you've gained the capacity for higher-ordered thought, which comes with pubertal change—if I can take you inside the human body and you can watch these changes unfold, I can get you really interested. "Wow, that's what goes on inside my body during puberty?" Then I can talk to you about the statistics on the falling age of puberty in girls and the ways in which the childhood of girls has actually been shortened over the last century, and maybe our exposure to endocrine-disrupting chemicals has something to do with that. And then I'm going to open up your mind to accepting, "Okay, really, that's true? Well, what are the numbers on this? How far has puberty fallen? In how many women? Is it different for white girls and black girls? What are the numbers on that?" If I as a writer can get you to ask those questions before I as a writer ask them, then I've anticipated what you're thinking next and am sort of feeding your curiosity, providing these little crumbs along the trail to lead you along in this line of inquiry that I'm going on. But hopefully, you're one step ahead of me and you're hungry for the information, so I'm not pulling you along. That's always my goal.

SCOTT: I find myself even thinking of a pharmaceutical metaphor: certain types of information can be absorbed by the mind better if they're supported by other kinds of information or language. If you combine information with story, they're both absorbed by the audience in a way that would not happen with either the information or the story if they were presented separately.

SANDRA: Right. There's also the issue of memory. Are you going to remember the statistic or not? I have no psychological basis for saying this—this is just my observation as a writer—but I think our ability to remember is related to imagery and storytelling. We will remember a number if it's attached to a story that we heard because we can remember the story. The number is part of the story and therefore we can remember it. Or if it's tied to an image, you know.

SCOTT: You mentioned earlier that you wouldn't even try explaining the issue of, what was it—Parkinson's and paraquat?—unless you had a particular case, an individual story, that you could combine with it. So when there is a scientific or a social issue you know you want to explore, to write about, are you looking for that image that will go along with it, the chief image? Or one particular person's story or a community story that you think will be kind of the dominant mechanism for helping people absorb and retain what you're saying?

SANDRA: Yeah, I am. And because I'm a creative writer rather than a journalist, although I've done some journalism, my preference always is to have a memoiristic approach and use the power of memoir, of my own experience, as the vehicle rather than to tell the story of another community or interview people. I mean, I certainly have done that. I wrote a big investigative piece, for example, in *Orion* magazine a couple of years ago—it took a year and a half of my life—where I went into a community where a polyvinyl chloride factory had blown up. I interviewed people there—you know, the person who was the last remaining survivor in the hospital with all these burn injuries and the person who was the emergency responder, the first on the scene. So I had this kind of constellation of other voices, which is sort of classic environmental journalism, where I've gone and interviewed all the people who were impacted by this incredible environmental disaster. I can do that, but for whatever reason, my signature style is to use the first person and my own life for characters and things like that.

SCOTT: This leads directly into the next question that I had. As I mentioned to you earlier, I've been asking a number of writers and artists more general questions about language and information, and I'm curious to know what you think of the assertion that for information to have meaning it has to be infused with affect, with feeling. Would you say that your work seeks to bring together information and emotion in particular ways?

SANDRA: Yeah, I mean, I would have no quarrel with anything that you just said. There are times, actually, when communities are so divided emotionally over an issue that I actually feel my task is simply to speak plainly about the science, and oddly enough that often happens most not in scientific venues but in communities, like communities of farmers, who are often my audience, who are torn apart by an incinerator siting or whether or not to use a certain kind of chemical pesticide. In those cases I actually keep affect out. I honor the fact that there are two sides to this argument and there are people in the room who have very strong opinions on both sides. I stick very close to the data, and I simply explain things to people about what we know. I've had farmers with eighth-grade education, and I've done some pretty sophisticated organic chemistry with them on dioxins and furans and what their half-life are, because that's what they need to know to make a decision for the referendum or whatever decision that's impending.

My biggest challenge in some situations, like with farmers, is that so many farmers are deaf because they're old, because farmers are old in our country, and because they've been working around combines and other diesel equipment for so long. And I'm often in a junior high school auditorium and the sound system is terrible, so I've got all these people with hearing aids, and I'm just trying to get them to hear the data. That's what they want. I don't always have an affective moment. There are times when there is so much affect in the room that the best thing to do is just be able to be a very good science teacher for people.

SCOTT: Your sensitivity to audience is very important. When you know you're writing for a particular venue or speaking to a very particular type of audience, you try to gauge how to draw emotion in or exclude emotion from your language.

SANDRA: I do, and sometimes there are false notes that I hit. I don't always hit it right, but it is certainly my intention to pay attention to those things. It's one thing if I'm invited in to speak because everybody in that room wants to be there for some reason. Even if it's some students who've been compelled to come because they have to write a paper, they have a motivation for being there, whereas, as an author who writes books or even white papers—because I often write technical white papers—your words go out and they have to stand on their own. You have to convince people to start reading, first of all, and then to keep reading. So the challenge is very different than in public speaking.

In the case of my white papers, in particular, usually I'm commissioned to write them either as background papers so that some organization can understand something about breast cancer or something like that. Once I wrote a white paper so the architectural community could understand the environmental health effects of polyvinyl chloride, which is a building material, from point of production all the way up through use and disposal. I had to learn all about the industrial chemistry of PVC manufacturing. Well, that can be a fairly dry topic, and architects are busy people, and I want them to keep reading, so there's a role not for affect necessarily but a role for really playful use of language because it's my sense that architects appreciate design and beauty, and so if I'm going to describe something like how vinyl acetate and vinyl chloride are mixed and problems that are created, blah, blah, blah, I want to create this sort of beautiful language as an eloquent way of getting people to see this very complex, messy organic chemistry. Because I think that will impress architects enough to keep reading.

I'm always thinking about who my audience is and how I can seduce them, essentially. That's my role, the seducer, because I talk about things nobody wants to hear about, you know, birth defects and learning disabilities and cancer. Nobody really wants to know this stuff, so I'm always thinking about how can I seduce somebody through this really hard genetics or this really hard organic chemistry, and sometimes it's through simply being plainspoken and almost nonpartisan, sometimes it's through eloquence. Sometimes it's through being funny. Humor is good. Sometimes it's through pure lyricism and beauty of language. So there are lots of arrows in my quiver, I think, and I try to figure out, okay, what's the seductive method this time.

SCOTT: One of the reasons why people cease to pay attention is that their minds freeze up, become numb. Certain subjects or kinds of information are sensitive, painful, or just like a glass wall that the mind can't attach itself to. One of them, as we were discussing earlier, is numbers— the presentation of information by way of numbers. Occasionally there are people with very important information to share with the world who think that if you just lay it out there plainly it will do its trick, but often the communication falls flat.

Sometimes when I'm talking with people about the difficulty the human mind has in fathoming quantitative information I quote a passage from Annie Dillard's *For the Time Being* where she says that all you need to do in order to capture the meaning of a huge number, such as the population of China, is to multiply yourself by that number. What do you think about that idea?

SANDRA: I don't know that passage. I love it.

I do know that numbers are definitely the battleground over which environmental health is being played out, so those who seek to deny, dispute, or discount connections between the health of our environment and human health use numbers, and then those of us who are trying to demonstrate that these connections are important are using the same numbers, but differently. So, for example, there are two very famous ientists, Peto and Doll, who wrote a very well-known paper in 1981 which alleges that only 2 percent of human cancers are caused by exposure to the environment.

Now, that was a long time ago, 1981, and they have a pie chart in that diagram that's been reproduced in almost every state and county health department report on cancer in the environment, so it's considered a very authoritative paper. And recently there was a big exposé that showed that one of those two guys, during the time that they were doing that research, was actually on industry payroll, working for the polluters, and answering questions about whether or not those pollutants could be playing a role in cancer. We didn't know that at the time the paper was written, and now we realize there was a lot of industry money behind generating those numbers. We suspected that for years, and now we finally know that it's true.

But when I wrote *Living Downstream* we didn't know that those were actually industry-supported numbers, so I simply took those numbers for what they were. Okay, let's just say that 2 percent of cancers are caused by exposure to the environment. Let's just say that's true. When you run the numbers, it turns out that's more than eleven thousand people a year. So then I actually calculated how many funerals a day that was, and that's like some thirty funerals a day, and I asked my readers to imagine going to that many funerals a day every day for a year. That's the number of Americans killed because somebody made a profit by putting a carcinogen into the environment that we all share. Are you comfortable with that? Are those eleven thousand deaths homicides? If you know something is a cancer-causing agent and you release it anyway just because you don't know who you're going to kill, do we still say those deaths are homicides? That's more than three times the number of people killed in the World Trade Towers, and the specificity of those deaths have caused us to fight a couple different foreign wars at this point because of our rage, almost blind rage and anger, about those deaths.

I think the problem is not that those eleven thousand deaths are trivial, that they're negligible and not important, but rather there's a lack of specificity. We can't put an individual name to each of those eleven thousand like we can with those who died in the World Trade Towers. That's the difference—lack of specificity. So that's the power of autobiography, I think, because I can say, "I'm one data point. I had bladder cancer when I was twenty. I'm one data point in the big registry of cancer for the year 1979, and what does that mean? Does that matter?" That's how human stories and math can kind of work together, I think.

SCOTT: So you actually think very methodically, very carefully, about how to frame information. That's in a sense what we've been circling around again and again during this conversation.

SANDRA: Yeah. I could have, for example, argued the numbers. I could have said, regarding that Doll and Peto paper, those numbers were probably cooked. But if you're my audience, you're going to filter that through your own belief system. And one of those guys was knighted. He's Sir Richard Doll, so who am I to question his numbers, right? So rather than question the numbers, I use the same numbers and I just ask people to think about whether 2 percent of cancer deaths a year, some thirty funerals a day, is a trivial thing.

SCOTT: I have one final question, which is, in a sense, *the* question. I wonder whether you have any way of knowing that the work you're doing, your writing and your public speaking, is having a positive impact on public health or on the protection of the environment. You mentioned speaking to a group at UCSF recently and people responding very viscerally to what you were talking about. But do you have any sense that this kind of work, your energetic efforts to popularize important social issues and scientific topics, is having the impact you would desire?

SANDRA: Well, no. It's not. I don't know what would be enough to make me say yes to that question. I think the things that Bill McKibben is doing with climate change are exactly dead on, and I think he's right. I think Al Gore and others are right to say that we basically have about ten years to turn this around. We used to think we had about half a century, but we really don't. And ten years is twenty semesters. That's how I think about it. And what could any one of us do in twenty semesters that would be sufficient? So, no, I have to say I don't see what I want to see yet. But, on the other hand, I'm aware that there are plenty of times when I've looked back in history at situations when people were working as hard as they could and it didn't seem like enough, but it was only a few years later that something tipped, something happened that made a big difference. So just because we can't see forward to the impact that our actions have doesn't mean we should stop. We can redouble our efforts maybe, but it doesn't mean they are futile.

CHAPTER 16

Introspection, Social Transformation, and the Trans-Scalar Imaginary

An Interview with Chris Jordan

SEATTLE, WASHINGTON, JUNE 8, 2011

SCOTT SLOVIC: So much of what we really need to understand about the world today comes in the form of numbers, and yet numbers are both useful and, in some way, tragically unhelpful in the sense that they leave us without the proper affect. We don't really know their true meaning, in a sense, and we often need other ways of reaching into that information and figuring out how it affects our lives and how we should think about it, how we should allow it to change us. So I'd like to talk about your work as a visual artist, which is a bit different from the work of the writers we've been working with in other aspects of this book—and yet much of your work is intensely related to this larger topic. I wonder if we could begin, by way of background, by talking about your professional and artistic roots. How did you start out doing this work? As I understand it, you actually trained as a lawyer and then took a step in a different direction.

CHRIS JORDAN: I come from a family of artists. My dad was an amateur photographer for many years, so I picked up an interest in photography pretty early on from him. My mom is a professional watercolor painter. She doesn't do cutting-edge work—it's more like traditional landscape painting. I was just around a lot of color and composition when I was a kid and developed an interest in photography. I've been photographing pretty seriously for probably twenty-five years or so. The whole legal career, for me, was more about my fear of living than a case of my really being interested in that. It was an unconscious process for me at the time, but I can look back and see that I was taking a safe route. All that time— all the years I was in law school and all the years I was a lawyer—I was passionately into photography. But my work at that time was really just about aesthetics. I was interested in composition and texture and color, and I didn't use photography or even *see* it as a way of engaging with the world. That only came to me quite a bit later, after I had left my legal job.

I started photographing piles of garbage, not because I was interested in mass consumption, but just because I thought they were beautiful. It was just purely a study in aesthetics. It was other people who looked at my work and started suggesting that there was a social component that makes this stuff relevant. I had been kind of vaguely aware that there were these cultural undercurrents, these frightening cultural undercurrents. I remember reading Neil Postman's book called *Amusing Ourselves to Death* quite a few years previously and being affected by that. It's a book about the television culture. And I was kind of aware of the mass consumption culture all of the years I was a lawyer, but I think I was living in exactly the state of denial that my work as a photographer has come to depict. I didn't want to know about any of this.

SCOTT: What was it about your growing understanding about the relevance of this beauty you were photographing to your own life of consumption that enabled you to accept that idea rather than pushing it aside as would be so typical in our society—this tendency toward denial? Was there something about the timing of this realization in your own life that enabled this awakening? Why were you able to challenge yourself to reconsider aspects of your own lifestyle?

CHRIS: I think it's the fact that I got myself into therapy around that time. It was actually a few years before I left the legal practice. I've been in therapy for going on twelve years now. I go three times a week and have made a really in-depth process of looking inwardly and asking myself questions like "Why am I angry all the time?" "Why am I mean to the people I love?" Back then I was asking myself "Why am I doing this work that I hate?" "And why do I feel so anxious?" "Why am I contemplating suicide when everyone's telling me I'm so successful?" As I began to look at those questions, I began to see the incredible, almost ecstatic experience of coming out of denial. In that process I saw that I had been living under this illusion that being in denial is the best way to live. It's become this long, slow experience. It wasn't an epiphany, but rather a long, slow process—one that still continues for me—of opening up my internal experience that has improved my quality of life.

SCOTT: So you've achieved this through years of self-reflection, aided by the
process of therapy. Would you say that in a sense your artistic work is
performing this kind of project for your audiences? In what way might
your art achieve the effect that you've accomplished in your own life
through different mechanisms?

CHRIS: No one's ever put it that way before, but yeah, that's exactly what
I'm trying to do with my work. It's really challenging because it's like
delivering a dose of medicine that people don't want. And the challenge
is to deliver it in a way that tricks them into taking it—I use a lot of

FIGURE 16.1 Plastic Bottles, 2007. Depicts two million plastic bottles, the
number used in the United States every five minutes.

FIGURE 16.2
Close-up Plastic
Bottles, 2007.

sleight of hand with my work, fooling the viewer into walking up and looking at an image. If they knew what it was all about, they wouldn't even go to the exhibition!

SCOTT: So in a sense the illusion, or the subterfuge, of your work may come by way of abstraction. A lot of your work, on a large scale, particularly the digital images—they look almost abstract. And then the concrete reality comes by way of the close-up and the title, right?

CHRIS: Yes.

SCOTT: So is that where the—however you prefer to phrase it—the subterfuge or the indirectness or the illusion comes from . . . because of the appearance of mere aesthetics, a delightful and moving image that operates primarily on the level of beauty? And then closer inspection reveals something with a moral component.

CHRIS: Yeah—you totally nailed it there. I billed each one of the pieces in my *Running the Numbers* series with that exactly in mind. It's like when you stand back at a distance it looks like something attractive or at a minimum something innocuous—you know, just six giant orange rectangles, one of those pieces of modern art that doesn't raise any defenses. It looks completely nonthreatening or it looks like something cool and beautiful. Wow, a beautiful painting of something! And it's only when the viewer gets up very close that he sees all the individual items that it's made of—by that time the person's peripheral vision is completely filled with the issue. He's comprehending something about the enormity of the number without even yet knowing what the issue is exactly. It's only when the viewer reads the plaque, which I put off to the left—and I hope the viewer puts off reading it until he has absorbed the piece—then he sees that it's, you know, the number of gallons of oil we burn around the world every second or the number of plastic bottles we use in the world every two minutes or whatever.

SCOTT: So in a way you've captivated the audience on a level at which most people are likely to be nondefensive, unguarded. You have this understanding that people are seeking pleasure, are seeking beauty. If they're attending an art exhibition, obviously they're there to be delighted in some way. And then the teaching process occurs after you've already lured the audience in and hooked them in a sense—then you're delivering a message. In a way, then, your beautiful images are serving as vehicles for moral messages. Some artists would be concerned about doing this, but you seem to have made an artistic choice that this is an important way of educating your audience or achieving a kind of social reform by way of art that would be beneficial to you and your family as well . . . if everyone were more informed and enlightened. Do you think of your work as a teaching process or as a way of advancing a particular ideology?

CHRIS: I chafe a little bit at the idea of it being teaching and also that it's moral. I suppose it probably is both of those things, but I don't like to think of myself as an activist because what I don't want to be doing is handing out answers . . . saying, "You're all bad and this is how you *should* be." I try not to go there. What I'm really interested in is not so much pointing to somebody's behavior and saying, "You're bad or you're wrong" with a moral judgment attached to it. It's simply to illuminate the fact of what we're doing, which itself might be unconscious. An analogy that I like to use is that I feel like I'm an alcoholic who's woken up to my own alcoholism, and now I'm sitting in a room with my whole family who are all metaphorically alcoholics. I'm not wagging my finger: "You guys are all bad." I'm just saying, "Hey, everybody, have we all noticed the giant pile of empty vodka bottles over in the corner there? Look how many there are. That's all ours." Period. And to let each person take that information and process it as he or she will. I don't want to impinge on people's freedom to make choices or wag my finger at the people who are making bad choices. I think that simply illuminating the fact of what we're doing is frequently enough. I don't need to add my own judgment to it because the fact itself is, in most cases, stunning.

SCOTT: What kinds of responses have you received from people who've viewed your work? Have they used the word "stunning," which implies to be stunned into silence, to be in a condition of shock, as if to say, "This is the reality that I'm living in, that I'm somehow complicit with"? What do you think is the thought process of people who view your work, who are surprised or stunned by this information?

CHRIS: It's been a really fascinating experience over a few years to receive lots of feedback and to see how it affects people.

SCOTT: Do people tend to write to you after they attend your exhibits?

CHRIS: I get tons of e-mail, yeah. When I had the exhibit in Eugene at the Jordan Schnitzer Museum, I went down and visited, and a flood of e-mails came in from there over a period of a couple months. But they come in all the time from all over the place because people see the work on my website and blogs and stuff.

SCOTT: So in a way you're able to use that to conduct research about how people react to certain kinds of images. I wonder if you can summarize the patterns of response you've noticed.

CHRIS: The pattern I find most troubling and that is most challenging to me is that people frequently tend to point to everybody else and say something like, "Boy, people really need to see this work. Everybody else needs to see it." There's a sort of feeling I get like people are digging me in the ribs as if to say that we're on the same team together. "I'm really glad to see that you get this, and I get this, too. And all those other people really need to get it now."

SCOTT: So they're deflecting in a way. Rather than performing the introspection that you seem to want to stir, people are deflecting the social problems, the problems with overconsumption, they're deflecting these toward those other "unenlightened people."

CHRIS: Yeah. There's this sort of us-versus-them thing. It's just another form of denial. One of my favorite times was when I was at the TED Conference in Monterey where people fly from all over the world to attend. It's this very hoity-toity event, where there's tons of consumption going on. People fly on transcontinental 747s to attend the TED Conference. And after showing my work, this guy comes up to me and says, "You know what I hate? It's when people don't turn off the water when they shave. You know, I turn off the water when I shave. You know how much water that saves?" It was sort of like high-fiving, and there's denial going on there.

But I think there's something else happening, and this is the piece of it that's really troubling to me, and that is when we behold the enormity of the cumulative effects of our behaviors it's disempowering. It's really hard to hold onto our sense of empowerment as an individual when you're standing in front of a visualization of 6.8 billion people's consumption. Because on one hand we all know that the collective is made up of lots and lots of individuals, and that each of us is individually contributing to the catastrophe of global warming, the destruction of life in our seas, or whatever. But each one of our contributions is infinitesimal— incomprehensibly small and abstract. We can't see it. Go buy a new iPod, and the sea doesn't rise a few feet. We can't in any way measure and perceive the effect that each one of us is having on the world. We can only see the cumulative effect. So there's a natural tendency to point toward the collective and say it's the collective's problem because it's true.

SCOTT: —and in a way not to register one's own membership in the collective. This us-versus-them impulse. So can you think of any of your images in particular, from any of your projects, that you feel have been especially effective in not allowing this sort of deflection or denial? Any works that may prompt viewers' sense of their own complicity to the subject that you're revealing?

CHRIS: Yeah. Well, the image of two million plastic bottles is by far the most effective one that way. I've had lots of people write to me and tell me that they've stopped drinking water or soda out of plastic bottles after seeing that image. I was at an exhibition in Boulder, Colorado, at the Boulder Museum of Contemporary Art with a friend of mine who's a really cool Boulder hippy, and we were standing in front of that piece, and he had a bottle of water in his hand and was drinking from this plastic bottle. And he said, "Just a second," and he went and threw the bottle in the garbage. Then he came back and stood in front of that piece again, and he got this sheepish look on his face and said, "Well, that was just one bottle." Then he looked back at my piece, and I saw him sort of reel back. His neck snapped back, his eyes opened, and he looked at me and said, "I just got your piece. That's two million-one bottles." And I said, "Yeah, that's exactly it." That's one of the issues I try to raise with all of the *Running the Numbers* pieces. I'm trying to raise the issue of the individual's role in the collective. With each piece, when you stand back, you see the collective. I scale it so that when you stand back at a distance, you can't see the individuals that make up the collective. You only see the homogeneous collective, and when you get up close you see all the individuals, but by the time you get all the way up close and you can see all the individuals, you can no longer make out the collective. It's a kind of Google Earth process. A friend of mind calls it "the trans-scalar imaginary." When you stand back at a distance, you can't see the details; and when you can see the details, you have to use your memory or your imagination to recall what the big picture looked like.

I'm trying to raise this question. It's not a simple thing. We're all indoctrinated with the green viewpoint that, yes, every vote counts. Your vote counts. "Get out there and vote!" Every individual matters. On the surface, we're all led to believe that. But when you look a little deeper at what our experience is of being one out of seven billion or so, when every single day two hundred thousand new people enter the population of the world—or in the United States, each of us is one out of three hundred million—I think we have this intuitive sense of *not mattering*. I feel that inside myself. It's like, fuck it—I don't need to recycle stuff. It's everybody else that needs to do it. If everybody else *does* do it, then the world will be healed, and I still don't have to.

SCOTT: What you're describing now is the idea of a lack of responsibility. It doesn't matter what each of us does as an individual. Our individual responsibility is relatively slight, but it's the flip side of what you mentioned earlier as this sense of disempowerment. "I don't have the power to accomplish much—either to cause much damage or to achieve much good—because I'm only one small individual." This relationship between empowerment and responsibility is quite interesting. I like the story you told about your friend in front of the picture of all the water bottles. Most responses to art probably don't happen in such a public situation, side by side with the artist, who's watching for a reaction. "Is this having the desired effect?"

Your mentioning the large number of people on the planet reminds me of something we sometimes bring up when we're talking to people about the difficulty that humans have in fathoming quantitative data. We quote a passage by the writer Annie Dillard, from her book *For the Time Being*, where she says, "There are 1,198,500,000 people alive now in China. To get a feel for what this means, simply take yourself—in all your singularity, importance, complexity, and love—and multiply by 1,198,500,000. See? Nothing to it."

CHRIS: [Laughs.]

SCOTT: She presents this passage without any detailed explanation. I wonder what your reaction is to this idea that there might be a simple multiplication process of the individual by the sheer number of other individuals in order to achieve an understanding of the collective.

CHRIS: Well, there's a visionary level of insight in that statement by Dillard. I think she really gets that when you talk about a billion, one hundred million of *anything* it's completely incomprehensible. It's strange and interesting. I've read what various writers have said about the incomprehensibility of large numbers. You've probably seen that book called *New World New Mind* . . .

SCOTT: I like that book a lot. I think it's a very important book.

CHRIS: Well, the nugget I pulled from there is that the human mind can't comprehend numbers beyond more than a few thousand. Recently I heard that there's another guy out there who says we can't comprehend more than about seven. As soon as you start getting into twenty-two or forty or sixty or something like that, you have to think in *groups*. That's two groups of ten, six groups of ten—but seven is the biggest number we can really feel in our hearts.

SCOTT: One of the reasons for the entire project of this book is to show the latest research in cognitive science in relation to what artists and writers are doing, and to reveal that sensitivity may actually begin to decline when we go from one to two.

CHRIS: Aw! Unbelievable!

SCOTT: Our sense of emotional engagement begins to blur already with two.

CHRIS: That's one starving child versus two starving children!

SCOTT: Exactly. This is what people are studying empirically these days.

CHRIS: Fascinating! Well, at the same time that that exists as a truth of our consciousness, every day we are reading numbers and talking back and forth to each other in numbers that are in the hundreds of thousands or the millions. And lately you must have noticed that numbers in the *trillions* are beginning to be used in our cultural lexicon. I never heard numbers in the trillions back when I was younger, except when we talked about astronomy: "trillions of stars in the universe . . ."

SCOTT: Right. To say the word "trillion" was like saying "google" or "infinity," but now this is our national debt, something we're supposed to understand in our practical lives and yet it's vastly beyond the apprehension of the human mind.

CHRIS: By many levels of magnitude.

SCOTT: And it's not even a matter of the ability to perform complex mathematical calculations. Even people who are fantastic mathematicians cannot understand such numbers on a visceral, emotional level.

CHRIS: And yet, that's the only information we have to attempt to comprehend and relate to the most profoundly important issues of our times . . . like global warming. The only number we've got is nine gigatons. Nine gigatons of carbon are being emitted into the atmosphere by the burning of fossil fuels yearly. Nine billion tons! That's nine billion times two thousand pounds! So eighteen *trillion* pounds of carbon. And there's nowhere where you can go see it. I believe if we could go stand in front of a pile of one-pound chunks of coal—eighteen trillion pounds of carbon reduced to a form in which we could see it—I think we would feel something extremely profound. Might not be a good feeling. I think we would be shocked. If we could go see all of the plastic bottles we're throwing away . . .

I'm doing a new piece that I'm making out of the Mayan calendar. It's the 925 million people in the world right now who are either starving or suffering from malnutrition. Nine hundred and twenty-five million, according to the World Health Organization. If we could actually fly over in a helicopter 925 million people all collected in one place, we would comprehend something, and I think it would drop down to the level of *feeling* in a way that just can't be accomplished by the numbers alone.

SCOTT: So is this what you're attempting to accomplish in this new piece? To create the sensation of flying over an enormous group of these people, all of whom are suffering from starvation or malnutrition? How are you going about depicting this? And obviously if they're arrayed like the Mayan calendar, it's not just a group of people on the ground as you're flying over them. There's something elegant and structured about the visual appearance of this group. In what sense are you representing the appearance of this assembled group as you fly over and what gave you the idea of using the Mayan calendar as the collective image?

CHRIS: All of my work attempts to visualize these statistics. That's the idea behind it. If you can *see* something, if you can stand in front of the number of barrels of oil that we're burning in a minute, if you can stand in front of them and see these things, then I think it would lead to a further comprehension than if we have the numbers alone. That's the point of the *Running the Numbers* series. With each one of the pieces, my challenge is to try to convey it in a way that does lead to some comprehension and that also attempts to honor the complexity of the issue. I could do 925 million dots on a great big canvas. I'm sure you've seen those experiments where they collect a million peanuts—a bunch of kids in a science class get together and collect a million peanuts. This helps you comprehend the number a little bit more. But I'm interested in comprehending more than just a giant number. I want to comprehend numbers that specifically relate to these catastrophic-level, unconscious behaviors that we collectively engage in as a culture.

SCOTT: How do you go about choosing the larger image that a viewer will see from a distance?

CHRIS: I've been interested in the Mayan calendar for quite a while because there's all this apocalyptic mythology associated with it as a result of a few misguided New Age people. Actual scholars of the Mayan calendar say it doesn't end in 2012. The thing that it predicts in 2012 is not the end of the world at all. It simply is the end of one of many cycles in that mathematical structure that the calendar is made of. I think it's a fascinating thing. The Mayans were brilliant astronomers. They knew the world is round and we're in the solar system. . . . There's this misguided idea that the Earth's about to end associated with the Mayan calendar. My belief is we're at risk of the world coming to an end in the very near future, but it's not going to be because of some deity out there or some event that comes to us. It's going to be our own doing. We are potentially causing the end of human civilization.

So I've been really interested in doing a piece about the Mayan calendar. It's not known why the Mayans declined the way they did, but one theory is that they exhausted their agricultural resources. I had those things in mind as I thought about doing a piece about the Mayan calendar. What I built this piece of is 92,500 plant seeds that I got from a seed bank, one of those Noah's ark seed repositories that's protecting seeds. I'm constantly frustrated by how limited my *Running the Numbers* work is in its ability to say what I want to say. This piece has 92,500 agricultural plant seeds, which is one-hundredth of one percent of the number of people today who live in a condition of starvation or malnutrition. To actually show the full 925 million people would take ten thousand of that print! The print is five by five feet when it's printed at its full size. Ten thousand of those prints would cover 8.3 football fields solidly. And if I made that many prints and put them out over a vast area, and people walked down and looked and realized that each tiny seed represents a person in the world who right now is suffering from malnutrition, then they might begin to comprehend the issue. But, really, my work in just the vaguest way points in the direction of what we can't comprehend by the numbers. But I think it only gets us a very short distance.

SCOTT: There's something dazzling about the statistics that you have at your fingertips, something overwhelming about the sense that even this complex and intricate design you've created represents only a minute

FIGURE 16.3 Maya, 2011. Depicts 92,500 agricultural plant seeds, equal to one-hundredth of one percent of the number of people in the world who suffer from malnutrition. To illustrate the entire statistic with 925 million seeds would require ten thousand prints of this image, covering more than eight football fields.

FIGURE 16.4
Close-up Maya,
2011.

fraction of the issue you're attempting to characterize. Your approach to revealing the plight of so many people around the world is quite different than approaches that attempt to show one individual—one malnourished child, for instance—and say, "Try to fathom this one suffering person and then magnify that through some kind of emotional calculus." I would say that your approach here is building upon the *New World New Mind* message that things are happening in the world today, often due to technological processes we've invented, that we have no way of fathoming. In a way, rather than spurring people to reach for their checkbook with this kind of image, you're *exploring* the phenomenon of our insensitivity. You're not giving people a simple solution to the problem.

CHRIS: That relates to another piece of feedback that I frequently get about my work. Virtually every time I do a public presentation, during the questions and answer part, someone always raises a hand and says, "You got me. So what should I do?" My answer has evolved over time. There was a time when I started giving people things to do. Look at this website, become vegetarian, . . . I had a list of things to do. Then I realized I was going down a road I didn't want to follow as an artist. I was getting preachy. My answer now to that question—"What should I do?"—is to think of that question itself as a form of defense because when we decide that we want to do something it's always going to be something that's not enough. Like change the light bulbs in your house or pump up your car tires so they're at full pressure so you'll get maximum gas mileage. It's always going to be a gesture because that's really all we can do as individuals. If we decide that we're going to do something, then I'm relieved of the anxiety that I feel for the fact that I'm powerless. And I think the desire not to feel that anxiety is frequently the motivation to ask the question, "What should I do?" I want people to *feel* that anxiety and to be with it because as citizens of the world who are trying to comprehend these issues, we have to learn to live with a huge amount of anxiety and bear it. Anxiety is the first step, and below that maybe we can begin to get to our anger or our fear, and maybe even deeper than that finally begin to get to our grief about what's being lost. When we feel those things, that's when we act decisively and at a level that's appropriate to solving these problems.

SCOTT: I wonder if we could conclude with just a few general questions. For instance, when you were talking about having the opportunity to visit with scientific experts on various topics, such as the plastic contamination of the ocean or climate change or biologists who specialize in albatrosses or other species, surely you're being inundated with information. You're listening to information, you're reading technical articles, and I wonder how you feel about the idea that for information to have meaning it has to be somehow infused with affect, with feeling. And when you're sitting there listening to these experts, are you thinking about how you might be able to use your tools—your camera—to convey this information meaningfully to your own audience?

CHRIS: It's a really interesting question because we're stuck with these numbers, with data, as the only information we have to try to make meaning, to try to comprehend and feel something that is profoundly important, whether it's global climate change or the number of women being raped in the Congo. All we've got is data and, in some cases, photographs that help us make meaning. But one of the things I keep hearing over and over again from scientists is how they're wringing their hands over their inability to convey to the public the gravity, the profound importance, of what they're discovering. It's so interesting to be behind closed doors with a climate scientist, this very measured person who writes in scientific language for peer-reviewed technical publications. I asked him, "So what are your feelings about global warming and the need to get this information out?" And all of this passion comes out! Scientists are furious about what's happening and their inability to communicate to the public in a way that the public gets how important what's happening actually is.

SCOTT: In a way, you're stepping into that communication gap and helping to interpret and reach out with that information. Is that the case?

CHRIS: Yeah! When I do a new piece, I want to really comprehend the issue. I don't want to be one of those photographers who goes to Africa and sits across the river with a two-thousand-millimeter lens and takes photographs of the native people. If I photograph native people, I want to go there and be with them. I feel that way about these issues, too, whether it's the number of plastic bottles consumed or anything else. I try to immerse myself in the issue, to read up on it, because it's always so complex, and I know that I myself am implicated in all of the issues— we all are—and it's so easy to get one-dimensional. I want to hear from the scientists and really understand an issue like the Pacific garbage patch before doing a piece about it. Usually during the learning process some ideas come to me about how I can create layers of meaning that I try to put into my pieces.

SCOTT: I wonder about the use of visual images, in particular, as a way of creating this meaning because some might suggest that language is more precise and nuanced in a certain way. It enables us to explain in detail what we think is happening in a situation or in a phenomenon, whereas the image is still, it exists in one moment, and although there might be many details that make up a visual image, the explanation or interpretation has to be captured in that one static moment. How do you see the difference between how a still image communicates and how verbal language communicates meaning?

CHRIS: Really interesting question. Well, if you think of what "meaning" really is—to me, meaning is about *feeling*. I know that I've found meaning when I feel something. Language can so frequently be abstract. This is something I talk about a lot with my wife because she's a poet. She would say language isn't abstract—language can be the most powerful thing to evoke meaning. That's when it's in the hands of poets. But when it's in the hands of scientists, frequently there's an abstraction in language that makes it really hard to grasp any *feeling*. Talking about something or reading a paragraph about something—it's almost like having a *map* that points toward the thing we want to understand, but the map is not the territory. It's just a map, and we want to get to the territory, which is the feeling.

There's something about visual images that allows us to comprehend a subject that enables feeling to occur. Language frequently misses the mark. I remember a seminal moment in my artistic career. I was in Washington, DC, on a legal project, but I took a day off to walk through the Holocaust Museum, and then I went across to Maya Lin's Vietnam War Memorial. Standing in front of that pile of eyeglasses in the Holocaust Museum and seeing those photographs of the piles of shoes—that was a visceral experience. And standing in front of that wall—there was a visceral comprehension on a deep, gut level. The preverbal part of our mind gets something at that point. No amount of reading of a book could convey this.

SCOTT: Were those experiences in Washington an important part of your own development as an artist?

CHRIS: Oh, yeah. The basic hope or intention of my work is to try to make these global issues personal to the viewer and for myself. I'm trying to figure out how to comprehend these issues on a personal level for myself, to allow myself to feel what they're about. I want my heart to grow big enough that I can go to a place like the Holocaust Museum and allow myself to really comprehend it, come fully out of the denial and allow myself to know what that feels like.

SCOTT: Robert Jay Lifton would argue that this tendency toward denial is actually a survival mechanism. He's the psychiatrist who coined the term "psychic numbing," particularly in response to the atomic bomb attacks on Japan at the end of World War II. Lifton would argue that we live today not just in places that have suffered some form of acute devastation, but all of us live in a condition of persistent numbness, persistent insensitivity on a psychological level, that enables us to continue with our lives in the face of what you might call intolerable phenomena, such as the extraordinary harming of albatrosses in the Pacific Ocean by ingesting plastic.

I wonder whether you'd say you yourself have experienced psychic numbing when you witness various disasters—when you go to New Orleans after Hurricane Katrina, when you repeatedly visit Midway Atoll in the Pacific and spend a lot of time learning about the harmful effects of plastic and the implications of climate change. You are the perfect candidate for absolute numbness, but that's *not* what has happened to you! If anything, as you just said a moment ago, you are pursuing ever greater sensitivity—the desire to open your heart to the real meaning of all of this. How have you somehow succeeded in sidestepping psychic numbing, or are you constantly trying to elude this obliterating numbness?

CHRIS: I definitely agree with Lifton's thesis, and I definitely feel the numbing experience myself. It's just that I don't agree with the idea that there's somehow a benefit. I think we can still go on, even if we remain sensitive to experience. All the people I know who have fully, deeply experienced an incredibly tragic event, like the death of a loved one from cancer, people who have *really* gone there, as opposed to living in denial like a lot of us do—like Terry Tempest Williams, for example; *Refuge* is an extremely instructive book on how to go all the way there when a loved one dies. The people I know who do that come out of it not in a condition of being unable to go on or in a state of collapse. They come out of it transformed. But I do see a pervasive tendency in our culture not to allow ourselves to feel bad stuff. Personally, I view it as my responsibility as a global citizen to face these issues because on the one hand maybe you could say it's better for us as individuals not to feel these things, to live in denial, but where that's getting us collectively is possibly to the annihilation of most of our biosphere and, at a minimum, the annihilation of us as a viable civilization.

It seems to me that the next evolutionary step for humanity is for us to get this stuff and to develop a kind of collective consciousness where we can become an enlightened society that manages its resources intelligently, that manages its population intelligently, and then begins to harness all of the resources of this planet. The first step of that process, as I see it, is, like the alcoholic, to face the fact that you're an alcoholic. I know a few people who've been through that process, and they say it's the most joyful experience of their lives—the moment they stand up and admit they have a problem and begin the healing. It's not a bad thing.

SCOTT: So, in a way, that's the project of your artistic work—to help people to come to terms with the fact that they as individuals or we as a society have certain problems. This project of accepting the condition we're in so that we can begin to undertake the kinds of transformations that are needed to do things in a healthier way.

CHRIS: Yeah, and as I said in my preface to the Katrina book, I don't do this work because I'm a fundamentally negative person or because I like pain. It's not an exercise in pain or self-punishment or something. I think of my work as an act of love. One of the things that has come to me in these Midway trips is that I'm now unafraid to say that I'm in love with this world and I believe in our ability to change. It just needs to happen . . . soon.

PART IV

Postscript

SCOTT SLOVIC AND PAUL SLOVIC

FRENCH-BORN CONCEPTUAL PAINTER ROMAN OPALKA (1931–2011) began his life's work, *OPALKA 1965/1-∞*, in the year 1965, eventually painting rows of ever more faint numbers across 233 canvases. By the time of his death, he was painting white numbers on a background he called "blanc merité" (well-earned white), accentuating the existential problematic of his exercise in probing the meaning (or non-meaning) of numbers. He stopped short of the number 6,000,000, but the precise figure seems not to matter. Although the painter himself suggested in 1987 that his work explores how time "embodies our progressive disappearance," other views of this methodical accrual of numerals might include the idea that numbers eventually attain not only invisibility, but a certain vacancy of meaning—numbers, numbers, numbers. Where does this get us in the end? The ultimate disappearance of Opalka's numerical rows into white upon white hints at the emotional numbness that occurs when human beings receive purely (or mostly) numerical information.

FIGURE 17.1 Roman Opalka's final numbers, handwritten on August 6, 2011, the day of his death.

As demonstrated by various articles presented in Part I of this book, psychologists and other social scientists have documented the cognitive obstacles to human apprehension of large-scale, invisible phenomena, even phenomena that may have catastrophic social and ecological implications— phenomena that are often described by way of numerical data. In fact, the larger and more significant the phenomenon is, the less likely we are to *feel* its meaning, its importance. This ironic failure of sensitivity may end up being the tragic (or comic) punch line to the human story: "They continued killing themselves off through war and starvation and environmental degradation, all the while reproducing, consuming, and growing their economies as if there were no threat to the survival of their species. They apparently had little sense of what was happening all around them." If mosquitoes, ants, and cockroaches could speak, this is what they might say to each other about us following our demise.

For many years, scholars have attached the adjective "slow" to the vast, distant, and otherwise invisible dangers facing our species and the rest of the planet. Back in 1989, Robert Ornstein and Paul Ehrlich concluded their book *New World New Mind: Moving Toward Conscious Evolution* by suggesting, "We cannot and should not completely change the responsiveness of the human system to sudden change. But . . . we could develop a new kind of 'news' report that first analyzes the slow dangers affecting humanity and then portrays them in a way that is understandable to the old mind." Innovative modes of communication might, they argue, bridge the gap between the insensitive human mind (which has evolved to be alert primarily to nearby, rapid events or changes) and the processes and events we now grapple with, many of them resulting from human technologies developed in just the past few centuries (much too recently for there to have been a biological evolutionary response). We need "certain kinds of information" to break through the limitations of "the old mind" (p. 246).

Two decades later, in *Slow Violence and the Environmentalism of the Poor* (2011), Rob Nixon described and called forth a new movement of "writer-activists" to help us "apprehend threats imaginatively that remain imperceptible to the senses, either because they are geographically remote, too vast or too minute in scale, or are played out across a time span that exceeds the instance of observation or even the physiological life of the human observer" (p. 15). For Nixon, the key question of our time is, "How do we bring home—and bring emotionally to life—threats that take time to wreak their havoc, threats that never materialize in one spectacular, cinematic scene?" (p. 14). He characterizes this problem as one of "apprehension" and points out that this concept entails "perception, emotion, and action." The solution to this quandary of apprehension may come in the form of "narrative imaginings" of writer-activists who "offer us a different kind of witnessing: of sights unseen" (p. 15). Nixon points to such writers as Jamaica Kinkaid, June Jordan, Njabulo Ndebele, and Nadine Gordimer, among various others, as exemplars of this writer-activist effort to witness and narrate the "unseen," particularly in the context of poor and disadvantaged communities throughout the world. While Nixon's approach highlights systemic violence in countries far away from North America, perhaps the deepest irony of *Slow Violence and the Environmentalism of the Poor* and other efforts to sensitize American readers to distant crises, such as Samantha Power's *A Problem From Hell: America and the Age of Genocide*, is that we are inured to problems located in our own neighborhoods if those problems are "slow" enough, if we feel unable to react with efficacy, if other factors outweigh our attention to these problems, if we trust media that have urged us not to care, or if the affected individuals are "too numerous." The psychophysics of brightness, mentioned in the Introduction, teaches us with startling simplicity that our sensitivity and compassion tend to wane much more precipitously than we'd like to think. Our moral schemes guide us to believe that the value of each life should be constant and more or less equal, but our minds function otherwise, allowing a slippage in value, in salience, already with the second life in jeopardy, whether that life is on another continent or just around the corner.

The effort to attach story and image to the unseen and perhaps unseeable is neither new nor limited to writers who have come from developing nations or impoverished backgrounds. As we have tried to suggest in this volume, our most inspired writer-activists hail from far-flung regions of the world—from India, Mexico, and the United States, to offer only a few representative examples (see the interviews in Part III and the various literary, artistic, and journalistic samples in Part II). Perhaps, above all else, these writers and visual artists function as "sensory translators," transforming abstract information into viscerally, experientially meaningful discourse that might trigger in audiences the impulse to act individually or collectively. In his 1997 volume *Data Smog: Surviving the Information Glut*, David Shenk complains that information technology "truly cannot replace human experience" and that its compounding of "available information" merely "helps devalue the meaning of each piece of information" (p. 199). He recommends "data-fasts," self-editing, and on the whole reducing our production of and exposure to vast quantities of information as a way of preserving the meaning of what we do have to process. This may be good advice. But one of the essential lessons of our book is that *how* information is communicated (whether in large quantities or small)—such as the intertwining of numerical and narrative descriptions or sometimes the extension of abstract numerical data into narrative or visual analogues—may be particularly essential to our apprehending (and perhaps counteracting) the dangers and injustices human beings impose upon ourselves and the planet.

Communicating the deeper meaning of quantitative information—its emotional and moral dimensions as well as its other dimensions—may help clarify how such information confirms or conflicts with our personal and cultural values and may facilitate the evolution of our values. This enhanced understanding of information does not guarantee that we will make good decisions, as individuals or as societies. However, appreciating the psychological factors determining how we draw meaning from information may enable us to mitigate cognitive tendencies (such as psychic numbing, pseudoinefficacy, the prominence effect, and the asymmetry of trust) that undermine rational decision making.

REFERENCES

Nixon, R. (2011). *Slow violence and the environmentalism of the poor.* Cambridge, MA: Harvard University Press.

Ornstein, R., & Ehrlich, P. (1989). *New world new mind: Moving toward conscious evolution.* New York, NY: Doubleday.

Power, S. (2003). *A problem from hell: America and the age of genocide.* New York, NY: Harper Perennial.

Roman Opalka. (2011, August 26). *The Telegraph.* Retrieved from http://www .telegraph.co.uk/news/obituaries/culture-obituaries/art-obituaries/8725751/ Roman-Opalka.html.

Shenk, D. (1997). *Data smog: Surviving the information glut.* New York, NY: Harper-Collins.

Contributors

BETTY ARIDJIS, with her husband, Homero Aridjis, cofounded El Grupo de los Cien (The Group of 100), an association of distinguished artists and intellectuals concerned with environmental protection in Mexico and throughout Latin America. In 2011, Aridjis, who also regularly translates her husband's work into English, spearheaded a campaign to raise awareness of the situation in Mexico's San Luis Potosí state, where a Canadian mining operation is threatening an area thought to be sacred by the Huichol Indians.

HOMERO ARIDJIS, who served as Mexican ambassador to the Netherlands and Switzerland, and from 2007 to 2010 as Mexican ambassador to UNESCO in Paris, is one of Mexico's leading authors. Among more than forty volumes of poetry and prose, he has published such works as the novel *1492: Vida y tiempos de Juan Cabezón de Castilla* (1985) and the poetry collection *Eyes to See Otherwise/Ojos de otro mirar* (2002). From 1997 to 2003, he was president of PEN International, the worldwide organization for writers. As an environmental activist, he is especially well known for his work on air pollution in Mexico City, the endangerment of gray whale breeding waters off the coast of Baja California, and the destruction of monarch butterfly wintering habitat in his native Michoacán.

RICK BASS, the author of more than thirty books of fiction and nonfiction, lives in Montana's Yaak Valley. Bass began his career as a petroleum geologist in Mississippi before moving to Montana in 1987 and devoting himself to writing and wilderness protection efforts. The recipient of numerous awards, Bass was a finalist for the National Book Critics Circle Award for

Why I Came West (2009). His recent books include *The Wild Marsh: Four Seasons at Home in Montana* (2009), *Nashville Chrome: A Novel* (2010), and *All the Land to Hold Us: A Novel* (2013), among others. The essay collected here comes from Bass's 1996 work *The Book of Yaak* and shows how the author both uses and transcends numbers in expressing his concern for an endangered landscape.

ANNIE DILLARD received the Pulitzer Prize for nonfiction in 1975 for her book *Pilgrim at Tinker Creek*. In a dozen books of poetry, fiction, and nonfiction, she has received acclaim for her poetic probings of topics ranging from natural history to eclectic spirituality. Dillard taught for twenty-one years at Wesleyan University; her most recent publication is a novel called *The Maytrees*, published in 2007. The article included in this book, first published in *Harper's*, comes from Dillard's 1999 volume *For the Time Being*, a book that explores how the human mind attaches meaning to objects, experiences, and information.

Medical anthropologist PAUL FARMER has dedicated his life to treating some of the world's poorest populations, in the process helping to raise the standard of health care in underdeveloped areas of the world. A founding director of Partners In Health (1987), an international charity organization that provides direct health care services and undertakes research and advocacy activities on behalf of those who are sick and living in poverty, Farmer, along with his colleagues, has demonstrated that quality health care is possible to deliver in resource-poor areas. Farmer has been honored with numerous humanitarian awards, as well as a 1993 MacArthur Fellowship. His latest publications include *To Repair the World: Paul Farmer Speaks to the Next Generation* (2013) and *In the Company of the Poor: Conversations Between Dr. Paul Farmer and Fr. Gustavo Gutierrez* (2013). His life and work are the subject of Tracy Kidder's 2003 book *Mountains Beyond Mountains*.

KENNETH HELPHAND is Knight Professor of Landscape Architecture at the University of Oregon. His books include *Colorado: Visions of an American Landscape* (1991), *Yard Street Park: The Design of Suburban Open Space* (1994), *Dreaming Gardens: Landscape Architecture and the Making of Modern Israel* (2002), and *Defiant Gardens: Making Gardens in Wartime* (2006). The former editor of *Landscape Journal*, Helphand is a fellow of the American

Society of Landscape Architects, an honorary member of the Israel Association of Landscape Architects, and chair of the Senior Fellows in Garden and Landscape Studies at Dumbarton Oaks.

CHRIS JORDAN is a Seattle-based visual artist (photography, digital composition, and film) who practiced law for a decade before resigning from the bar and devoting himself to photography. His works, in collections such as *Intolerable Beauty: Portraits of American Mass Consumption* (2003–2006), *Running the Numbers I: An American Self-Portrait* (2006–2009), and *Running the Numbers II: Portraits of Global Mass Culture* (2009–2010), prompt viewers to think about themselves and their lifestyles in relation to the collectives (the societies) to which they belong—in other words, his art explores the phenomenon of scale.

NICHOLAS D. KRISTOF has been a columnist for the *New York Times* since 2001. After joining the *Times* in 1984, initially covering economics, he served as a *Times* correspondent in Los Angeles, Hong Kong, Beijing, and Tokyo. He later was associate managing editor of the *Times*, responsible for Sunday editions. In 1990 Mr. Kristof and his wife, Sheryl WuDunn, won a Pulitzer Prize for their coverage of China's Tiananmen Square democracy movement. Kristof won a second Pulitzer in 2006, for what the judges called "his graphic, deeply reported columns that, at personal risk, focused attention on genocide in Darfur and that gave voice to the voiceless in other parts of the world."

ROBERT JAY LIFTON is a psychiatrist and "psychohistorian." His book *Death in Life: Survivors of Hiroshima* received a National Book Award in 1969. He has served on the faculties of Yale and Harvard Universities and the John Jay College of Criminal Justice and is recognized as a leading scholar of the Holocaust. He has also published two books of humorous cartoons about birds: *Birds* (1969) and *Psycho-Birds* (1978).

MARCUS MAYORGA is a doctoral student at the University of Oregon and research coordinator at Decision Research. He has interests in decision making, emotion, prosocial behavior, moral psychology, and philosophy. His primary area of research is charitable decision making, studying how individual differences can affect motivations for prosocial behavior.

BILL MCKIBBEN, the Schumann Distinguished Scholar at Middlebury College, is a leading American environmental activist and journalist, particularly well known for his work on global climate change in such books as *The End of Nature* (1989), *Fight Global Warming Now: The Handbook for Taking Action in Your Community* (2007), and the collection *The Global Warming Reader* (2011). Selections of his own work have been gathered in *The Bill McKibben Reader: Pieces From an Active Life* (2008).

GREG MITCHELL writes the Media Fix blog at *The Nation* and is the author of more than a dozen nonfiction books, including *Journeys with Beethoven, Atomic Cover-Up, The Age of WikiLeaks*, and *Bradley Manning*. He was the longtime editor of *Editor & Publisher* and, before that, executive editor at *Crawdaddy*.

ROBERT MICHAEL PYLE has written or edited more than a dozen books of natural history and personal narrative, including such works as *Wintergreen: Listening to the Land's Heart* (1987), which received the John Burroughs Medal for distinguished natural history writing. Based in Grays River, Washington, Pyle holds a Ph.D. from Yale's School of Forestry and Environmental Studies and has published numerous scientific papers in addition to his prolific literary essays, stories, and poems. Known particularly for his love of butterflies and his efforts to support invertebrate conservation (he founded the Xerces Society for Invertebrate Conservation in 1974), his recent books include *Sky Time in Gray's River: Living for Keeps in a Forgotten Place* (2007) and *Mariposa Road: The First Butterfly Big Year* (2011), both of which received Washington State Book Awards.

VANDANA SHIVA, who received her Ph.D. in physics from the University of Western Ontario in Canada, is a philosopher and social/environmental activist based in New Delhi, India. The author of more than twenty books and hundreds of articles, her work addresses issues including agriculture and food, intellectual property rights, biodiversity, biotechnology, women's empowerment, and the plight of rural people in India and other parts of the world. Her books include *Monocultures of the Mind: Biodiversity, Biotechnology, and Agriculture* (1993), *Stolen Harvest: The Hijacking of the Global Food Supply* (2000), and *Earth Democracy: Justice, Sustainability, and*

Peace (2005), among many others. Her many honors include the 1993 Right Livelihood Award.

PAUL SLOVIC is president of Decision Research and a professor of psychology at the University of Oregon. He studies human judgment, decision making, and risk perception and has published extensively on these topics, including such books as *The Perception of Risk* (2000) and *The Feeling of Risk: New Perspectives on Risk Perception* (2010). His most recent work examines "psychic numbing" and the failure to respond to mass human tragedies. He is past president of the Society for Risk Analysis and in 1991 received its Distinguished Contribution Award. In 1993, he received the Distinguished Scientific Contribution Award from the American Psychological Association, and in 1995 he received the Outstanding Contribution to Science Award from the Oregon Academy of Science. He was elected to the American Academy of Arts and Sciences in 2015.

SCOTT SLOVIC is professor of literature and environment and chair of the English Department at the University of Idaho. The author, editor, or coeditor of twenty-two books in the field of literature and environment, his recent works include *Going Away to Think: Engagement, Retreat, and Ecocritical Responsibility* (2008), *The Future of Ecocriticism: New Horizons* (2011), *Nature and the Environment: Critical Insights* (2013), *Ecoambiguity, Community, and Development: Toward a Politicized Ecocriticism* (2014), *Currents of the Universal Being: Explorations in the Literature of Energy* (2015), and *Ecocriticism of the Global South* (2015). He served as the founding president of the Association for the Study of Literature and Environment (ASLE), and since 1995 has edited the journal *ISLE: Interdisciplinary Studies in Literature and Environment*.

SANDRA STEINGRABER is sometimes thought of as the literary daughter of American scientist, author, and environmental activist Rachel Carson. A cancer survivor herself, Steingraber, who has a master's degree in English and a Ph.D. in biology, published the story of her own cancer experience in the context of industrial pollution and human health risks in the 1997 book *Living Downstream: An Ecologist Looks at Cancer and the Environment*. Her other literary works concerned with environmental contamination and human health include *Having Faith: An Ecologist's Journey to Motherhood* (2001) and *Raising Elijah: Protecting Our Children in an Age of Environmental Crisis* (2011). She is currently distinguished visiting scholar in the Division of Interdisciplinary and International Studies at Ithaca College in New York.

DANIEL VÄSTFJÄLL is a research scientist at Decision Research and professor of cognitive psychology at Linköping University in Sweden. He is the director of the Linköping Center of Behavioral and NeuroEconomics. His research examines how affect influences judgment and decision making—in particular, the role of emotion in charitable giving.

TERRY TEMPEST WILLIAMS, well known for her antinuclear, antiwar, and pro-wilderness activism, is a prolific author of more than a dozen popular books, including the loosely linked trilogy *Refuge: An Unnatural History of Family and Place* (1991), *Leap* (2000), and *Finding Beauty in a Broken World* (2008). Her meditations on the Rwanda genocide of the 1990s in this book were initially published in *Orion* magazine. Williams currently divides her time between Utah, Wyoming, and New Hampshire, where she teaches at Dartmouth College.

Editors
Scott Slovic and
Paul Slovic

Index